Centerville Library
Washington-Centerville P[...]
Centerville, Oh[...]
DISCARD

D1197459

THE
**OHIO STATE
UNIVERSITY**

Leabharlann Library
Maigh Nuad/Maynooth
Coláiste Ollscoile

THE
OHIO STATE
UNIVERSITY

AN ILLUSTRATED HISTORY

Raimund E. Goerler

 THE OHIO STATE UNIVERSITY PRESS • COLUMBUS

Copyright © 2011 by The Ohio State University.
All rights reserved.

Library of Congress Cataloging-in-Publication Data
Goerler, Raimund E. (Raimund Erhard), 1948–
   The Ohio State University : an illustrated history / Raimund E. Goerler.
      p. cm.
   Includes bibliographical references and index.
   ISBN-13: 978-0-8142-1154-0 (cloth : alk. paper)
   ISBN-10: 0-8142-1154-2 (cloth : alk. paper)
   1. Ohio State University—History. I. Title.
   LD4228.G64 2011
   378.771'57—dc22
                  2010043954

Cover design by Jeffrey Smith of Designsmith
Text design by Jennifer Shoffey Forsythe
Type set in Adobe Minion Pro
Printed by Thomson-Shore, Inc.

∞ The paper used in this publication meets the minimum requirements of the American
National Standard for Information Sciences—Permanence of Paper for Printed Library
Materials. ANSI Z39.48-1992.

9 8 7 6 5 4

CONTENTS

LIST OF ILLUSTRATIONS

CHAPTER ONE

CHAPTER TWO

CHAPTER THREE

CHAPTER FIVE

CHAPTER SEVEN

CHAPTER TEN

PREFACE AND ACKNOWLEDGMENTS

Universities blend past, present, and future in several ways. Institutions of higher education teach knowledge developed by past generations to students of today. They also use the wisdom of the past to create original ideas that lead to new ways of thinking and doing that will impact the future. Buildings and streets named after people prominent in the university's history serve as landmarks that guide present and future generations. Traditions—institutional, social, and athletic—abound. It is no exaggeration to say that one cannot fully experience OSU today without referencing the past and looking toward the future.

This book provides a condensed history of The Ohio State University for its students (present and future), faculty, staff, and alumni. Its purpose is to provide an understanding of the present campus and university as it has evolved from its past. As university archivist of Ohio State for more than three decades, I have a keen appreciation of how the present relates to the past and how important the past is in preparing for the future. In my interactions with students, faculty, staff and alumni, I have become aware of how little many know about the history of their university. A one-volume history that is comprehensive from the beginning of OSU to the present has not appeared since 1952. Only recently has the university been teaching students about its own history.

In writing this book, I decided to look at the history of the university as if it were a prism that has many sides. If I were to ask people what aspect of the University is most important to them, I know that I would receive many different answers. Some would say its physical environment, the buildings and places on the campus. Others would point to its academic life, its teaching and its research. Many would argue for the social life, the student experience outside the classroom. No doubt more than a few would claim that athletics and traditions make the university what it is. If a university has importance in different ways, then its history should reflect its multiple sides and how they came into being.

This book is unlike most histories. Its purpose is to orient, not to present fact after fact marching through time. Certainly it is more like a guidebook to the past than an encyclopedia. Most of the chapters look at different aspects of the university and how they developed. More often than not, the chapters begin with the present and explain the major milestones of the past that led to the present.

This book has also taken shape from an unusual resource of the university itself, OSU's photo archives. As one of the earliest universities to teach photography, Ohio State probably has more photographs of itself—literally more than a million—than any other college or university in the United States. Previous histories have barely used the vast visual resources available to illustrate the past of OSU. Michelle Drobik of the OSU archives, along with Kevlin Haire, was particularly helpful in alerting me to appropriate photographs and to digitizing them for this work.

In writing this book, I benefited from the help of many. My colleagues with whom I taught "OSU History and Its World"—Dean Emeritus Tom Minnick (University College), Vice President Emeritus John Mount, Professor George Paulson (Medicine), Professor Paul Young (Architecture), and Professor Christian Zacher (English)—provided intellectual stimulation and encouragement for me to undertake this book. So, too, did the many guests who lectured in the class. Designed for undergraduates, the course faced the challenge of presenting the history of OSU in a ten-week quarter, while exploring OSU's continuing activities in teaching, scholarship, and service. The nature of this course blended historical narrative about the origins of OSU with current information. Put another way, this course addressed the university's present in the context of its past and provided commentary about facing the future.

I owe a special thanks to my readers: John Bruno, Robert Butche, Tamar Chute, Mabel Freeman, Bertha Ihnat, George Paulson, Dick Thomas, Paul Young, and Chris Zacher. They saw drafts of the manuscript and helped to shape the progress of the text. The Ohio State University Press and its director, Malcolm Litchfield, encouraged this project at its beginning and guided it toward completion. Chris Zacher and Tom Katzenmeyer of OSU helped to make this publication possible. Finally, the OSU Libraries and its former director, Joseph Branin, approved the research leave needed to accomplish the book.

THE
OHIO STATE UNIVERSITY

AN ILLUSTRATED HISTORY

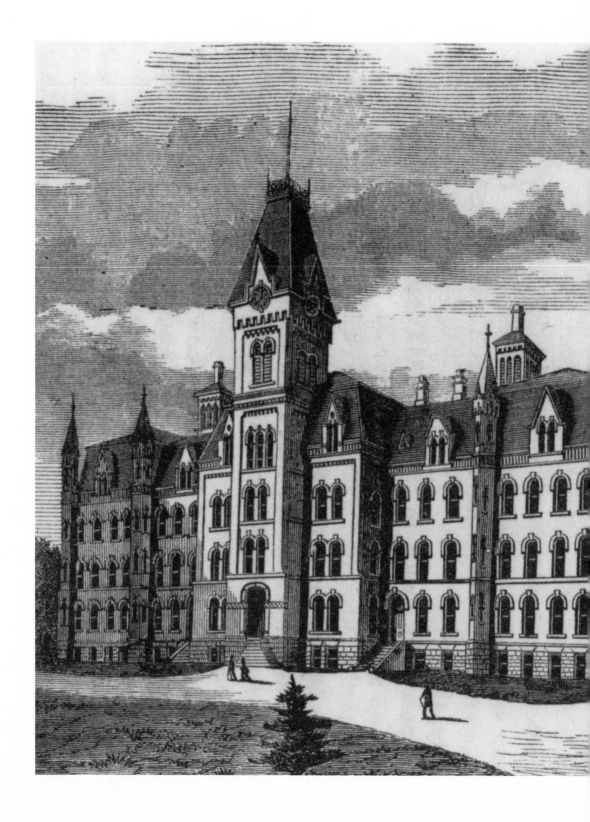

CHAPTER ONE

OSU'S EARLY YEARS

From the Founding to the First Graduating Class, 1862–1878

*The Agricultural and Mechanical College
Bill passed yesterday. I am satisfied that
an institution of great importance to the
State may be founded. . . . "*
—From the diary of Ohio Governor
Rutherford B. Hayes, 1870

*To me personally, these years, the first
ten of the life of the institution, were the
most stimulating and evolutional of all my
life.*
—Professor Thomas Mendenhall (member
of the first faculty)

THROUGHOUT its history, The Ohio State University has had lofty ambitions. Today, the university's vision, its statement of what it seeks to be, declares: "The Ohio State University will be recognized worldwide for the quality and impact of its research, teaching, and service" and that "The Ohio State University will be among the world's truly great universities."[1] As early as 1874, President Edward Orton, predicted that the founding of the university and its "education for the industrial classes" would be a turning point in the history of civilization that "would justly divide the new from the old."[2]

Lofty ambitions aside, the early years of Ohio State were actually ones of lofty aspirations in the midst of adversity. The university struggled at a time when only a minority of Ohioans—or residents in other states—cared much about higher education. Certainly, the State of Ohio did not invest readily in its new institution. In 1876, for example, the secretary of the university's board of trustees complained that Ohio supported its prisons and insane asylums but did nothing for its university.

1.1 Senator Justin Morrill (1810–1898) had never attended college, but through the Morrill Act, which created land-grant colleges and universities, he had an enormous influence on higher education in the United States and on the beginning of The Ohio State University. Through time and change, OSU's identity as a land-grant college has been a constant feature.

THE MORRILL ACT, 1862

As early as 1859, Congressman (later Senator) Justin Morrill of Vermont had proposed that the federal government sell public lands and from the revenue provide the states endowments for special colleges and universities. These land-grant colleges were to provide special programs of education in engineering and agriculture at a low tuition, because of the federal support.

Heated debate followed, because Morrill's proposal would create an unprecedented participation of the national government in higher education. James Mason of Virginia called the bill "one of the most extraordinary engines of mischief." Ohio congressman George Pugh denounced the bill "as atrocious a violation of the organic law as if it were the act of an armed usurper."[3] Although Congress passed Morrill's bill, President James Buchanan vetoed it.

In 1861, the beginning of the Civil War presented Morrill with another opportunity. Much of the earlier opposition had come from Southern Democrats in Congress, many of whom left the capital as their states seceded from the Union. Moreover, the new president, Abraham Lincoln, was a Republican who supported Morrill's bill. President Lincoln signed the Morrill Act on July 2, 1862.

1. See Academic Plan, Vision Statement, http://www.osu.edu/academicplan/preface.php

2. Edward Orton inaugural address, 1874, in "Third Annual Report of the Trustees of the Ohio Agricultural and Mechanical College to the Governor of the State of Ohio," 25.

3. William Kinnison, *Building Sullivant's Pyramid: An Administrative History of the Ohio State University, 1870–1907* (Columbus: The Ohio State University Press, 1970), 7–9.

1.2 Named in 1965 as construction began, Morrill and Lincoln Towers (left to right) memorialize Senator Justin Morrill and President Abraham Lincoln, author and signer, respectively, of the act that provided for the creation of land-grant colleges. Along both buildings runs Cannon Drive, which memorializes State Senator Reuben Cannon, who wrote the act creating the Ohio Agricultural and Mechanical College (later The Ohio State University).

The Morrill Act had several requirements for states to meet if they were to receive revenue from the sale of public lands as an educational endowment. The act granted each state public lands equal to thirty thousand acres for each senator and representative from the state in Congress. States that wanted to participate in the Morrill Act had to arrange for the sale of the land themselves. Revenue from the sales was an irreducible endowment to: "the support and maintenance of at least one college, where the leading objects shall be, without excluding other scientific and classical studies, and including military tactics, to teach such branches of learning as are

1.3 *The Morrill Act required that colleges and universities that received money from the sale of public lands offer military training to students. At The Ohio State University, military training has been a lengthy tradition, as this photograph from the 1870s shows.*

related to agriculture and the mechanic arts, in such a manner as the legislatures of the states may respectively prescribe, in order to promote the liberal and practical education of the industrial classes in the several pursuits and professions of life." If the endowment, through poor investments, should diminish, a state had to replenish it from its own funds. In addition, the act declared that "No portion of said fund, nor the interest thereon, shall be applied directly or indirectly under any pretense whatever, to the purchase, erection, preservation or repair of any building or buildings."

Aside from requiring training in military tactics (a reaction to the crisis in military leadership caused by the withdrawal of Southerners from the professional military academies), the Morrill Act granted states much discretion in applying the land-grant monies. It did not require the states to create new colleges. In fact, the act made it more difficult to found new colleges by forbidding the use of the endowment to buy or erect or repair any buildings. Nor did it stipulate that the beneficiaries of the endowment should teach only, or even primarily, courses in agriculture and the mechanical arts. Some states created new institutions; others divided the endowment among existing colleges to support new programs in agriculture and engineering or the mechanical arts.

The Morrill Act in Ohio

In November of 1862, Ohio's Governor David Tod urged the state legislature to accept the conditions of the Morrill Act. However, some Ohioans opposed it. The auditor of state feared that the act was a bad deal for Ohio for two reasons. First, it burdened the state by having to manage the sale of federal lands at state expense. Second, it held the state liable for protecting the endowment for an undertaking that, in his opinion, seemed destined to fail. As he put it, "The idea that a college for teaching such branches of learning as is related to agriculture and the mechanic arts can be successful seems to be visionary. . . . It seems to me that the teaching of agriculture and the mechanic arts in a college where military science is also taught would be almost as difficult as their peaceful pursuit in a country occupied by an army."[4]

Again and again, efforts to accept the Morrill Act failed in the Ohio legislature. Groups did support the Morrill Act, but for different reasons. The State Agriculture Board, which the legislature had set up to promote agriculture, saw the Morrill Act as so useful to farmers that members wanted a new college dedicated principally to the mission of educating farmers and mechanics. However, other colleges and universities—Miami at Oxford, Ohio in Athens, and Farmers College near Cincinnati—wanted a share of the endowment and promised to begin programs in agriculture and engineering. Not until February 9, 1864 did the legislature agree for Ohio to accept the Morrill Act in general,without deciding which institutions were to receive the endowment funds.

To create the endowment the State had to manage the sale of its share of land-script, nearly 630,000 acres largely west of the Mississippi River. Ohio created a commission and charged it to sell the land at a minimum price of an acre for a total of at least $504,000. After some effort, the commissioners reported that other states were selling their lands for less than Ohio required and sales of Ohio's scrip had been disappointing. Soon, the State empowered the commissioners to sell at the best price and to do so quickly. By the end of 1867, Ohio had sold its share at an average of .50 per acre and created an endowment of $340,894.70.[5] Years later, Alexis Cope, secretary of OSU's board of trustees from 1884 to 1904, lamented: "When we remember that the grant to the state of New York under Ezra Cornell has to this date yielded nearly seven millions of dollars to the endowment of Cornell, we are filled with unavailing regret that the munificent grant to our state was so wasted."[6]

THE CANNON ACT

Although disappointing when compared to New York's, the endowment created from the Morrill Act provided a handsome fund for higher education in Ohio. According to one estimate, it exceeded the endowments of the wealthiest colleges

---

4. Alexis Cope, *History of the Ohio State University,* vol 1: 1870–1910 (Columbus: The Ohio State University Press, 1920), 5.

5. Cope, 10–11.

6. Cope, 12–13.

in Ohio—Ohio Wesleyan, Oberlin, and Kenyon. Miami and Ohio, the oldest in Ohio—had endowments of only $100,000 and $80,000.[7] Not surprisingly, the contest among Ohio's colleges and universities for the rich Morrill endowment continued for nearly three years of debate until the passage of the Cannon Act of 1870.

In 1865, the State Commissioner of Common Schools proposed dividing the Morrill funds. One part would create a centrally located college where military instruction and applied sciences would be taught; the other would go to three colleges already established but in different parts of Ohio. Governor John Brough (1864–1865) opposed dividing the fund or giving it to an existing institution. Norton S. Townshend, who was president of the State Board of Agriculture, supported the governor and signed a memorial to the Ohio General Assembly, declaring "your memorialists are deeply anxious that the noble fund now entrusted the State for the purpose of instruction in Agriculture and the Mechanic Arts should not be misapplied or perverted to any other use.[8]

1.4 In the Ohio House of Representatives, Reuben P. Cannon, of Portage County, introduced the Cannon Act of 1870 that led to the Ohio Agricultural and Mechanical College. It created a powerful board of trustees to settle such controversial issues as location and curriculum, which previous legislatures had failed to address.

Ralph Leete, a lawyer from Ironton, stirred even more controversy when he published an article that recommended that the State of Ohio seize the assets of state-chartered Ohio and Miami Universities and combine their funds with the Morrill endowment. From this treasure, he would create a premier and central institution where agriculture and the mechanic arts and all subjects were taught.

Supported by Governor Rutherford B. Hayes (1868–1872), the Cannon Act was one of a series of bills that won enough votes to resolve the vexing opportunity provided in the Morrill Act. First, the Ohio General Assembly passed an act which allowed municipalities to organize, support, and control their own institutions of higher education. In other words, these municipalities could develop their own colleges and universities, even if they did not receive money from the Morrill Act. A second act approved investing the sale from the land scrip, with interest secured at 6 percent as part of the irreducible debt of the state. This satisfied those who feared the state would mismanage the Morrill funds and burden the taxpayers. Another act allowed

1.5 Ralph Leete, outspoken member of the first board of trustees

7. Kinnison, 22.
8. Cope, 16.

H. B. No. 29.

Mr. CANNON.

A BILL

To Establish and Maintain an Agricultural and Mechanical College in Ohio.

SECTION 1. *Be it enacted by the General Assembly of the State of Ohio*, That

2 a college for the benefit of agriculture and mechanic arts is hereby established

3 in the state of Ohio, in accordance with the provisions of an act of congress of

4 the United States, passed July 2d, 1862, entitled an act donating public lands

5 to the several states and territories which may provide colleges for the benefit

6 of agriculture and mechanic arts, said college to be located as hereinafter pro-

7 vided.

SEC. 2. The government of said college shall be vested in a board of trustees

2 to consist of nine persons, one from each of the present judicial districts of the

3 state, who shall be appointed by the governor, by and with the advice and

4 consent of the senate. The president of the state board of agriculture and

5 the president of said college shall be ex officio members of said board. The

6 president of said college shall be its chairman. Three of those first appointed

7 shall hold their office for two years, and three for four years, and three for six

8 years, to be determined by lot, and thereafter each member shall be appointed

9 for the term of six years, except in cases of appointments to fill vacancies

10 occasioned by death, resignation or removal from office, in which latter case

11 the appointment shall be for the unexpired term. The trustees shall receive

12 no compensation for their services, but shall be entitled to reasonable and

13 necessary expenses whilst in discharge of official duties.

SEC. 3. The trustees and their successors in office shall constitute a body

1.6 First page of the Cannon Act, which established The Ohio Agricultural and Mechanical College, in 1870

OHIO Agricultural AND Mechanical COLLEGE.

The OHIO AGRICULTURAL AND MECHANICAL COLLEGE will be opened for the admission of Students, September 17 of the present year. The building will be ready for occupation at that time, and a Faculty, consisting of a President and six Professors and Assistant Professors, will be upon the ground.

The College will open with excellently equipped Laboratories in Chemistry and Physics, with well selected Cabinets in Mineralogy, Geology, and Zoology, and with ample means for teaching, in the best methods, such other branches as are to be at present provided for.

Two COURSES OF STUDY will be established at the opening of the College—an *Agricultural Course* and a *General or Scientific Course*. The Agricultural Course will extend through three years, and its successful completion will be attested by a special diploma of the Institution. Candidates for admission to this Course must be fourteen years of age, and must sustain examination in the ordinary branches of Common School Education, viz: in Reading, Orthography, Penmanship, English Grammar, Descriptive and Political Geography, Arithmetic, and in Algebra to Quadratic Equations.

The *General Course* will extend through four years, and students passing successfully through it will receive the degree of Bachelor of Science.

In addition to the requirements already named for entrance upon the Agricultural Course, candidates for admission to the General Course must sustain examination in Elementary Physics, Chemistry and Botany, in Physical Geography, in Algebra to General Theory of Equations, and in Plane Geometry. In other words, as the Agricultural Course is adjusted to the needs of students coming from the Common Schools, the General Course is designed, in the main, to take up the work of education where it is left by the High Schools of the State.

1.7 Excerpt from a circular distributed to newspapers in Ohio that announced the opening of the Ohio Agricultural and Mechanical College on September 17, 1873

counties to sell bonds, which they could use to buy land and erect buildings if they wished to compete as a site for the new institution. The Cannon Act was the fourth and final part of the legislative initiative. Introduced by Reuben P. Cannon, the bill created a nineteen-member board of trustees—one from each Congressional District in Ohio—whom the governor proposed and the Senate confirmed. In addition, the president of the State Board of Agriculture served as an ex officio member. These trustees would make all decisions necessary to begin the Ohio Agricultural and Mechanical College: its location, its curriculum, its faculty, and its administration.

Although it created a powerful board of trustees, the Cannon Act also set limits. It directed the trustees to select a site of not less than one hundred acres; the site had to be central in the state and accessible by railroad from different parts of Ohio. Finally, the Cannon Act required selecting a site quickly, by October, 15, 1870, and by significant consensus, a three-fifths vote of all members, not by a simple majority.

The Cannon Act mandated other requirements. The college had to have at least four departments (agriculture, mechanic arts, military science, and literature). The college had to be open "to all persons over fourteen years of age, subject to such rules and regulations and limitations, as to numbers from the several counties of the state, as may be prescribed by the board of trustees." It also required that the chief geologist of Ohio, who was surveying the geological resources of Ohio, deposit in the college a set of specimens from the survey. Years later, the volume and quality of deposits make a geological museum—Orton Hall—a priority for the new college.

1.8 Civil War hero and three times governor of Ohio, Rutherford B. Hayes played a critical role in fostering the Cannon Act that established the Ohio Agricultural and Mechanical College. Hayes believed that making higher education affordable for many would create economic opportunities for all.

GOVERNOR RUTHERFORD B. HAYES AND THE FOUNDING OF OSU

Governor Hayes, a Republican, signed the Cannon Act and confided to his diary: "The Agricultural and Mechanical College Bill passed yesterday. I am satisfied that an institution of great importance to the State may be founded under it if the management is in good hands." However, the *Cleveland Herald* referred to the passage of the Cannon Act and its creation of an independent college and declared ominously: "The [land-grant] fund, so far as answering the object intended by Congress, might as well have been cast into Lake Erie or the Ohio River.

We make the prophecy that time will prove the College to be a failure and the fund to have been wasted."[9]

Within two months, Hayes had selected nineteen nominees for the board of trustees and delivered the names to the Senate for confirmation. To make the board as bipartisan as he could, Hayes tried to choose Democrats as trustees from districts represented by Democrats and Republicans where Republicans predominated. Twelve of the nineteen had been in the legislature. Seven had been lawyers. Four were members of the State Board of Agriculture, including Norton S. Townshend, who had been so supportive of scientific farming and the Morrill Act specifically. Fewer than half of the board had attended a college, a fact not surprising when success in life seemed unrelated to academic credentials.[10]

1.9 Joseph Sullivant, a prominent citizen of Columbus and a son of the man who surveyed Franklin County, was a member of the first board of trustees of the university and had a profound influence in locating the new institution in Columbus and in shaping its curriculum. Sullivant believed that the land-grant university should have a broad curriculum not limited principally to agriculture and engineering.

Politics and constituencies aside, Hayes had his own ideas for what the new college should be. A graduate of Kenyon and of Harvard, Hayes was a well-educated man who had an expansive or "liberal" philosophy of education. Evidence of his preference for a comprehensive college near an urban area was his effort to recruit Joseph Sullivant of Columbus. Sullivant was a son of Lucas Sullivant, the first surveyor of Franklin County. Educated at Ohio University and at Center College in Danville, Kentucky, Joseph Sullivant took an interest in agricultural education and joined the state board of agriculture. Since he was known for being outspoken and for having such liberal views, Sullivant's nomination stirred so much opposition in the Ohio Senate that he asked Hayes to withdraw his name. Hayes refused and persuaded Sullivant to allow the Senate to confirm him.

Another controversial appointment that Hayes supported was the outspoken Ralph Leete. He had been a critic of Miami and Ohio Universities and took a dim view of colleges and professors in Ohio generally: "The State of Ohio is now the center of population of the United States. There are no intellects of high order in her many colleges nor in any manner connected with her educational system. . . . Most of the professors of our literary institutions are bitter sectaries and not infrequently narrow-minded country politicians. As a class they are generally incompetent."[11]

Hayes had helped to pass the Cannon Act and hosted the first meeting of the board of trustees in his office on May 11, 1870. Although Governor Hayes was not

---

9. Cope, xii.
10. Kinnison, 38.
11. Cope, x–xi.

1.10 *Facing High Street, Sullivant Hall memorializes the contributions of Joseph Sullivant in the founding of the university.*

a member of the board, he was invited to attend its meetings and, in the words of one account, "He was deeply interested in the location and organization of the College, and on many important matters the Board had the aid of his wise counsels."[12]

DECISION: THE PLACE

At their first meeting in Governor Hayes's office, the trustees charged its executive committee to prepare an address to the people of Ohio. In it, the board of trustees was to state as clearly as possible the purposes and wants of the college and to ask for offers of sites and financial support. A site of at least three hundred acres was required. Curiously, the Cannon Act itself had stipulated only a minimum of one hundred acres. In all likelihood, this greater acreage appeased those on the board who would have preferred a more emphatically agricultural purpose for the new college

1.11 *Valentine B. Horton was president of the first board of trustees. A lawyer, successful businessman, and three-term member of Congress, he was a commanding figure on the board.*

12. Cope, 47.

Six days after the meeting, Joseph Sullivant of Columbus tried to rally the citizens of Franklin County to bid for the new college. On May 17, even before the executive committee had drafted its address, Sullivant issued appeals in newspapers to the citizens of Franklin County and asked for a meeting of all interested parties, especially the county's farmers and mechanics: "The advantages accruing to any county which secures this institution are so obvious that I need not here present any arguments to prove them. It is not proper that the citizens of Franklin County should move immediately in behalf of their own interests? Shall we, by indifference or supineness, neglect this opportunity, and permit the superior liberality and enterprise of another county to care away a prize which we can and ought to preserve for ourselves?"[13]

On June 4, two weeks after the energetic Sullivant made his appeal, the executive committee of the trustees issued its request for proposals. Besides the requirement of three hundred acres, the announcement encouraged counties to offer more than the minimum of $100,000 that the board required. Because the Morrill Act forbade the use of the land-grant endowment for land or buildings, the trustees looked for a county that offered generous amounts of land and money. The deadline for the offers was September 1, because the Cannon Act required a decision in October.

The appeal from the board drew only four proposals—Clark, Champaign, Franklin, and Montgomery counties. One historian who studied the votes in the four counties pointed out that in areas in which farmers predominated, attendance at elections to vote on bond issues was low and in some areas farmers voted against the bonds. Seemingly, the State Board of Agriculture and the strongest advocates of an agriculturally focused curriculum for the Ohio Agriculture and Mechanical College failed to stir enthusiasm among a great number of actual farmers.[14]

On September 6, 1870, the board assembled in the rooms of the State Board of Agriculture to review proposals received from three counties and then a late fourth. Voters in Champaign and in Clark County had offered $200,000 in 8 percent county bonds while Franklin County offered $300,000 in 7 percent bonds and private subscriptions of cash at $28,000. Rather than decide from the proposals alone, the trustees resolved to visit likely sites.

Before adjourning, however, the board requested Mr. Sullivant to "read an elaborate paper" in which he presented his views about the purposes of an agricultural and mechanical college. Joseph Sullivant, who had given the purpose of the Ohio Agriculture and Mechanical College much thought, listed ten departments which should make up the organization of the college, even though the Cannon Act required only four. Sullivant added mathematics and physics, general and applied chemistry, geology, mining and metallurgy, zoology and veterinary science, botany, horticulture, and vegetable physiology, and modern and ancient languages and a

---

13. James E. Pollard, *History of The Ohio State University: The Story of Its First Seventy-Five Years, 1873–1948* (Columbus: The Ohio State University Press, 1952), 9.
14. Kinnison, 43.

department of political economy and civil polity to the needed curriculum.[15] While no action followed Sullivant's address, his ideas of a broad and diverse curriculum for the new college would reappear later.

On September 20, the board, which had visited sites in four counties, reassembled to hear proposals. Montgomery County, which had bid late, had made the highest offer, a donation of $400,000, while Franklin County had the second highest bid of $300,000. The trustees spent the entire day as each side presented the merits of their proposal. Advocates for Franklin County argued that Montgomery County was not central enough to satisfy the Cannon Act. Supporters of Montgomery County pleaded their case while others spoke for Champaign and for Clark counties.

Franklin County had several advantages. Clearly, it was geographically the most central. Also, it could be the most accessible of the counties because of its railroad connections to all parts of Ohio; two of the railroads already serving Franklin County offered $28,000 if the site were there. Another argument in favor of Franklin County was that the new college could make a better case of support from the legislature if it were near the state capital. Trustee Ralph Leete was in favor of not only placing the college in Franklin County but having its main building in Columbus, near the State Library.[16] In addition James Comly, editor of the influential newspaper, *Ohio State Journal*, in Columbus, who had called for a university with a broad curriculum, spoke and wrote in favor of Franklin County.[17]

Finally, on September 21, the board reassembled to choose a county for the new college. At the first ballot, the vote was so indecisive that the board resolved to settle the issue by conducting a series of ballots. After each ballot, the county with the fewest votes fell from consideration. Twenty-six ballots later, only the offer from Franklin County survived after a close contest with Clark County, which had a large delegation that included the leading industrialists of the community. The most agricultural of the counties, Champaign, had been the first to lose. On October 12, when the trustees turned to considering several sites in Franklin County, a resolution to reconsider selecting Franklin County failed, 10 to 5.

Next, the trustees voted to use the bid and donation from Franklin County to buy the Neil Farm from Robert Neil, a tract that had formally belonged to the family patriarch William Neil. (The Neil family, for whom Neil Avenue, which runs through the campus is named, became prominent in Columbus by investments first in stagecoaches and a hotel and then in real estate.) This transaction came after four votes, as some of the trustees voted for another site in nearby Worthington. In the voting for the Neil Farm and for Franklin County, Rutherford B. Hayes may have asserted some quiet influence; years later, Hayes revealed that he took credit for locating the college where it is today: "If anybody was its founder, in the words of

---

15. Cope, 37.

16. Minutes of the Board of Trustees of the Ohio Agricultural and Mechanical College, January 5, 1871 (hereinafter Board minutes).

17. Kinnison, 41.

Governor Corwin, 'a great part of it I am which.' The land I worked so hard to get, now in the city of Columbus, is already worth twice as much as the land grant fund, and will be in a few years worth millions."

1.12 Handwritten notes by Joseph Sullivant concerning the curriculum and organization of the Ohio Agricultural and Mechanical College

DECISION: THE CURRICULUM

Today, The Ohio State University offers an extraordinary range of educational opportunities. In 2008, the university taught some 12,000 courses, 167 undergraduate majors, 130 programs leading to masters degrees and another 103 to doctorates. In 1870, no one who supported the founding of this land-grant college could have envisioned that the new college would have so broad an educational mission. Some thought that the Ohio Agricultural and Mechanical College should focus primarily on teaching agriculture and engineering.

Others disagreed. They argued that the federal Morrill Act that created the land-grant colleges significantly stated " . . . the leading objects shall be without excluding other scientific and classical studies, and including military tactics, to teach such branches of learning as are related to agriculture and the mechanic arts. . . . " The Cannon Act that established the Ohio Agricultural and Mechanical College simply quoted the Morrill Act: "The leading object shall be, without excluding other scientific and classical studies, and including military tactics, to teach such branches of learning as are related to agricultural and mechanic arts."

How much of the curriculum should be "liberal" and how much should focus on "practical education"? One outcome of the debate led to the change of the institution's name in 1878.

Soon after deciding the site of the college, the trustees settled the matter of its educational character and the courses it would offer. Discussions about the curriculum had already taken place at the first meeting of the trustees on May 11, 1870. At its meeting on January 5, 1871, Dr. Townshend argued, "That the course of instruction in the Ohio Agricultural and Mechanical College should embrace not only the sciences that especially pertain to agriculture and the mechanical arts, but whatever practical instruction will make the labor of every industrial class more successful and elevating." Townshend thought the new college should do what other colleges in the state did not, namely, provide education directly related to the agricultural, mechanical, and vocational needs of Ohio.

Trustee Thomas Jones countered that the new institution should not be primarily a technical institution, but should include all the features of a general and classical

1.13 A man who favored many social movements, including anti-slavery and women's rights, Norton S. Townshend was a relentless advocate for agricultural education. While serving as a member of the first board of trustees, his fellow trustees elected him as the first professor of agriculture in 1873. He remained at OSU until his death in 1895. His daughters, Harriet and Alice, were the first to enroll at OSU in 1873.

education. Similarly, Valentine Horton, president of the trustees, commented that the board could not exclude the classics because the Morrill Act stipulated that they should be in the curriculum. In the end, Horton argued that the purpose should be "to educate American citizens—not farmer's servants, as in England; nor as

1.14 Shown here as it looked in 1906, Townshend Hall, which is on Neil Avenue near the Thompson Library, memorializes the contributions of Professor Norton Townshend

machines, as in Prussia; but for every kind of life. From the first, the new college should be of the highest character."[18]

Joseph Sullivant followed by referring to the model of ten departments that he had proposed at the first meeting on May 11. Sullivant explained that if finances allowed, he would teach "all that was worth knowing," but his priority was to teach that "which seemed best calculated to fit our pupils for the practical duties of life. What the farmer and mechanic needed, like all other men, was good education; and in proportion as that was general and liberal, would they be best fitted for their special vocations."

Sullivant's words and plan carried much weight with the board. When it resumed discussion on January 6, 1871, a special committee of the board returned "after only a few minutes" of deliberation and approved Sullivant's proposal of ten departments of instruction. The board as a whole agreed, with only one dissenting vote. Years later, Sullivant would defend the choice of a broad curriculum for the land-grant college by writing, "Trained and educated minds ever have, and ever will take precedence over ignorance and limited knowledge, in all the affairs of life, and it is a mistaken notion that a narrow and technical education is all that is required in the industrial pursuits of men."[19]

That the trustees accepted Sullivant's plan so quickly suggests that they shared a vision about the mission of the Ohio Agricultural and Mechanical College. Sullivant himself, in presenting his educational plan for the second time, noted that

---

18. Board minutes, January 5, 1871.
19. Pollard, 18.

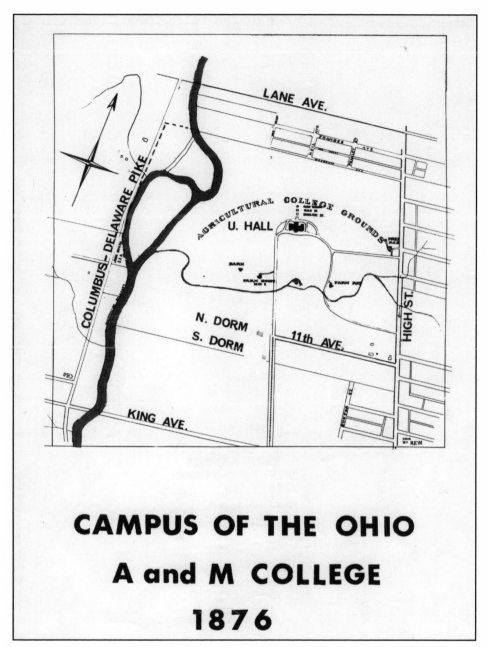

CAMPUS OF THE OHIO

A and M COLLEGE

1876

1.15 Campus map 1876

he was "gratified that, at last, there would be no substantial difference amongst us, as to the character to be impressed upon our institution."[20] In all likelihood, many of the members of the board itself, so carefully chosen by Governor Hayes, shared Sullivant's broad and inclusive educational outlook.

---

20. Board minutes, January 5, 1871.

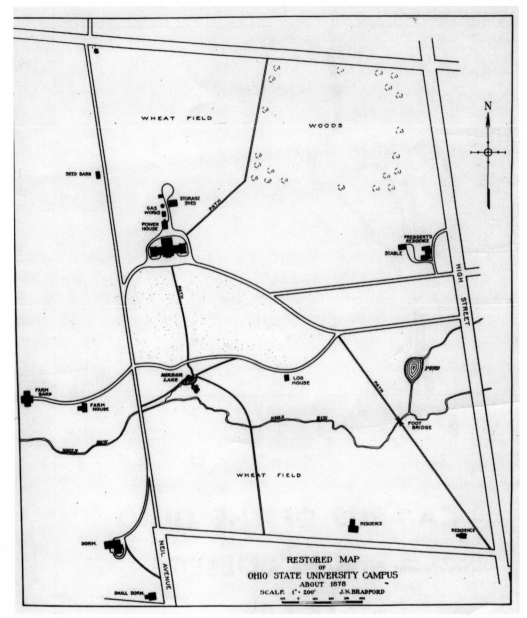

1.16 Campus map, ca. 1878

HIRING THE FIRST FACULTY

While there was agreement about the intellectual character of the new college—a broad curriculum that included the liberal arts—the board divided sharply on strategy. Specifically, should the college, with the richest endowment of any institution in Ohio, try to offer a broad curriculum from the beginning? On the other hand, should it focus on agriculture and mechanical engineering first and add other subjects later? These were questions not only of educational mission but of practicality,

OHIO AGRICULTURAL AND MECHANICAL COLLEGE.

1.17 Engraving of University Hall 1873

and they were significant. Colleges and universities had failed because they had exhausted their financial assets. Ohio in Athens had closed its doors from 1845 to 1848; Miami in Oxford would do so from 1873 to 1885.[21]

On January 2, 1873 the board voted on which chairs of instruction to fill and then began recruiting faculty for the opening of classes in September. Its committee on faculty, which included Sullivant, recommended that only six of the ten chairs in Sullivant's original proposal be filled in the first year of the college.

Norton Townshend moved to amend the report and drop the professors of English and of languages, modern and ancient. He feared the college was trying to do too much too early and that the agricultural and vocational programs would suffer from the dispersion of financial resources. As recorded in the minutes, "A warm discussion followed" and the board divided eight to seven in favor of filling those positions. Sullivant had won and Townshend lost, but both men would continue to work together.

DECISION: CHOOSING A PRESIDENT

At first, the trustees looked to political figures as candidates for president. In 1871, some of the trustees invited General Jacob D. Cox, who had been governor of Ohio

---

21. Thomas N. Hoover, *History of The Ohio State University: Vol. II: Continuation of the Narrative from 1910 to 1925* (Columbus: The Ohio State University Press, 1926), 92; Walter Havighurst, *The Miami Years, 1809–1959* (New York: Putnams, 1958), 133.

from 1866 to 1868, to be a candidate, but Cox declined.[22] Ohio Governor Edward F. Noyes (1872–1874) encouraged trustees to consider a former U.S. Senator, James Patterson of New Hampshire. Patterson had been a professor at Dartmouth College, where Governor Noyes had been a student and had befriended him. On October 9, 1872 in the governor's office, the trustees voted for Patterson, ten to one over Norton Townshend, the candidate favored by the State Agricultural Board. Patterson visited the campus and seemed interested in accepting. By April, however, a national scandal had tainted president-elect Patterson. As a senator, he had bought stock in the Credit Mobilier, the construction company of the Union Pacific Railroad. When newspapers reported that some senators had received stock in the construction company as an incentive and reward for their support of subsidies for the Union Pacific Railroad, a torrent of public outrage followed. Patterson therefore withdrew his candidacy.

Finally the trustees turned to Edward Orton, president of Antioch College. Previously, the trustees had offered Orton a professorship in geology an offer that Orton declined. After Patterson withdrew from consideration as president, the trustees again contacted Orton and renewed its offer of a professorship in geology, mining and metallurgy as well as the presidency. This time, Orton accepted.

THE FIRST FACULTY

Even before hiring a president, the trustees had selected the faculty at their meeting on January 1, 1873. Thomas Corwin Mendenhall, a teacher in the High School of Columbus and known to Joseph Sullivant as a member of the board of education, was to teach physics and mechanics. Sidney A. Norton of Cincinnati became professor of general and applied chemistry. Joseph Millikin of Hamilton, Ohio had charge of English and modern languages and literature, and W. G. Williams of Delaware was to teach ancient languages and literature.

An important appointment was that of trustee Norton Townshend, who became professor of agriculture. Although he failed in previous votes on the board, Townshend kept his faith in the future of the Ohio Agricultural and Mechanical College and accepted the offer to become its first professor of agriculture. There he remained for nearly nineteen years, until January of 1892. His decision to leave the board and accept their employment, which the trustees could end arbitrarily in this era before tenure, showed that the disagreements in the board happened in the context of a general consensus about the character of the new college.

In recruiting some faculty, the trustees faced both unexpected difficulties and opportunities. When W. G. Williams decided to remain at Ohio Wesleyan University, the trustees turned to John Henry Wright to teach ancient languages and literature. Finally, in the summer of 1873, the trustees had an unexpected opportu-

---

22. Board minutes, March 8, 1871.

1.18 Shown here is the first faculty of OSU, 1873–1874. At the center is President Edward Orton, who also taught geology, mining, metallurgy, and mineralogy. Moving from the top and clockwise, Professor Thomas C. Mendenhall taught physics. Joseph Millikin gave instruction in English and modern languages and literature; Norton Townshend took responsibility for agriculture, while John H. Wright taught ancient languages. In the lower left, Albert Tuttle was hired in 1874 for anatomy and zoology. Sidney Norton taught chemistry while Robert W. McFarland taught mathematics and engineering.

nity to add a department of mathematics and engineering. Miami in Oxford, Ohio had closed because of financial circumstances and Robert W. McFarland became available.

Then, as now, it was difficult to generalize about faculty. At the twenty-fifth anniversary of the founding, Thomas Mendenhall recalled that they shared a common vision about a "new education." As Mendenhall described it,

1.19 *Shown in 1918 as a trustee of the Ohio State University, Professor Thomas Corwin Mendenhall had a distinguished career in physics. He served as the first professor of physics, from 1873 to 1884.*

This new education was one in which science should have its share, and in which observation and experiment should displace time-honored methods of instruction, not only with scientific subjects but with all others as well. A small number of American colleges and universities were turning

1.20 *Built in 1904, the Physics Building, which sits on the south side of the Oval, was named in honor of Professor Mendenhall in 1925.*

their faces in this direction, including, very naturally, the newly created institutions which owe their existence to the Land-grant Act of 1862. The men who were chosen to constitute the first faculty of the Ohio Agricultural and Mechanical College were already known to be warm advocates of the new education and their selection was doubtless due in large measure to this fact . . . they were united in their enthusiasm for the work and an overwhelming determination to win success.[23]

Critics of higher education, like Mendenhall, thought that learning in higher education should engage students in observing and in questioning. They believed that traditional instruction, as in Ohio's denominational colleges and at Ohio and Miami universities, focused only on passing on ancient knowledge as unquestioned facts and memorization as a means of disciplining the mind. Teaching and learning, by this method, which dated back to medieval times, required memorization and repetition of facts memorized, not discussion and questioning. The 1870s, however, were years of great intellectual excitement. People inspired by changes in science, especially the work of Charles Darwin, and in industry challenged traditional institutions and accepted views. Thus, it was argued by many that colleges and universities should emphasize observation and experimentation and a general spirit of inquiry in all disciplines.[24] This was the spirit and outlook that inspired Thomas Mendenhall and others of the first faculty. As Mendenhall recalled,

> The actual possession of knowledge was not the chief characteristic of the members of the first faculty; indeed some of them would hardly have taken high rank in this respect. It was not their love of learning, but rather their *loving to learn* [sic] which was their prominent intellectual trait. In other words, the spirit of investigation dominated them. They were disposed to seek the laws of nature in the various phenomena in which nature concealed them, rather than in the tomes of a library.[25]

This was particularly fortunate because the new college had few books and would develop its library very slowly.

THE OPENING

Although the new college would become a university of international stature, its beginnings were modest. University Hall had not been fully completed by the autumn of 1873 and a dormitory was far off schedule. Although the campus was not finished as planned, the faculty had been hired and notices had been posted in newspapers announcing the start of classes. The Trustees decided to enroll students

---

23. Mendenhall, Thomas C., ed., *History of The Ohio State University, Vol. III: Addresses and Proceedings of the Semicentennial Celebration, October 13–16, 1920* (Columbus: The Ohio State University Press, 1922), 191–92.

24. Kinnison, 69–70.

25. Mendenhall, *Semi-Centennial Celebration*, 190–91.

at the Ohio Agriculture and Mechanical College on September 17, 1873 as planned.

The registration book for opening day bears the names of twenty-four students who presented themselves as candidates for admission. All were from Ohio and nine were from Columbus, including the three children of Professor Norton Townshend. Even the Columbus residents had difficulty in reaching the old Neil farm and its one college building because the only road, known as Worthington Pike (later High Street), was "hopelessly worn out, deeply guttered, and much of the time perilously deep with mud."[26] In the following days, more students appeared to apply for admission and by the end of the first academic year enrollment had reached ninety.

The opening of the college attracted little public attention. The *Cleveland Leader* reported, somewhat erroneously, "The Agricultural College began its first term yesterday, with twenty-five students in attendance. One of these is a young lady from this city." The *Columbus Dispatch* reported on September 18 that "They say a small beginning makes a good ending."[27] One reason for the lack of attention was that the day after September 17, the United States entered one of the worst financial periods in its history, with the Panic of 1873. Another was that the new college had not arranged for any speeches or receptions to draw attention to the occasion because of the uncertainty of the date of the opening.

The lack of journalistic scrutiny may have been fortunate because much was

1.21 Note in this photograph of the library in University Hall in 1889 the number of women students, the formal attire, and the card catalog in the center.

---

26. Cope, 45.
27. Pollard, 31.

1.22 This photograph shows students of the first dormitory, the North Dormitory on Neil Avenue near W. 11th. Originally, the trustees had expected that the dormitory would be available when the college opened in 1873. However, delays in planning and construction caused the North Dorm to open in 1874. The delay meant that some students had to live briefly in University Hall. In 1908, the North Dorm was razed.

not in readiness. One student remembered that on opening day the roof had not been completed, the inner doors were not hung, and the floor of the lecture-room chapel had not even been started: "in short, the noise of the saw and plane of the carpenters, and the rattle of the plumber's hammer were heard daily, if not hourly, for months after the opening of the school."[28] Professor Mendenhall remembered that the one building was " . . . in the midst of a muddy field, surrounded by the noise, dirt and confusion of the unwillingly departing workmen. . . . As a lecture table, Mendenhall used a carpenter's bench and recalled that his dinner pail was the only piece of equipment available, which he attached to the ceiling of the room for use in illustrating principles in physics."[29]

---

28. Pollard, 33.
29. Pollard, 32.

1.23 *Completed in 1873, University Hall served as the only classroom building, the office building, the library, even as the dormitory for some students and faculty.*

The inauguration of President Edward Orton did not take place until January 8, 1874, more than three months after classes began, and the setting was the Ohio Senate chamber, not University Hall. Edward Orton presented his views on the educational objectives of the new college. In doing so, Orton voiced themes that would continue as leitmotivs into the present. One was the goal to provide access to higher education for many at a time when tuition at private colleges made them inaccessible to all but the wealthy few. As he put it, "To the mass of the industrial classes of this State, the privileges of Harvard, Yale, or Vassar are practically as inaccessible as those of Cambridge or Heidelberg."

Another theme was breadth of educational opportunity. In Orton's words, "The farmer's or mechanic's son is not obliged to sign away his liberty when he enters the doors of this institution. If when he comes to himself under the genial influences of culture, he finds capacity and aptitude for serving the world best in law, theology, or medicine, he is violating no obligation, expressed or implied, by using the discipline and knowledge here attained as an equipment for any one of these professions."

Finally, Orton voiced the views of his faculty that education at the new land-grant institution would be different, stressing observation and the practical application of knowledge. Rather than rely on memory and reading alone, the student

Ohio Agricultural and Mechanical College.

Faculty Records.

I.

Sept. 17th., 1873. Wednesday. Minutes of the meeting of the Faculty.

The meeting was called by the President, and held in his room at the College, at about 3 o'clock P.M.

On motion Assist. Profr. Wright was appointed Secretary of the Faculty for the ensuing term.

Present were: the President; Dr. Townshend; Professors MacFarland, Norton, Millikin, Mendenhall, and Assist. Profr. Wright. Jas. Sullivant Esq., of the Exec. Com. of the Board of Trustees was present as a visitor.

After a discussion participated in by all the members of the Faculty, the following provisional arrangement for hours & classes was made.

1. That there be one daily session; from 8 to 1, or 9 to 2 o'clock.

2. The following particulars.

Provisional Programme Names.	9. A.M	10. AM	11. AM	12. M		3. PM
Pres. Orton						
Dr. Townshend						Agriculture
Prof. McFarland	El. Algebra	Trigonometry		Adv. Algebra		
" Norton				Chemistry		
" Millikin	German	Ele. English		Adv. English		
" Mendenhall			Adv. Physics	Ele. Physics		
Assist. Profr. Wright	Latin		Greek			

In conversation subsequent, the Faculty

1.24 *Minutes for the first faculty meeting of The Ohio Agricultural and Mechanical College*

must be "brought face to face, as far as possible, with the facts and principles with which he deals. His own eye must see, and not another's." In contrast to the traditional teaching that depended upon memory and mental drill, Orton declared that land grant colleges must teach " . . . in a truly scientific way—by induction, by experiment—instead of in the dogmatic method which has so largely prevailed hitherto."

FIVE YEARS LATER

By 1878, much had changed from the humble beginnings in September of 1873. Even the name of Ohio Agricultural and Mechanical College had been changed, to The Ohio State University. Although Orton had favored the change as more reflective of the broad scope of education on the campus, the actual initiative came from a legislator, State Senator George W. Wilson of Madison County.[30] The same act of 1878 also changed the number of trustees for a third time to seven, which endured until 1963, when the board added two members. (Since then, the state legislature has made two significant changes to OSU's board of trustees. In 1989, it added two nonvoting members to the board; in 2006, the legislature raised the total number of trustees to seventeen.)

The campus had changed also. Enrollment had reached one hundred and ninety-eight from fifty-two counties of Ohio.[31] The faculty, who had grown to twelve in number, taught in fourteen departments, including military science and tactics. Students had moved out of University Hall and into two dormitories. Within a year, some academic departments would also move out of University Hall into more specialized buildings, beginning with engineering, which moved to a new building in 1879.[32]

In June 1878, President Orton presided over the first commencement, a class of six, and gave the graduation address in the chapel, the largest room, in University Hall. Entitling his address "The Liberal Education of the Industrial Class," Orton repeated the themes of his inaugural. The industrial classes were almost everyone, the new education was scientific in character and higher education for the public was a new undertaking. Orton concluded " . . . it is to public education that we must look for the chief power in welding and unifying the discordant elements of our national life, and of that public education, the State, properly expanded and equipped is the summit and the crown."

By 1878 the university had fixed an identity for itself, including what would be an enduring name and other symbols, such as colors and seal. Its first graduates would be harbingers for many generations of students. By 2007, OSU's alumni, living and dead, numbered more than 550,000. However, the university of 1878 bore little likeness to the mission statement adopted by OSU in 1992: "The Ohio State has as its mission the attainment of international distinction in education,

---

30. *History of The Ohio State University,* vol. 1: 107–8.
31. "Annual report for 1878 of the Board of Trustees of The Ohio State University," 16.
32. *Ringing Grooves of Change* (Columbus: The Ohio State University, Division of Campus Planning, 1970), 12.

1.25 Shown here is the first graduating class of 1878. Members of this class desired ribbons with which to wrap their diplomas. A committee of students first selected orange and black as colors. After discovering that these colors belonged to Princeton, they then selected scarlet and gray. Following graduation, members returned in 1879 and formed the OSU Alumni Association.

scholarship and public service." Even the goal of education for the public masses articulated by Orton in 1874 and again in 1878 did not include any people of color (even though a group of African Americans in Columbus had championed Joseph Sullivant's call for a bid from Franklin County to host the new college) and very few women.[33] The founding was done; the future would be the work of generations of trustees, presidents, faculty, staff, students and alumni.

---

33. *History of The Ohio State University*, vol. 1: 22.

CHAPTER TWO

THE PRESIDENTS OF OSU

We are looking for a man of fine appearance, of commanding presence, one who will impress the public; he must be a fine speaker at public assemblies; he must be a great scholar and a great teacher; he must be a preacher, also, as some think; he must be a man of winning manners; he must have tact so that he can get along with and govern the faculty; he must be popular with the students; he must also be a man of business training, a man of affairs; and he must be a great administrator. Gentlemen, there is no such man."[1]

    —Rutherford B. Hayes when OSU was searching for a president in 1892

---

1. Alexis Cope, *History of The Ohio State University: Vol. 1: 1870–1910* (Columbus: The Ohio State University Press, 1920), 158.

MORE THAN A hundred years later, a modern search committee could add several requirements to this already lengthy list. The ideal candidate should have a talent for courting private donors; for representing the university to governmental agencies; for advancing cultural and racial diversity; and for inspiring winning athletic programs which recruit young people who excel as athletes, students, and citizens. Finally, a president should be equally impressive in many settings, from commencements to small parties.

Selecting a president has always been a momentous decision, one made by the board of trustees. OSU's presidents have shaped the history of the university; portraits, histories, and buildings memorialize their service and contributions. However, the process of recruiting and choosing has evolved. The modern custom of a search committee that represents constituencies of the university community is a relatively recent innovation. In May of 1971, President Novice Fawcett, at the request of the board, developed procedures to select his successor. Fawcett put together a search committee that included trustees, faculty, a dean, students, nonteaching staff, the chair of the Development Fund, the president of the alumni association, and the past chair of the board of trustees.[2] This has served as a model for the present day. Previously, the trustees alone had conducted a search and made the final selection.

Despite the lofty expectations from a modern president, the office has evolved gradually in gaining administrative authority over OSU. Not until the administration of William Oxley Thompson (1899–1925) did the office of president at OSU achieve its modern significance. In his first year as president, Thompson persuaded the trustees that the president, with a trustee, the secretary, two members of the faculty, and two from the College of Law were "to have charge of all matters presented to the incoming legislature in which the university may be interested." In 1909 the trustees rewrote their bylaws and defined the president as "the executive head of the University."[3] Previously, presidents of OSU had been first among the faculty, taught classes, met with faculty in curricular matters, and regulated student life as best they could. Meanwhile, the board of trustees and its secretary managed the university, monitored its finances, and distributed budgetary resources.

Whether as chief executive or chief of the faculty, harmonious relations with the trustees have always been critical to the tenure and effectiveness of any president of OSU. Typically, governors of Ohio have not consulted with OSU presidents when appointing new trustees. Some trustees of OSU, such as Rutherford B. Hayes, Julius Stone, John Bricker, and Leslie Wexner, have had social, financial, and political importance that rivaled and even exceeded that of the president. Two presidents— Harold Enarson (1972–1981) and Edward Jennings (1981–1990)—timed their own

---

2. Paul Underwood, *History of The Ohio State University, Vol. X: The Enarson Years, 1972–1981* (Columbus: The Ohio State University, 1985), 10; John B. Gabel, *History of the Ohio State University, Vol. XI: The Jennings Years, 1981–1990* (Columbus: The Ohio State University, 1992), 7–8; Francis P. Weisenburger, *History of The Ohio State University, Vol. IX: The Fawcett Years, 1956–1972* (Columbus: The Ohio State University, 1975), 234.

3. James E. Pollard, *History of The Ohio State University: The Story of Its First Seventy-Five years, 1873–1948* (Columbus: The Ohio State University Press, 1952), 204.

retirement to take place when the last board member who had participated in their hiring retired.

From 1873 to 2009, the university has had thirteen presidents (E. Gordon Gee has had two administrations). All but one was male. Four (Edward Orton, Walter Quincy Scott, William Henry Scott, and William Oxley Thompson) were ordained ministers; a fact explained by the circumstances that ministers were among the most educated people in the nineteenth century. Four presidents were attorneys (James Canfield, George Rightmire, Howard Bevis, and E. Gordon Gee) and all but four (William Henry Scott, Rightmire, Bevis, Novice Fawcett, and Karen Holbrook) attained the presidency after service as president at other institutions of higher education. Only two (Rightmire and Fawcett) had been students at OSU, and only George Rightmire reached the presidency after serving as a professor and a dean at OSU. None of the OSU presidents had careers in politics, before or after their administrations. Finally, the presidents remained in office at OSU an average of 10.75 years (a figure inflated by the lengthy tenures of three presidents—Thompson for twenty-six years and Fawcett and Bevis for sixteen years each). By comparison, Walter Quincy Scott had the briefest administration, only two years.

EDWARD ORTON (1873–1881)

Born on March 9, 1829 in Deposit, New York, the first president of OSU was the son of a religious family. Both his father and his uncle were Presbyterian ministers and Edward Orton himself sought a career in the ministry at first. He attended and graduated from Hamilton College in New York in 1848 and later attended Lane Theological Seminary in Cincinnati.

Orton became interested in science, which brought controversy to his life. Charles Darwin's *Origins of Species* excited

2.1 President Edward Orton (1873–1881)

his appetite for science and competed with his ambitions for the ministry. Orton withdrew from Lane Theological Seminary to study chemistry and botany for six months at Harvard's Lawrence Scientific School, but then returned to religious studies at the Andover Theological Seminary. He was ordained as a Presbyterian minister in 1858.

2.2 *Built in 1856 as part of the Neil Farm, the first presidential residence stood at 1873 North High Street, near the current location of Mershon Auditorium. It housed OSU's presidents until 1926, and it was torn down in 1949.*

After a brief career in the ministry, Orton turned to science again, first as chair of natural science in the New York State Normal School at Albany, where he also led a Sunday school class, although some controversial remarks about religion and science and his interest in Charles Darwin's *The Origin of Species* led to his resignation.[4] Next, Orton accepted an offer to become a principal of an academy, at Chester, New York, where he befriended Austin Craig, pastor of a nearby church. Years later, in 1865, Craig served as acting president of Antioch College and offered Orton the leadership of Antioch's preparatory department. A year later, Orton became professor of geology, botany, and zoology and then advanced to become president of Antioch College in 1872.

At Antioch, Orton attracted attention in Columbus. Governor Rutherford B. Hayes, who had been a leader in establishing the Ohio Agricultural and Mechanical College, had appointed Professor Orton as an assistant in the second geological survey of Ohio in 1869. In 1870, trustees of the new Ohio Agricultural and Mechanical College first offered Orton a professorship in geology, mining, and metallurgy, which he declined. However, Orton did accept a second offer from the trustees as president and a professor of geology and mineralogy. Orton served as president until 1881, but continued as professor of geology and as state geologist.

Orton had a profound influence during the formative years of the university,

---

4. Pollard, 20–21.

2.3 Now the Kuhn Honors and Scholars House, this building on West 12th was the home for Presidents Rightmire, Bevis, and Fawcett.

which were filled with both hope and controversy. After all, land-grant colleges were still new, and the Morrill Act of 1862 as well as the Cannon Act of 1870 gave trustees much discretion in curriculum. Articulate and forceful, Orton spoke of the land-grant college as a turning point in the history of higher education. As president, Orton advocated for a broad curriculum beyond agriculture and engineering, and was not dismayed when the state legislature changed the name from the Ohio Agricultural and Mechanical College to The Ohio State University. Some in the State Board of Agriculture and in the legislature, to put it mildly, were disappointed by this decision because it seemed to diminish the prominence of agriculture and engineering as priorities for the university.

Periodically, the trustees and the president had conflicts. Orton disagreed when the trustees dropped algebra from the admissions test in 1877. Orton saw the matter as one that faculty should decide; trustees felt that dropping algebra would make access easier for potential students. A particularly vexing matter that stoked passions for several years was that the trustees wanted the president and faculty to require students to attend chapel services on campus. Orton and many of the faculty knew that such exercises were common at many institutions, but thought them inappropriate for the new and nondenominational land-grant college.

As a testimonial for his president and colleague, Thomas Mendenhall, one of the original faculty, recalled, "As a teacher [Orton] was most inspiring. His literary and linguistic powers were unusual and he easily made any topic attractive, even to

2.4 First and foremost, Edward Orton was a geologist of prominence, as well as the first president of OSU and a minister. In this photograph from the 1890s, Professor Orton is taking students on a tour of geological samples displayed in Orton Hall.

2.5 A photograph from the 1880s depicts Professor Orton with students on a geological field trip. Note the rock picks and picnic baskets.

the dull. From hundreds of his pupils comes the testimony that to him they owe the first quickening of their intellectual life, the earliest revelations of their own moral obligations and responsibilities."[5] In 1891, OSU's trustees honored Orton by naming the new geological museum in his honor. Edward Orton died in 1899.

WALTER QUINCY SCOTT (1881–1883)

At thirty-six years of age, Walter Quincy Scott was not only the youngest of the presidents but also the most controversial. Born in 1845 in Dayton, Ohio, the sixth of thirteen children, Walter Q. Scott's father was a lawyer and a leader in the community. At eleven years old, the family moved to Fairfield, Iowa. Six years later, as a seventeen-year-old, young Walter enlisted in the Fourth Iowa Cavalry, took part in General Sherman's campaign through Georgia, and served until the end of the war in 1865.

Following his military service, Scott entered Lafayette College and graduated at the head of his class. So outstanding was his scholarship that Scott continued at Lafayette, first as a tutor and then as professor. Later, he studied theology at the Union Theological Seminary in New York City, and in 1874 became pastor of the Arch Street Presbyterian Church in Philadelphia. In 1878, Scott returned to Ohio as professor of mental and moral Philosophy and political economy at Wooster College.[6] By one account, "Doctor Scott was a man of great personal charm; an eloquent speaker and possessed of such accomplishments, scholarly and otherwise, that he speedily became popular with the student body and with the people of the city of Columbus with whom he came in intimate contact."[7]

2.6 *Walter Quincy Scott*

Scott's credentials as a minister and as a professor attracted OSU's trustees. According to Secretary Alex Cope, the selection of Dr. Walter Quincy Scott was "due to the fact that he was an ordained minister of the Gospel whose orthodoxy, although at one time under suspicion, had been attested by the result of an investigation and 'trial' during his connection with another institution of learning." Unrelenting criticism by other colleges in Ohio pressured OSU's trustees to find another president who was also a minister. In addition, Edward Orton had resisted the

5. Pollard, 25; Thomas C. Mendenhall, ed., *History of The Ohio State University, Vol. II: Continuation of the Narrative from 1910 to 1925* (Columbus: The Ohio State University Press, 1926), 195.

6. Pollard, 74–75

7. Cope, 80

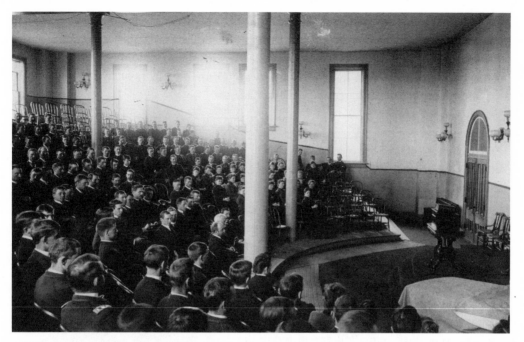

2.7 *Chapel service, as shown here in University Hall in the 1880s, when it was daily and compulsory, was a flashpoint between students, faculty, and trustees.*

wishes of the trustees to have mandatory attendance at chapel services, a practice common to other colleges and universities.[8]

However, Walter Quincy Scott's views and his outspokenness soon alarmed the trustees. His inaugural address agitated some in the audience when he agreed with Charles Darwin that "Man's origin must be pushed back to a place as little known as it is remote."[9] As a public speaker, Scott seemed too vigorous and too radical. His favorable remark about Henry George, author of *Progress and Poverty,* which proposed using tax policies for social as well as economic development, alienated people with more traditional economic and political philosophies.[10]

Meanwhile Scott disappointed the trustees in the pressing, albeit controversial, matter of daily and compulsory attendance at the chapel in University Hall. Supported by the faculty's reluctance to engage a secular institution in religious exercises, Scott did not carry out the board's wishes.[11] As a result of the president's intransigency, the trustees sought and received an opinion from Ohio's attorney general that trustees had the authority to require chapel attendance. Still, the president and the faculty resisted.

The delays in compulsory attendance at chapel, the controversial lectures about Henry George and political economy, and the seeming lack of responsiveness to the

8. Cope, vol. 1: 80

9. William Kinnison, *Building Sullivant's Pyramid: An Administrative History of The Ohio State University, 1870–1907* (Columbus: The Ohio State University Press, 1970), 91.

10. Kinnison, 97.

11. Kinnison, 92–93.

trustees brought a quick end to the presidency of Dr. Scott. On June 18, 1883, when the trustees considered renewal of faculty appointments for the next year, normally a routine event, Scott failed of reelection. In the public controversy that followed, the trustees explained that Scott had not been renewed because he had neglected to carry out the expressed wish of the trustees, that he had promulgated unsound and dangerous doctrines of political economy, and that he lacked executive ability.[12]

After leaving OSU, Scott had a varied career, first as president of Phillips Exeter Academy in Massachusetts, at pastorates in New York and Pennsylvania, and at the Bible Teachers' Training School in New York City, where he taught church history and ethnic religions.[13] By 1909, the controversy at OSU had become a faint memory. The trustees awarded Scott the title of president emeritus and arranged for a portrait by George Bellows.

2.8 Although OSU does not have a building named in honor of the controversial President Walter Quincy Scott, it did commission George Bellows, noted artist and former student, to paint this portrait of him in 1912 to hang in the new Main Library that opened in 1913.

2.9 University president William Henry Scott (1883–1895)

WILLIAM HENRY SCOTT (1883–1895)

To succeed Walter Quincy Scott, the trustees found another Scott, William Henry Scott, who at the time was president of Ohio University. The son of a miller, Scott was born in 1840 in Athens County and graduated from Ohio University in 1862. In 1865, following study in the Methodist ministry, he became a pastor first in Chillicothe and then in Columbus. In 1869 Scott returned to Ohio University as professor of Greek. Three years later, in 1872, he became its president. He served

12. Pollard, 81.
13. Kinnison, 109.

2.10 *Scott Hall on West Campus is named in honor of President William Henry Scott.*

there for eleven years before accepting the invitation to serve as president of OSU first and then as its professor of philosophy.

Unlike his predecessor, the second Scott proved quiet, even timid, and had conservative points of view. Scott enforced the will of the trustees for compulsory daily service at chapel. Typically, the service included singing, some instrumental accompaniment, the reading of Scriptures, and a prayer.[14]

Scott had a more difficult time with students, who resented the dismissal of the first Scott. In Scott's first year as president, student behavior towards him was so rude that the faculty wrote a letter to the board and defended William Henry Scott.[15] Even as late as 1888, when Scott had been president for six years, students still expressed their dissatisfaction. When students of the senior class tried to pass a resolution calling for electing a new president, the faculty threatened to exclude them from commencement exercises.[16]

Despite his relative unpopularity among the students, the presidency of William Henry Scott continued for twelve years and was a period of stability, growth, and accomplishments. Unlike his predecessors, Scott had more opportunity to maintain good relations with the trustees. On July 26, 1883, the trustees resolved that OSU's president could attend all board meetings whenever his duties as "President of the Faculty" allowed.

14. Pollard, 86–87.
15. Pollard, 93.
16. Pollard, 93.

Scott's administration benefited also when in 1887, a commanding figure of significant political influence, Rutherford B. Hayes, joined the board. In 1895, after rejecting several previous efforts to resign as president, the trustees accepted Scott's resignation, although he continued as chair of philosophy for another fifteen years. In accepting his resignation, the board praised Scott: "For twelve years he has guided its [OSU's] development with faithfulness, patience, kindness, firmness, fairness, and broad and true sagacity. The qualities have borne fruit not only in a strong and united faculty, a large and enthusiastic student body, in increased appropriations and endowments from state and nation and in the beginnings of private munificence, but in every detail of the strong and healthy growth of this great institution in all its departments."[17]

JAMES H. CANFIELD, (1895–1899)

As OSU's fourth president, the university trustees selected an educator who was not a minister. Born in Delaware, Ohio, the birthplace of Rutherford B. Hayes, in 1847, James Canfield grew up in New York City where his father was rector of a church. He graduated from Williams College, worked in a construction firm for a railroad, and then studied law in Jackson, Michigan. While practicing law in St. Joseph, Michigan, Canfield became a member of the local school board, a service that sparked his lifelong interest in education. A former

2.11 James Canfield

faculty member at Williams helped Canfield in 1877 gain appointment to the University of Kansas in Lawrence. There he taught English, history, political science and civics. Despite the heavy teaching load, he published three books concerning taxation, rural opportunities for higher education, and local government. In 1891, Canfield accepted an offer to become chancellor of the University of Nebraska.

In 1894, OSU's trustees asked Canfield to accept the presidency. A significant exchange of letters followed, which described Canfield's views of the mission of a land grant university and the role of the president. In a letter of December 31, 1894, Canfield asked the trustees if OSU intended to become the leader of Ohio's public schools and declared that strengthening the public schools in the state should be

---

17. Board minutes, July 1, 1895.

2.12 *Built in 1940, Canfield Hall on West 11th Avenue served as a dormitory for women. President Canfield himself was an advocate for women in higher education, and so naming the building in his honor was fitting.*

a priority for the university. Also, Canfield wanted to know if OSU intended to be a balanced institution in which the humanities, languages, and literatures were as strong as the industrial or vocational side. Finally, Canfield asked, "Are you an institution thoroughly and heartily committed to coeducation in the broadest and truest sense of the word?" Thus, Canfield revealed himself to be a man of progressive views who was dedicated to coeducation and to leading an educationally ambitious university.[18]

In replying to each of Canfield's concerns, Alexis Cope, secretary of the board of trustees, attempted to reassure Canfield. Referring to the Morrill Act and its purposes, Cope noted, "of course you will have observed that there is a *narrow* [*sic*] and a *liberal* [*sic*] construction of this grant. Our Trustees have in practice favored the latter construction." Cope declared that OSU's trustees had taken a great interest in the public schools. They had sent professors to high schools in Ohio to better prepare students for OSU. He reassured Canfield that OSU, with the help of Rutherford B. Hayes, had already strengthened its industrial and agricultural areas. Now, the liberal arts would have priority. Finally, Cope declared that "There is no one who has more to say, quietly, about University matters, than the Board or the President." Cope also stated, "The Board of Trustees is absolute master of the situation and would quickly resent any dictation from any quarter." He finished by stating that

18. Cope, 193–96.

" . . . if you come you will have the cordial support of the Trustees and faculty in making this institution one of the foremost in the land."[19]

On July 1, 1895, the presidency of James Canfield began, and it proved to be colorful and controversial. As Secretary Cope put it, "Surely no president of a college or university, in his first year of administration, was ever attended by more auspicious conditions and circumstances than was President Canfield."[20] Canfield took unprecedented steps to advertise the university to Columbus and arranged for posters about OSU to be hung on the city's streetcars. Evening concerts for the public took place on campus. Early in his administration Canfield promoted reorganizing the university into colleges rather than schools, each with its own secretary, faculty, and dean.[21] He supported librarian Olive B. Jones in calling for a separate library building, but proposed that the library be located in a grand building in the center of the Oval. As an advocate for educated women, Canfield encouraged creating a department of domestic economy, a move considered progressive for the time, and called for a women's dormitory building. Finally, the president proposed adding a medical school to OSU by acquiring Starling Medical College and Ohio Medical University.

Canfield's vigorous leadership, however, stirred controversy among the trustees and the faculty. Speaking for the trustees, Secretary Cope described Canfield as seeing his presidency as " . . . the same relations to the Board of Trustees, as the President and manager of a railroad, or other great corporation, sustains to its Board of Directors. The government was to be no longer representative but autocratic."[22] In 1897, the trustees overruled his efforts to change the responsibilities of a professor whom the board had appointed. In 1898, Canfield, without consulting the trustees, had his friend, Ohio senator James R. Garfield, a fellow graduate of Williams College, introduce a bill to create a college and university council. It was to review all institutions of higher education in Ohio and to revoke the charters of those institutions that failed to provide a quality education. The bill caused so much turmoil in the Senate that some members of the chamber threatened to withhold financial support from OSU unless Canfield disavowed it. Other legislators warned the trustees to keep Canfield away from state legislators in the future.

These controversies, and the continued opposition to adding a medical school, which opponents feared would be too expensive for OSU, led Canfield to resign. In his letter of resignation dated May 9, 1899, Canfield explained the reasons behind his decision: "I have been conscious for some time that the service which I am permitted to render the University and the State, under existing conditions and precedents at this University, is not commensurate with the possibilities of executive work under other and more usual conditions."[23] After leaving OSU,

---

19. Cope, 197–200.
20. Cope, 239.
21. James Pollard, OSU Archives, vertical File.
22. Cope, 229.
23. Cope, 278–79

Canfield became librarian at Columbia University, where Seth Low, a boyhood friend, had become president.

WILLIAM OXLEY THOMPSON (1899–1925)

No president of OSU has received more honors from the university than William Oxley Thompson. His statue overlooks the Oval and is a landmark of the campus. The library behind his statue was named in his honor in 1948. Inside is a bust of Thompson, whose nose students rub for good luck, and a portrait.

Actually, Thompson had achieved distinction even earlier as president of Miami University at Oxford, Ohio from 1891 to 1899. Particularly noteworthy was his success in the state legislature where he had argued for the Sleeper Bill in 1896. This awarded Miami a special tax levy, similar to what the Hysell Act did for OSU in 1891. Under his leadership, Miami, which had closed during the financial depression of 1873, experienced a period of financial stability and growing numbers of students and faculty. When Thompson's candidacy for OSU became known, the *Ohio State Journal* in Columbus referred to his accomplishments at Miami as "little short of extraordinary" and declared enthusiastically: "Dr. Thompson possesses all the required qualifications of a successful college president. He is not only a scholar of recognized ability but a splendid executive."[24]

2.13 *William Oxley Thompson*

Thompson would achieve distinction as OSU's fifth president and its first chief executive, but he took pride in being an ordained minister. Born in 1855 at Cambridge, Ohio, Thompson began life as the oldest son of a shoemaker and farmer in a family of ten. Working as a farm laborer, as a teacher, and even as a janitor, Thompson earned enough money to pay for his education at Muskingum College, where he graduated in 1878. The following year, he entered the Western Theological Seminary in Allegheny, Pennsylvania, where he was ordained as a Presbyterian minister in 1881. His first ministerial appointment took him to in Iowa as a home missionary. In 1885, Thompson sought a more favorable climate for his ailing wife and accepted an appointment as president of the newly organized Synodical College of the Synod of Colo-

---

24. Pollard, 166

rado. Six years later, he returned to Ohio as president of the chiefly Presbyterian Miami University. At Miami and later at OSU, Thompson kept up an active ministry, attended meetings of the Presbyterian Synod, gave sermons as a guest of local churches, married students, and baptized children at his home.[25]

The OSU that developed during the twenty-six years of the Thompson admin-istration was, in many respects, the modern, large, and multidimensional university—including a hospital and a college of medicine—envisaged by his predecessor, James Canfield. One of the primary reasons why Thompson succeeded and Canfield did not had to do with their personalities and styles of communication. Of Canfield, President Eliot of Harvard once wrote that he was "breezy in manner and sometimes in matter."[26] In contrast, people commented that Thompson listened to each person, weighed all sides to an issue, and set out on a reasonable and cautious path.[27]

2.14 Bust of Thompson by OSU professor and artist Bruce Saville, located in the Main Library. Students rub his nose for good luck.

As president, Thompson invested much time in talking to and working with people. One anecdote describes his habit of walking from his house at 15th Avenue and High Street to his office, tipping his hat to everyone and speaking to many. Another was Thompson's response to a professor's complaint about a janitor: "If you would treat him like a man you'd have no trouble with him."[28] Students liked Thompson so much that the graduating class of 1904 commissioned a portrait of the president, who had been at OSU for only five years.

The trustees appreciated President Thompson from the beginning. As Secretary Cope put it, "A different atmosphere pervaded the institution. The new President's modest assumption of his duties and his tact in the performance of them, soon inspired a confidence which was felt in all the departments."[29] The trustees appointed Thompson to the committee of the board of trustees which represented OSU and its needs to the state legislature. In 1909, the trustees adopted a revision of their bylaws and declared that the president was to be "the executive head of the University."

It would be wrong to credit the success of Thompson to personality alone. The president and the university both benefited from social forces that were national

25. Refer to oral history interview with Maryanne R. Thompson in OSU Archives.
26. Cope, 230.
27. See oral history interview with Maranne R. Thompson; also Thompson vertical file, OSU Archives.
28. Pollard in Thompson VF, OSU Archives.
29. Cope, 292.

in nature and reached all campuses. One was the development of high schools across the state that enabled OSU to close its preparatory department, a special program for those who could not pass the entrance examination, in 1896. Another was a new expectation, especially in middle-class families, that children should prolong their educational years after high school. Parents and children linked college education with career success and social mobility. Beginning in the 1890s, and increasingly after World War I (1914–1918), student enrollment increased tenfold, leading to the expansion of the university's physical plant and its academic programs.

During the many years of the Thompson administration, the expectation developed that universities could, and should, provide research, expertise, and services needed to address modern challenges. In the early 1890s, Canfield had envisaged that OSU would provide the experts for state government; under President Thompson this became a reality. In 1910, OSU began granting research leave to faculty. The federal Smith-Lever Act of 1914 expanded OSU's extension services in agriculture and home economics across Ohio. World War I quickened research, especially in aviation and in chemistry. Beginning in 1919, OSU created research centers to gather data for business, education, and social research.

2.15 Unveiled in 1930, the statue of President Thompson is a landmark on the campus. The statue is shown with its sculptor, OSU professor Irwin F. Frey.

When Thompson retired in 1925, at the age of seventy, OSU was a major university. As early as 1910, the Carnegie Foundation for the Advancement of Teaching had concluded that OSU was the only institution in the state that was in fact, as well as in name, a university.[30] Between the beginning of Thompson's presidency and 1929, OSU added a College of Medicine, a College of Education, the Ohio Cooperative Extension Program, and a graduate school as well as one of the largest stadiums in the United States. Nationally, OSU had achieved distinction as a major university that could make national contributions. During World War I, OSU had provided not only soldiers but also domestic leadership in agriculture and industry;

30. Kinnison, 191–92.

its president, faculty, and alumni played a large role in crafting the law that created the Reserve Officers Training Program (ROTC).

Perhaps the most eloquent summary of the impact of President Thompson came from his successor, George W. Rightmire, on the occasion of the unveiling of Thompson's statue in front of the Main (now Thompson) Library in 1930:

> It has been said that an institution is merely the lengthened shadow of a man! This may be true of an educational as well as an industrial institution but it is not so likely to be. Teachers, students, and circumstances help mold the educational edifice but it nevertheless remains true that the president for a quarter of a century [William Oxley Thompson] is the only one in the institution who continuously sees all of its activities and projects in his view through the years, thereby enabling him to have a vision, and as mean and means coordinate, to bring the vision to fruition. This aphorism is beautifully applicable to our noble friend whose achievements we appreciate today.

GEORGE WASHINGTON RIGHTMIRE (1926–1938)

To succeed President Thompson, the trustees selected a former student and professor at OSU, George Washington Rightmire. Like Thompson, Rightmire, born in 1868 at Center Furnace, Ohio, came from a humble background. His father was a foundryman who died when the boy was eight, leaving a widow and five children. Like Thompson also, Rightmire worked to pay for his higher education, first as a schoolteacher, then in a bank and even in a mine. His financial needs required him to interrupt his college career at OSU, where he graduated in 1895. After that, Rightmire taught at Columbus North High School and reentered OSU to earn a degree in law, specializing in patent, trademark, and copyright law. In 1902, he returned to OSU, this time as an instructor in the College of Law, where he achieved the rank of full professor in 1906 and became acting dean in 1908. At the same time, Rightmire took an interest in city politics and government, serving as president of the Columbus City Council from 1906 to 1910.[31] Following Thompson's retirement, Rightmire first served as interim president and then was elected president in 1926.

As a former student, Rightmire was especially sensitive to improving the transition of students from high school to the much larger and more complex university environment. First, in 1927 OSU began a five-day Freshman Week during fall quarter to provide a general orientation to OSU and its expectations as well as an opportunity for physical and other examinations. Second, each of the colleges created junior deans, who guided freshmen and sophomores. In providing special attention to entering students, OSU hoped to retain enrollments for the junior and senior years.[32]

---

31. Pollard, OSU Archives vertical file.
32. Pollard, 287.

Certainly, the greatest achievement of the Rightmire years was that OSU sustained itself, and even grew, in the midst of such hard economic times. To cope with the financial difficulties, especially after the State of Ohio withdrew some of its financial support, the university reduced its clerical and maintenance staff, and even lowered salaries in 1932 and 1933. Two faculty committees, the Committee on Courses, Activities, and Programs and the Committee on Urgent Needs, guided OSU in identifying priorities and reducing courses and programs.

Others also helped OSU in hard times. The federal government aided the university by providing money for students to work on campus, for

2.16 George Washington Rightmire

2.17 Stillman Hall

2.18 and 2.19 The Great Depression, which began in 1929, shaped much of the administration of President Rightmire. Located on College Road, Stillman Hall was built entirely from federal aid. In Stillman Hall are murals painted by artist Emerson Burkhart, shown in the photograph, explaining the murals that depict historical periods in efforts to alleviate poverty. Stillman Hall and the Burkhart murals are two legacies of the Great Depression on the OSU campus.

2.20 Rightmire Hall, on West Campus, across the Olentangy River and near Bevis Hall

construction projects such as Stillman Hall, the OSU Golf Course, and an addition to University Hospital as well as the Faculty Club. At this time, the university also called upon private citizens and business for financial support. The Alumnae Council sponsored inexpensive and cooperative housing to women students by opening the Alumnae Cooperative House on West 10th Avenue.[33] Appeals to private businesses for support in scholarships had noteworthy success. Kroger Company and Sears Roebuck supported twenty student scholarships each.[34] In 1934, OSU established the University Research Foundation in order to connect faculty with opportunities for research financed by external sponsors, especially in business.[35] Four years later, in 1938, the university established the University Development Fund as an organized and continuing "effort to create funds for the University's needs outside of, and in addition to, state and federal appropriations."

In looking back to the period of the Great Depression as a special time in OSU history, several points stand out. First, enrollment between 1929 and 1939 remained stable and even increased, from 14,495 in 1929/30 to a low of 12,468 in 1933/34 to 18,067 in 1938/39. Second, the years left a number of tangible legacies for the future: Stillman Hall, the Stadium dormitory (moved to Mack Hall in 1998 and then to the Scholars Houses on 10th Avenue in 2005), the OSU Golf Course, and Converse Hall. Third, the crisis created the concept of the OSU faculty engaged in identifying programmatic priorities for the university. Fourth, the Depression resulted in the formation of the University Development Fund and the University Research Foundation. Both would have continuing impor-

33. Pollard, 326.
34. Pollard, 335.
35. Pollard, 320.

tance not only in coping with the financial crisis but with garnering opportunities for future development.

2.21 Howard L. Bevis

HOWARD LANDIS BEVIS (1940–1956)

In 1938, once he had reached the age of seventy, George Rightmire followed the example of his predecessor, William Oxley Thompson, and announced his retirement. To serve as acting president, the trustees appointed Dr. William McPherson, dean of the graduate school, a temporary appointment that lasted eighteen months.

Finally, in January 8, 1940 the Trustees agreed to elect an attorney and educator, Professor Howard Landis Bevis, of Harvard University. Born in Bevis, Ohio, near Cincinnati, he completed his undergraduate studies at the University of Cincinnati in 1908 and then earned a degree in law in 1910. After practicing law in Cincinnati and then leaving for a doctorate of juristic science at Harvard University, Bevis returned to the University of Cincinnati as a professor of law from 1921 to 1931. At the

2.22 Bevis Hall on West Campus, near Rightmire Hall

same time, he took leadership in the Republican Party in Cincinnati and in municipal affairs. In 1931, Ohio governor George White appointed Bevis as Director of Finance for the State of Ohio and then to a vacancy on the Ohio Supreme Court in 1933, where he served until 1935. After a brief service as Director of Finance for Ohio governor Martin Davey, Bevis returned to Harvard as professor of law and government in the Graduate School of Business Administration.

Almost all of Bevis's administration concerned itself with preparing for war, participation in World War II, and with managing the outcomes of that war. His administration's duration was second only to that of President Thompson in length. At the age of seventy, Bevis announced his retirement.

NOVICE G. FAWCETT (1956–1972)

In 1955, OSU's Trustees passed a rule that a president must retire at the age of seventy. Both Presidents Thompson and Rightmire had done so previously, and President Bevis himself, whose health had been failing, announced his retirement when he reached that age. The search for a successor to Bevis proved to be lengthy and difficult. A special faculty committee presented nearly one hundred names for the trustees to consider.[36] Finally on June 25, 1956, they elected Novice G. Fawcett.

Many faculty and staff at OSU were surprised because Fawcett, who was well known in Columbus, had not been a professor or an administrator in higher education. Born in Gambier, Ohio in 1909, Fawcett graduated from nearby Kenyon College in 1931. While teaching and coaching and then serving as superintendent of schools at Gambier, Fawcett earned a master's degree in Education from OSU in 1937. His experience as an administrator and his master's degree let to a meteoric career as a chief administrator of public schools in Ohio. From 1938 to 1943, Fawcett was superintendent of schools in Defiance, Ohio, and in 1943 became superintendent of Bexley schools near Columbus. Four years later, Fawett accepted

2.23 *Novice Fawcett*

---

36. Weisenberger, 2.

an offer to become assistant superintendent of schools in Akron. However, in 1949, he returned to Columbus as superintendent of schools, the youngest superintendent to date of a large city public school system in the United States.[37]

In Columbus, Fawcett achieved much recognition in the community and at OSU. In 1954 Fawcett served with President Bevis on the Ohio Committee on Expanding Student Population, which dealt with the challenges of Ohio's growing college enrollment. Although not a college president (nor had Howard Bevis been in 1940), Fawcett had attracted attention as an able administrator who had led large educational organizations.

President Fawcett had a formal inauguration in the newly opened St. John Arena on April 29, 1957. In his inaugural address entitled "Toward a New Level of Greatness," Fawcett developed six themes: an integrated research program encompassing all disciplines, from the humanities to engineering and the social and physical sciences; more attention to continuing education, especially through educational media such

2.24 President Fawcett was the first of the modern era of OSU presidents in his attention to raising money from private donors and foundations. His administration brought about the President's Club within the OSU Development Fund as an effort to link the president directly with major donors. Endowed chairs, named professorships, and student scholarships increased greatly at OSU because of his efforts.

as radio and television; reviewing the curriculum and exploring the use of new technologies in the classroom; improving educational leadership and administration by developing a talented cabinet; and continuing the university as a place of discovery. At the end of the festivities, the audience adjourned to attend the dedication of Mershon Auditorium.[38]

In many ways, Fawcett proved himself to be an able administrator, one who changed the organizational structure of OSU significantly. As an example, President Bevis had only three vice presidents (Academic Affairs, Student Relations, and Business). To improve communication and coordination, Fawcett added vice presidents

37. Weisenberger, 3–4.
38. *History of The Ohio State University, Vol. VII: Addresses and Proceedings of Novice G. Fawcett; Dedication* of *Mershon Auditorium, April 29, 1957* (Columbus: The Ohio State University Press), 31–40.

2.25 *The Fawcett Center for Tomorrow on Olentangy River Road represented OSU's programs in continuing education, telecommunication, and hosting conferences.*

and created a cabinet of vice presidents and directors, an administrative structure that has continued. In 1962, Fawcett added a vice president for research, a position that acknowledged the growing importance of sponsored research to OSU.

Another innovation in administration was the leadership of the president in meetings of the board of trustees. In the Bevis era, the president had not been involved in setting the agenda for the meetings. Fawcett, however, had years of experience with school boards and took charge of the agenda. After that, succeeding presidents had a leadership role in planning the meetings.[39]

Finally, President Fawcett, with his President's Permanent Planning Committee, and an energetic John Corbally, who was vice president for academic affairs and OSU's first provost, brought about a major and enduring reorganization of OSU's colleges and departments. Much of the change involved reducing the number of

39. Fawcett oral history in OSU Archives.

2.26 *One of the lasting accomplishments of the Fawcett years was the development of OSU campuses at Marion, Newark, Lima, and Mansfield (the latter is shown here). In creating those campuses, OSU was responding to a general demand for higher education in those areas and for a desire in the communities to have a link to OSU. A distinguishing feature of the regional campuses was that students could transfer all their credits directly to the campus in Columbus, without loss.*

departments in the College of Arts and Sciences. This created the College of the Arts, the College of Biological Sciences, the College of Humanities, the College of Mathematics and Physical Sciences, and the College of Social and Behavioral Sciences, and finally a special University College as a portal of entry for freshmen and sophomores. Although new colleges have been created or reshaped since 1968 (e.g., Human Ecology, Social Work, and Nursing) and University College came to an end, the academic landscape developed in the Fawcett years has largely endured for nearly four decades.

In March 1971, President Fawcett, who had had a series of medical setbacks, announced his intention to retire in 1972. His sixteen years of leadership had been ones of unprecedented growth in people, programs, and physical plant. They had also been times of much social turbulence on the campus.

HAROLD ENARSON (1972–1981)

In April of 1972, OSU's trustees announced that Harold Enarson, president of Cleveland State University, would succeed President Fawcett. Enarson was the first president of OSU to have earned a Ph.D., as all presidents after him will have done. In fact, Enarson was one of the most scholarly of OSU presidents, one who wrote his own speeches with much time and care.

Born in Iowa in 1919, Harold Enarson was the grandson of a Norwegian immigrant who broke the sod and built the house in which the future president would live. He grew up in both misfortune and poverty. The youngest of three children, Enarson saw sickness and death at an early age. As a child of four, Enarson saw his father gravely ill with tuberculosis; four years later a brother would die of the disease and then his sister. In 1929, the Enarson's sold the family farm and moved to Albuquerque, New Mexico in the hope that the hot and dry climate would improve their health. Enarson's mother worked as a maid because his father was too weak to work. Meanwhile, young Enarson earned money delivering newspapers and working in a neighborhood drug store.

2.27 *Harold Enarson*

After graduating from high school, Harold Enarson enrolled at the University of New Mexico, receiving a degree with honors in 1940 and earning a graduate scholarship to Stanford. World War II interrupted his academic career, first with employment in the Bureau of the Budget in Washington D.C. and then in the Army and Air Force. After the war, he resumed his work at the Office of the Budget, completed his MA at Stanford, and enrolled in the Ph.D. program in political science at the American University in Washington, D.C.

The national election of 1952 that brought the Republicans to power ended Enarson's position with the Wage Stabilization Board. He therefore accepted a position first as Assistant Director of Commerce for the City of Philadelphia and then as an executive secretary to the mayor. Academic life and administration, however, interested him more and in 1954, Enarson accepted an offer to be executive director of the Western Interstate Commission for Higher Education in Colorado. Six years later, he returned to the University of New Mexico as a vice president. In 1966, he became the first president of Cleveland State University. His success there—and the fact that Cleveland State University was one of few public universities to remain open during the student uprisings of 1970—attracted the attention of OSU's trustees.[40]

---

40. Underwood, 3–10.

2.28 *President Enarson with students*

2.29 *The original Student Union, located on 12th Avenue, was renamed Enarson Hall in 1986.*

One of the characteristics of Enarson's administration was a special sensitivity to people who had not figured prominently at OSU or, in fairness, at most other universities. Women made strides, including membership in the prestigious OSU Marching Band and in Ohio Staters. Enarson appointed the first two women vice presidents, Kathryn Schoen in Educational Services and Ann Reynolds as Vice President for Academic Affairs and Provost. He added an African American to university leadership by naming Madison Scott as Director of Personnel Services in 1971 and then as the first Vice President for Personnel Services in 1975. Meanwhile enrollments of African American students increased 38.2 percent in this period, and the university began an aggressive program, the Minority Masters Fellowships, to increase the number of African American graduate students. At the same time, OSU during the Enarson years became more helpful to nontraditional students by holding more classes in the evenings and even a "weekend university" at several shopping centers.

All of this took place at a time of financial difficulty. War in the Middle East, energy shortages, rampant inflation, and stagnant economic growth ended the "boom" period in higher education of the 1950s and 1960s. In a stagnant economy, finding money to maintain the campuses and buildings that had been constructed during the years of expansion was a problem. Also exasperating for Enarson was the State of Ohio's open admissions policies that forced OSU to accept unprepared students from the state's high schools and spend university resources on remedial programs.[41] Periodically, Enarson complained that federal and state bureaucracies required so much reporting that the work of gathering data and writing the reports distracted from the primary missions of teaching, research, and service.[42]

Ironically, President Enarson's wish to impose a regulation on OSU's College of Medicine caused one of the greatest stirs (second only to his firing of legendary football coach Woody Hayes in 1979) during his administration. During the 1950s, as OSU's College of Medicine and Health Center expanded, the university had encouraged medical faculty to add to their OSU salaries, which were not competitive with other institutions, by supplementing their income by seeing private patients in OSU facilities. As early as 1964, President Fawcett had attempted briefly to oversee the fees earned and divert a portion to OSU. Following the recommendations of external consultants, Enarson resumed the effort and medical faculty at OSU resisted. A bitter conflict in the courts followed until a compromise medical practice plan was agreed to in 1979, after five years of effort. The plan required that a portion of practice revenue went to support medical research in the departments that earned it.

In 1980, President Enarson announced his intent to resign in 1981. He cited no specific reason for leaving at age sixty-two but stated " . . . I think the thing one cannot afford is exhaustion and fretfulness, and I watched this in some of my col-

---

41. Underwood, 90, 181–82.
42. Underwood, 184.

leagues, so I concluded that I'd better leave while I was still—in my, eyes, at least—in good humor."[43] Later, he admitted that weariness, as well as worsening relations with the trustees and the Medical Practice Plan, had made retirement seem especially attractive.[44]

EDWARD JENNINGS (1981–1990)

In 1981, with the national economy in a severe recession, OSU faced a likely reduction in tax subsidies from the State of Ohio and much financial uncertainty. The continuing concern over financial affairs was an important reason in selecting Dr. Edward Jennings as president. Born in Minneapolis, Jennings came from a family of educators. His mother taught school while his father was a professor of law at the University of Minnesota. He attended the University of North Carolina at Chapel Hill and graduated with a major in industrial management. For two years Jennings

2.30 *Edward Jennings*

worked as an industrial engineer in South Carolina but left to earn an MBA from Western Reserve University in Cleveland, concentrating in finance. A Ph.D. in finance from the University of Michigan soon followed. In 1960 he accepted an assistant professorship at the University of Iowa. By 1976 he had become a full professor and vice president for Finance and University Services. From there, he moved to the University of Wyoming as president in 1979. The expertise of Jennings in finance and his record as president of the University of Wyoming prompted OSU to offer its presidency to Jennings in 1981.

Quickly, President Jennings addressed the budgetary crisis at OSU in several ways. He created a faculty committee to define when a financial emergency existed and to develop appropriate procedures for the release of tenured faculty. The University Senate and the board of trustees approved the documents in 1982.[45] At least, OSU had a policy to follow if the financial crisis

43. Quoted in Underwood, 197.
44. Underwood, 197.
45. Gabel, 32–35.

2.31 President Jennings with students

worsened. In addition, OSU added an early retirement incentive for senior faculty and staff so that the university would save money in salaries as units added more junior people to fill the vacancies. Another accomplishment was the creation of a standing committee of the University Senate, the University Fiscal Committee, to provide advice from faculty, students, and administrative staff.

OSU rebounded from fiscal distress. The national economy recovered and grew during much of the 1980s. In the relative prosperity, the State of Ohio initiated special programs to support higher education. Among these were the Eminent Scholar Program to bring new faculty with outstanding research records to Ohio's state colleges and universities, the Academic Challenge Program which provided additional state support to reward the state's best academic units, and the Research Challenge Program that provided additional state support based on the success of the public college or university in attracting research support from private and federal sponsors.[46]

Jennings sought new sources of revenue, especially from private sources. In 1981, OSU ranked lowest in fund-raising among its peers.[47] As early as 1982, planning began for a major change in the ambitions and scale of OSU's efforts based on the recommendations of a consulting firm. In April 1985, the trustees approved a national fund-raising campaign with a minimum goal of $225 million in five years, which grew to $350 million in September. After five years, OSU exceeded its goal and raised $460,173,693 for scholarships, chairs, named professorships,

46. Gabel, 68–72.
47. Gabel, 116.

buildings (including the Wexner Center), research labs, and more. Aside from the money, OSU had developed the infrastructure to plan and carry out fundraising at an unprecedented level, which it would use again in the near future.[48]

At any university, money should be only a means to an end and in the Jennings administration, that end or goal was to raise the academic quality of OSU. There were at least four major accomplishments. Moving to selective admission was one. Another was expanding and developing the University Honors program for undergraduate students. In 1981, this had been a loosely coordinated set of programs dispersed through the colleges and regional campuses; by the late 1980s, as a result of a committee's recommendations, the honors program became centrally led and much broader in scope. It included recruiting honors students, and establishing honors-based scholarships and honors residences. A third accomplishment was that the faculty reviewed the instructional landscape and developed the General Education Curriculum in each of the colleges. Finally, the Jennings administration significantly advanced the diversity of the campus by setting up a grants program to encourage pioneering efforts. As an example, Distinguished Affirmative Action Awards recognized and rewarded departments and colleges that met goals of recruitment and retention of minorities.

2.32 The Botany and Zoology Building at 1735 Neil Avenue was renamed to honor President Jennings.

---

48. Gabel, 116–35.

Despite a very successful presidency by any measure, Edward Jennings announced his intention to resign in October 1989. The daily pressures of the presidency, along with challenges in his private life, moved him to return to his life as a professor, this time as professor of finance at OSU. He became only the third elected president in OSU history (following Edward Orton in 1878 and William Henry Scott in 1895) who resigned office to continue on the faculty.

E. (ELWOOD) GORDON GEE (1990–1997)

As Edward Jennings looked forward to resuming his career in teaching and in research, a search committee and the trustees found a colorful successor in E. Gordon Gee. He enjoyed public attention—and added to it—perhaps more than any other president of OSU since James Canfield (1895–1899). Born in the small town of Vernal, Utah to a financially successful Mormon family, Gee graduated high school as student body president and then enrolled at the University of Utah. Graduating with honors in 1968, he continued his education as a graduate student at Columbia University. There, he made a pivotal decision in selecting an academic program, which led to both a degree in law and a Ph.D. in education, specializing in legal and

2.33 E. Gordon Gee

administrative problems in institutions of higher education. To combine both, he thought, would prepare him for leadership in academic administration.[49]

Opportunities in law and in higher education appeared quickly. In 1973, Gee accepted a position as assistant dean for administration at the University Of Utah College of Law; in 1974 he became a judicial fellow and staff assistant to the United States Supreme Court. A year later, he was an associate professor and assistant dean of law at Brigham Young University, the alma mater of his parents. After achieving the rank of full professor and associate dean, Gee served as dean of the law school at West Virginia University and became its president in 1981. Four and a half years later he moved to Colorado as president of the University of Colorado, where he served until accepting the offer to become president of OSU.

49. Malcolm S. Baroway, *History of The Ohio State University, Vol. XII: The Gee Years, 1990–1997* (Columbus: The Ohio State University, 2002), 11–12.

2.34 President Gee helping students move in to dormitories

Dressed in his traditional bow tie and suspenders and gifted with an infectious and often self-deprecating humor, Gee quickly became a popular figure. The new president had an extraordinary ability to remember names and faces. After commencements, he posed with the new graduates and their families for photographs As president, Gee and his staff invested much time in developing public relations strategies—invitation lists, press coverage, meetings with the media, direct mail programs—that focused attention on President Gee and his agenda for OSU.[50] More than any other president, with the possible exception of William Oxley Thompson, Gee came to personify OSU.

Although President Gee had his own distinctive style, he developed further some of the themes from the Jennings administration. He built on the fund-raising infrastructure to launch another campaign that raised more than one billion dollars from 1995 to 2000 (as well as a new campus for the Fisher College of Business). The "excellence" watchword that had been so prominent in the Jennings administration translated into "Continuous Quality Improvement" and "Total Quality Management" initiatives that were popular in industry. Academic units developed measurement for academic quality, while the university itself took an active interest in the national rankings of public universities as posted in issues of *U.S. News and World Report*.[51] In the search for more high-quality students, Gee invested more university resources into full and partial scholarship packages that attracted a greater number

50. Baroway, 152–53
51. Baroway, 136.

2.35 *President Gee at fund-raising event*

of National Merit and Achievement students to OSU. In addition, the Gee administration involved the OSU Alumni Association more than ever before in visiting schools and marketing OSU as the destination place for good students.[52]

In addition to recruiting new students, the Gee administration sought to improve the undergraduate experience for all. As an example, Gee created an Academy of Teaching from winners of the Alumni Teaching Award to reward and inspire good teaching.[53] Particularly significant was the work of the Committee on the Undergraduate Experience. Charged to study the undergraduate life and to recommend changes, the final report of the committee set a working agenda for the future. Many of its recommendations became realities and programs—the first year Experience Program, the direct admission of specially qualified students to colleges, and residential scholars programs, to name a few.

In other ways, President Gee expanded on the initiatives developed in previous administrations. OSU created offices that specialized in Hispanic student programs, in Asian American programs, and in veterans affairs. Recommendations from the President's Commission on Women pointed to the need to create more opportunities for women, especially in teaching and administration. Meanwhile, Gee met with and tried to respond to concerns from African American student groups and continued the Freshman Foundation and Minority Scholars programs. By the end of

52. Baroway, 40–43
53. Baroway, 134.

the Gee administration in 1997, minority and women representation in the faculty increased by 12 percent and minority students grew 6 percent from what it had been in 1987.[54]

Since he was nationally known, it was not unusual for President Gee to draw attention and receive offers from other universities. In 1995, he almost accepted an offer to become chancellor of the University of California. Two years later, in 1997, the Gee administration ended when he accepted the presidency of Brown University.

WILLIAM ENGLISH (BRIT) KIRWAN (1998–2001)

The twelfth president of OSU was the first from the South. Born in Louisville, Kentucky in 1938, William English Kirwan earned a bachelor's degree from the University of Kentucky in 1960. Graduate study at Rutgers led to masters and doctoral degrees in mathematics in 1962 and 1964. An extraordinary career at the University of Maryland followed. In 1964, he became an assistant professor and advanced to full professor in 1972. Shortly after that, in 1977, Kirwan began his administrative career as chair of the department of mathematics. Four years later, he became first chancellor for academic affairs and then provost in 1986. Finally, in 1988 he became first acting and then president of the University of Maryland, a position he retained until accepting the offer from OSU.

2.36 *President Kirwan*

In the four years of his presidency, Dr. Kirwan achieved a reputation as a good listener and an articulate spokesperson, especially in the areas of academic achievement and diversity. Unexpectedly, an offer to return to Maryland as chancellor of the University of Maryland System and the opportunity to be close to his family and grandchildren ended his service at OSU in 2001.

Despite the brevity of his administration, Kirwan's leadership did have noteworthy achievements. In 2000, OSU adopted an academic master plan that voiced the goal of "becoming one of the world's great public teaching and research universities." The plan identified strat-

---

54. Baroway, 185.

2.37 *President Kirwan with students*

egies to reach that goal: to build a world-class faculty; to develop academic programs that define Ohio State as the nation's leading public land-grant university; to enhance the quality of the teaching and learning environment; to enhance and better serve the student body; to create a diverse university community; and to build Ohio's future. The plan served to prioritize the allocation of financial resources in times of economic difficulty. (Among those priorities was the massive renovation of the Thompson library, completed in 2009.) Even though Kirwan left shortly after the adoption of the plan, the plan itself served as the roadmap for OSU and his successor, President Karen Holbrook.

2.38 *President Karen Holbrook*

KAREN A. HOLBROOK (2002–2007)

Following the resignation of President Kirwan, a search committee recommended another president from the South, Dr. Karen A. Holbrook, at the University of Georgia. Born in Des Moines, Iowa in 1942, Holbrook graduated from the University of Wisconsin in Madison with undergraduate and masters degrees in zoology. She taught biology at Ripon College for three years and then resumed her graduate education at the University of Washington School of Medicine. In 1972, she earned a Ph.D. in biological structure, and then took up postdoctoral training in the department of dermatology. At the University of Washington, she became an instructor and advanced to the rank of professor of biological structure and medicine. In addition, Holbrook gained administrative experience, first as an associate chairperson and then as associate dean for scientific affairs.

Holbrook's career in science and in academic administration advanced quickly. In 1993, she became vice president for research and dean of theUniversity of Washington's graduate school. Meanwhile her scientific career continued and led to honors and awards, including election as a Fellow of the American Association for the Advancement of Science. In 1998, Holbrook accepted an appointment at the University of Georgia as vice president for academic affairs and provost. Her leadership there as well as in professional organizations attracted the attention of OSU's search committee.

At OSU, President Holbrook worked to bring the Academic Plan to fruition: "The Academic Plan is the University's agenda to enhance our academic quality, diversity, and stature as a world-class research university. It is imperative, therefore that each year we pause to assess our progress and then move forward with informed action toward our goals. . . . "[55] In her first state of the university address in October 2003, Dr. Holbrook named three actions that would characterize the leadership agenda within the context of the Academic Plan: pursue cutting-edge, interdisciplinary research for short-and long-term societal benefits; provide distinctive educational experiences and opportunities for undergraduates; and develop a twenty-first century model of outreach and engagement.

In fact, the Academic Plan served as the road map for OSU and President Holbrook. Her administration reached several milestones. OSU rose in national rankings and in scientific research. As examples, in 2006 *U.S. News and World Report* raised OSU to nineteenth among the top fifty public universities, a steep rise from the twenty-fourth ranking in 2002, when the Holbrook years began. For two consecutive years, in 2004 and 2005, the university added more faculty to the prestigious American Association for Advancement of Science than any other university. Finally, in 2005 the National Science Foundation reported that OSU had become the tenth leading public research institution when measured by total research spending.

OSU's undergraduate experience improved also. The university enhanced their first-year experience by starting a "freshman success" series of seminars. In small classes, new students joined with faculty in learning about current issues in research and scholarship and many became excited about learning. President Holbrook took special pride in fostering undergraduate research by setting up the Undergraduate Research Office and in highlighting the accomplishments of undergraduates in the annual Denman Forum. Near the end of her administration, OSU reduced the number of credit hours for an undergraduate degree, a decision that matched other institutions and that was expected to lessen the financial cost to students. These significant accomplishments aside, more than a few students and alumni resented

---

55. From Office of President website; quote from October 2003 State of the University Address.

Holbrook's efforts to restrain the heavy drinking and inappropriate behavior of some football fans.

In 2006, President Holbrook decided not to seek a renewal of her five-year contract and ended her service at OSU on June 30, 2007. After the brief interim presidency of Dean Joseph Alutto of OSU's Fisher College of Business, a search committee recommended Dr. E. Gordon Gee, chancellor of Vanderbilt University, as the fourteenth president of OSU.

E. GORDON GEE (2007–)

Rarely in higher education does a president return to a campus for another term of office. A former president of OSU once remarked, "Take a lesson. They like you better when you are gone."[56] At OSU, both presidents Edward Orton and William Henry Scott seemed eager to step down to return to the faculty and submitted resignations that were not accepted. Never in the history of the university had a president returned until E. Gordon Gee accepted an offer from the board of trustees in July of 2007. In an emotional acceptance speech, President Gee stated:

> Yesterday I wrote to the Vanderbilt community, and its board, and I said the following: "I am not leaving Vanderbilt. Rather, I am following my heart and returning to a place that I consider home." So I'm sorry this is an emotional moment for me. So I thank all of you for letting me come home. I really do.
>
> In Luke 15, some of you can remember that New Testament story of the prodigal son. Well, I am that son. I left. I experienced the world. I made my way in a different way and a different time, but this place, this father, this magnificent institution never forgot me, and has now forgiven me and welcomed me home.
>
> . . . . .
>
> I want you to know, and what I said before, I am returning to be part of one of the most exciting, and let me just say this—I want to underscore this; I want everyone to hear this—I am returning to be part of the most exciting academic environment in American higher education.[57]

After taking office in October, Gee presented six strategic goals for OSU, many of which affirmed the Strategic Plan of his predecessors. First was to forge one university in which all of its colleges and administrative units share one identity and work harmoniously towards common goals. Another was to put students first as a priority and to provide them with unique and compelling educational experiences both inside and outside of classrooms. A third was to focus on fac-

---

56. Remarks by Edward Jennings at the dedication of Jennings Hall, May 2, 2008.
57. Remarks of Gordon Gee at The Ohio State Board of Trustees meeting July 12, 2007.

ulty success, a goal that required retaining, attracting, and rewarding world-class teachers and researchers. Fourth, OSU was to recast its research agenda to stimulate not only new theoretical knowledge but also new applications. A fifth goal was to make a difference in the well-being of the state and the world by employing the assets of the university to the benefit of communities. Finally, OSU should simplify its systems and structures to work more efficiently and effectively, without sacrificing transparency or accountability.[58]

Although the goals were ambitious, few who knew President Gee from his first administration doubted his energy, his leadership, or the likelihood of success. Even before his administration began officially, Gee was a frequent visitor

2.39 President E. Gordon Gee

to the campus and as president attended a mind-numbing number of functions. Hardly a student could graduate OSU without having met or seen President Gee more than once.

58. "Six Tragic Goals for Making the Coming Years Ohio State's Time." OSU Archives.

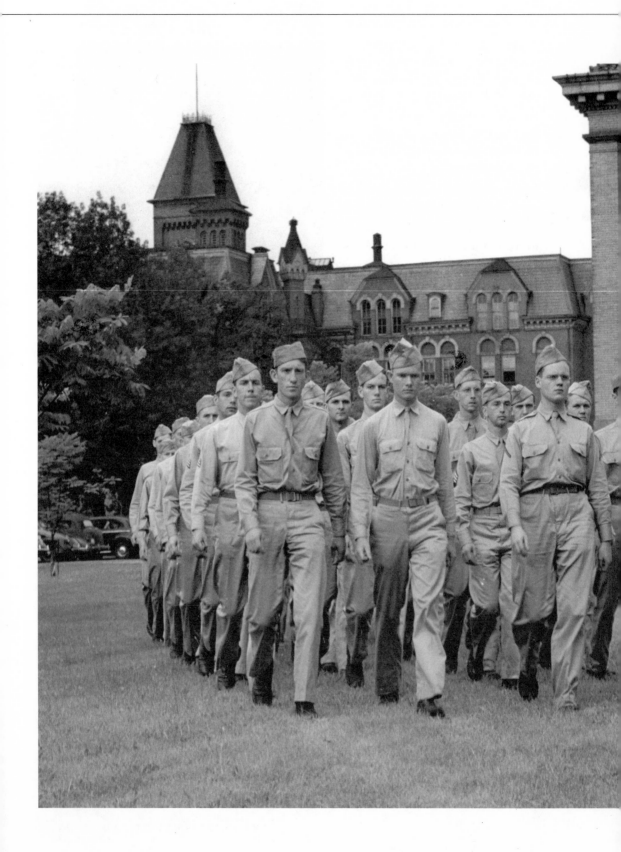

CHAPTER THREE

FIVE KEY TURNING POINTS OF OSU HISTORY

The University will be a glory to the State, a light and an inspiration to all who value and seek after the things of the mind.

—President William Henry Scott,
Annual Report 1895

To advance the well-being of the people of Ohio and the global community through the creation and dissemination of knowledge.

—OSU's Vision Statement, 2001

THE OHIO STATE UNIVERSITY grew from a humble land-grant institution to one of the most prominent and largest universities in the nation, one that is recognized throughout the world. In 1878, the year in which the college changed its name from The Ohio Agricultural and Mechanical College to The Ohio State University and graduated its first students, OSU had only 198 students and twelve faculty. President Edward Orton himself questioned the appropriateness of naming the new institution as a "university" when it offered so few programs. In contrast, the university of 2008 had 61,568 students on its five campuses and more than 5,000 faculty.[1] Since 1997, *U.S. News and World Report* has consistently included OSU among the top twenty-five public universities in the country.[2]

Turning points are important for understanding the history of OSU. A handful of times or events have quickened the pace of change on the campus and deserve special attention. Five pivotal events are: Trustee Rutherford B. Hayes's resolution of a rift between OSU and agricultural leaders in Ohio in 1887; the Hysell Act which in 1891 provided a state subsidy for OSU; World War II; the student demonstrations of 1970; and finally the advent of selective admissions in 1987 that changed the character of the student population and possibly of the university itself.

RUTHERFORD B. HAYES, OSU, AND SERVICE TO AGRICULTURE

At the founding of the Ohio Agricultural and Mechanical College in 1870, its most enthusiastic supporters were the spokesmen for scientific agriculture, such as Norton Townshend. They believed that applications of science, especially in mechanical engineering and in new fertilizers and experimental methods, would improve farming as a more profitable and more attractive way of life, an alternative to moving to new land in the West. This, the advocates argued, was the fundamental mission of the land-grant colleges founded by the Morrill Act.

By 1878, however, some Ohioans charged that the Ohio Agricultural and Mechanical College had strayed from its agricultural mission. Judge T. C. Jones, a former trustee, declared that "the college had got as far as possible away from God and agriculture."[3] Controversial, too, was that the state legislature had removed both agriculture and engineering from the name of the state's land-grant institution. More evidence was that only eighteen students were enrolled in the agricultural classes. Additionally, the college farm on the campus appeared to be in poor condition, with inadequate machinery and livestock of poor quality. On March 6, 1877, the trustees,

---

1. See http://www.osu.edu/osutoday/stuinfo.html.

2. Malcolm S. Baroway, *History of The Ohio State University: The Gee Years, 1990–1997* (Columbus: The Ohio State University Press, 2002), 294.

3. Alexis Cope, *History of The Ohio State University, Vol 1: 1870–1910* (Columbus: the Ohio State University Press, 1920), 458.

reacting to criticism, visited the college farm and agreed that its "management had been very unsatisfactory and required a radical change."[4]

Professor Norton Townshend had charge of the farm as well as agricultural education in the classroom. To help him and to add practical expertise, OSU Trustees appointed Charles E. Thorne to manage the farm and to supervise its operations. Thorne had grown up on a farm, had attended the Michigan Agricultural College at Lansing, Michigan, and was an acquaintance of President Edward Orton.[5] Thus, everyone expected improvement.

Thorne became increasingly frustrated with the lack of improvements—in livestock and in equipment—and blamed OSU for failing to provide adequate resources for farming. In 1881, he resigned and shortly thereafter became editor of *Farm and Fireside,* which had developed a national readership of farmers. Headquartered in Springfield, Ohio, which had lost in its bid to host the new college in 1870, the magazine published news about new implements and machinery for farmers. Under Thorne, the magazine became a persistent—and annoying—critic of OSU's administration, especially its trustees. Periodically, it charged The Ohio State University with neglecting its agricultural mission: "No college or university of general education in the United States will show a smaller proportion of its graduates engaged in agricultural pursuits than this agricultural college of Ohio."[6] In 1887, Thorne pointed out that although the university had graduated ninety-three students, only two had received the bachelor of agriculture degree.

Another matter further aggravated relations between the university and the outspoken advocates for agriculture in Ohio. In 1881, a day before Thorne's resignation, the trustees hired Professor William R. Lazenby, a graduate of Cornell University, to become chair of the newly established Department of Botany and Horticulture. When the trustees did not approve his requests for a new building, a residence, and more equipment for horticulture, Lazenby took matters into

3.1 Persistent critic of OSU and an intense advocate for agriculture, Charles Thorne became director of the Ag Experiment Station, later the Ohio Agriculture and Development Center.

3.2 Lazenby Hall on Neil Avenue near the Thompson Library is named after the industrious Professor William Lazenby, the zealous advocate for agriculture and horticulture. It sits on the site of the original Agricultural Experiment Station, which moved to Wooster, Ohio in 1892.

---

4. Cope, 452.

5. Cope, 453.

6. William Kinnison, *Building Sullivant's Pyramid: An Administrative History of the Ohio State University, 1870–1907* (Columbus: The Ohio State University Press, 1970), 131; Farm and Fireside, 10, no. 11 (March 1, 1887): 181.

3.3 Located at 1827 Neil Avenue, the site of the present Lazenby Hall, the Agricultural Experiment Station was a prominent point of conflict on campus between its board of control and the OSU trustees.

his own hands. He lobbied members of the State Board of Agriculture and the State Grange, who in turn persuaded the state legislature to create the Agricultural Experiment Station at OSU in 1882. However, the Station's own governing body, the Board of Control, governed the program on the campus, not OSU's Trustees. Although the board and the trustees developed operational agreements for the Station and the campus, the division of responsibility caused tensions.[7]

In 1886, OSU Trustees and the Agricultural Experiment Station clashed over funding and representation. A bill in the U.S. Congress, the Hatch Act, provided for annual subsidies to states to support agricultural experimentation at the land-grant universities. OSU's trustees looked forward to receiving the subsidies and administering them, as they governed and represented the university to the legislature. However, Charles Thorne and his *Farm and Fireside* urged readers to write to their representatives in Congress and press for an alternative. He wanted to amend the Hatch Act so that state legislators could steer the federal subsidy directly to the agricultural experiment stations, not to university trustees.

Thorne's advocacy for the station prevailed in Washington, D.C. and again in Columbus, Ohio. OSU's President William Henry Scott pleaded with the legislature

---

7. Cope, 479.

for OSU to receive the federal subsidies of the Hatch Act and to empower the board of trustees and the university to administer them. However, state legislators directed the federal money from the Hatch Act directly to the Ohio Agricultural Experimentation Station.

Matters worsened when the outspoken Charles Thorne became the first fulltime director of the Ohio Agricultural Experimentation Station in 1887.[8] An angry letter from Charles Thorne to Secretary of the Board of Trustees Alexis Cope illustrated the intensity of the disagreement and mistrust:

> I do not demand that the University dispense with *all* [sic] teaching of the classics, but I do insist that such teaching should not be made directly or indirectly the *leading feature* [sic] of the school. You claim that the university system is the real adherence to the Magna Charta of the institution. I claim that it is in direct defiance of that charter, for as your system of instruction is now arranged, your courses in Agriculture and the Mechanic Arts are not made the leading feature as required in this charter.[9]

In the end, Rutherford B. Hayes, the most prominent stateman in Ohio, bridged the chasm between OSU and agricultural leaders. When he left the White House in 1881, Hayes was fifty-nine years of age and a man of health and vigor. Education was Hayes's special passion. He believed that access to education, including higher education that fostered economic development, was the way to expand opportuni-

3.4 The Ag Experimentation Station, as it was on the Columbus campus. In 1891, it moved to Wooster, Ohio, where it had more space.

8. Kinnison, 136–39.
9. Cope, 506.

ties, financial and social. At a time of increasing conflict between industry and labor in the United States, Hayes advocated and worked for expanding educational opportunity and to making industrial or vocational education more available as ways of achieving social harmony.

As the governor who helped OSU come into being in 1873, Hayes maintained a keen interest in the university after his political career ended. In 1887, Hayes accepted an offer from Governor Joseph Foraker (1886–1890) to become a member of the board of trustees of The Ohio State University. During his brief service as a trustee, Hayes would have a remarkable impact. No other person on the board of trustees or the board of control had his stature in Ohio.

In November 1887, Hayes persuaded the trustees to invite the board of control, the governing body of the Agricultural Experiment Station, to a meeting. That joint and historic meeting took place on December 7, 1887. According to one witness,

> President Hayes at once took control. He did not propose to have an outbreak if he could prevent it. In a quiet, forceful way, he at once took up the subject by saying that the two boards had one great object in view, the service of the public, that their aims were similar, if not the same, that it was their mutual desire to so provide for the application of the annuity provided by the Hatch Bill that would yield the largest benefits to the agricultural interests of the State, that as gentlemen having such common interests they could not afford to quarrel, and that he was sure his colleagues on the Board of Trustees would join him in every effort to aid the Station in its laudable desire to enlarge and extend the field of its operations. Under his frank and broad treatment of the subject at issue, an onlooker saw the warlike lines in the faces of the antagonists rapidly disappearing.[10]

Guided by Hayes, both parties agreed to a memo of understanding. OSU's trustees shared property, acknowledged the station's independent status and increased the University's support for agricultural experimentation. In turn, the station agreed to use University faculty members in its research and to employ undergraduate and graduate students in its work when possible.

Having healed the rift with the agricultural community, Hayes used his political stature to raise the financial support for land-grant colleges. In 1890, U.S. Senator Justin Morrill proposed a bill to add to the land grants awarded the colleges in the original Morrill Act of 1862, a maximum of another $25,000 per year. At the request of President Scott, Hayes wrote to Ohio members of the U.S. House and the U.S. Senate and to all senators and representatives whom he knew to encourage them to support the bill. That effort succeeded: in 1891, the General Assembly granted the financial support from the second Morrill Act to The Ohio State University.

So important was Hayes to OSU that the news of Hayes's death prompted President William Henry Scott to order an adjournment of classes and hold a special

---

10. Cope, 125.

meeting of the faculty. In University Hall, the chapel on the first floor at the north side, which served as the largest meeting room on campus, was draped in black. The board of trustees held an emergency meeting and passed a lengthy resolution, part of which stated: "The members of this board feel deeply the irreparable loss the university has sustained in the death of President Hayes and share in the general sorrow of the state and nation." Finally, a special issue of the student newspaper, *The Lantern*, appeared on February 3. Its editorial concluded: "There will never come a time when the loyal sons and daughters of O.S.U. will not feel pride in the glory which the devotion of Rutherford B. Hayes shed over our young but sturdy University."

In retrospect, the accomplishment of Hayes in reconnecting OSU with its agricultural supporters was a critical chapter in the history and well-being of the university. As the only land-grant institution in Ohio, OSU had a stake in maintaining ties of friendship and service to the agriculture industry in the state. Agriculture then, as now, was important economically and politically in Ohio and the fledgling university needed its support in the state legislature

After Hayes's death, OSU's program in agriculture and in agricultural research achieved statewide, national, and international recognition. In 1891, the Agricultural Experiment Station left campus for more spacious facilities in Wooster, Ohio but retained its ties with OSU; in 1921, following the retirement of the combative Thorne, the board of control consisted of members of the OSU board of trustees and the Ohio director of agriculture. Finally, in 1982, the Ohio Agricultural Research and Development Center, formerly the Ohio Agricultural Experiment Station, merged administratively with OSU and the separate board of control ceased to exist.

THE HYSELL ACT, 1891

In 2008, the legislature of the State of Ohio appropriated $620 million of OSU's $4.1 billion dollar budget. Such support from the taxpayers of Ohio developed gradually and not in the early years of the university. During most of the nineteenth century, the State of Ohio did not provide any support in taxes to higher education. Neither Ohio University in Athens nor Miami University in Oxford, which had begun decades before OSU, received financial support from the state. In fact, opposition to state support for OSU came from many sides: those who favored frugality in government, the advocates of Ohio University and Miami University, and disappointed critics who believed that OSU had failed to support agricultural education.

As OSU grew in numbers of people, physical plant, and programs, its revenue from the land-grant endowment of the Morrill Act became increasingly inadequate to cover operating expenses, such as salaries for faculty and staff, equipment, utilities, and supplies. As early as 1876, trustee Joseph Sullivant complained truculently: "Something more substantial and material than a mere legislative enactment was here demanded: grounds, buildings, libraries, apparatus, furniture, and conveniences for teaching were necessary for the existence of a college. What of all this has the State of Ohio provided? Nothing!"[11] Two years later, when the legislature changed the name to The Ohio State University, President Orton commented that the word "university" would be appropriate only if the legislators would be willing to add the financial support needed to broaden and strengthen the academic program to make OSU a real university.

In 1879, six years after the opening of the college, the effort of trustees and president to win legislature support brought about a small success. One of the trustees, Hon. T. Ewing Miller, and President Orton arranged a trip to the University of Illinois and invited members of the finance committees of the legislature to join them. According to President Orton, the legislators admired the facilities of that land-grant school, including its art gallery, its library, the chemical laboratory, the green house, the machine shop, and the livestock: "All these things the members of the finance committees saw, and . . . they came back from their journey filled with new light and with a changed attitude towards their own struggling and neglected university." Shortly thereafter the legislature appropriated $15,800 for OSU but directed that most of the money go for a mechanical laboratory and for farm improvements.[12] Succeeding legislatures voted additional money to support OSU's farm, supplies for its school of mines, and walls and table cases for its geological museum.[13] All of these enhancements strengthened OSU's education in agriculture and in engineering, but did nothing for its arts or humanities.

In 1883, OSU President William Henry Scott requested a general subsidy from the legislature. To make his case, Scott pointed to Michigan and Wisconsin, where the legislatures had awarded the land-grant colleges a one-twentieth of a mill levy on the state tax rolls for the last ten years. As Scott put it, " . . . the University would benefit greatly not only from the total amount collected but in knowing in advance how much money would be available to it, rather than relying on the whims of legislators."[14]

In June 1890, a meeting of the alumni of OSU passed a resolution urging another application to the legislature. A committee asked alumni, ex-students, students, and friends of OSU to contact legislators and ask them to support a tax levy especially for the support of OSU. Some newspapers joined in support. In January of 1891, Governor James Campbell, (1890–1892) declared in his annual message:

> The University has made notable progress, and through your generous, although somewhat fitful, aid it has become a credit to the State. The number of students now crowds its capacity, and they are in need of increased facilities. It is mortifying to admit, that in the encouragement of higher education, Ohio stands twenty-sixth [of 38] upon the list of states. Some effort ought to be made to elevate the state to its proper rank in this

---

11. James E. Pollard, *History of The Ohio State University: The Story of its first Seventy-Five Years, 1873–1948* (Columbus: The Ohio State University Press, 1952), 69; trustees report for 1876.

12. Pollard, 70.

13. Cope, 110–111.

14. Cope, 137.

3.5 Ohio governor James Campbell became an advocate for increasing financial support for The Ohio State University and called for an annual subsidy to support OSU.

3.6 Campbell Hall, shown below in 1954, is located on Neil Avenue and was named for the wife of Governor James Campbell in 1921.

3.7–3.8 The Hysell Act enabled OSU to begin construction on two landmark buildings, Hayes Hall, shown above and completed in 1892, and Orton Hall, which was finished in 1893.

respect. A permanent and uniform income, large enough to stimulate healthy growth, is the most effective aid.[15]

Speaker Nial R. Hysell introduced the successful bill to create this special levy, and it became law on March 20, 1891. On the campus, the faculty and students held a party in University Hall. Professor Edward Orton, who attended the celebration, remembered that Professor Henry Detmers, the German-born professor of veterinary medicine, had declared "Und der name of Speaker Hysell shall be inscribed on the valls of the University in indelible ink."[16] Although Hysell's name was never inscribed on campus—no hall or street carries his name—the editors of the *Makio* for 1891 dedicated this student yearbook to Governor Campbell and to Nial R. Hysell as friends of education. Portraits of each appear in the yearbook.[17]

3.9 Nial R. Hysell, who was speaker of the Ohio House, had a significant impact upon OSU because the bill providing for the first annual tax levy in support of the university is in his name.

The Hysell Act, a critical turning point in the history of OSU, had both symbolic and practical importance. The act meant that the State of Ohio had finally accepted a continuing financial responsibility for the well-being of its state university. This had been the quest of the trustees since Joseph Sullivant voiced it in the 1870s.

The annual tax levy continued as the university's until it was replaced when the university became part of the state budget process in 1915.[18] In addition, the Hysell Act enabled the university to issue bonds against anticipated tax revenues. This empowered OSU to finance the construction of two buildings that would later be on the National Register of Historic Places: Hayes Hall and Orton Hall. In retrospect, a building named in honor of Hysell would have been appropriate.

WORLD WAR II AND OSU

Wars can have a traumatic impact on all aspects of life but such conflicts are not necessarily turning points in the history of institutions. During World War I, for example, OSU hosted a School of Military Aeronautics, sent students and faculty to military and governmental service, and participated significantly in the program of the Student Army Training Corps which enrolled 2,018 students on the campus

---

15. Cope, 139.
16. Cope, 143.
17. Kinnison, 167.
18. Pollard, 229.

3.10 *Engineering class building pontoon bridge, 1943*

3.11 *B-17s fly over OSU campus, 1943.*

and was the forerunner of the Reserve Officer Training Corps (ROTC). However, the war was so brief (for the United States at any rate, its engagement lasting from April 1917 to November 1918) that it had relatively little impact when compared with World War II, which began for the United States on December 7, 1941.

World War II and the years following had great impact in transforming OSU into the university of today. When America entered the war, student enrollments fell, as males left campus for military service. After the war's cessation, however, the number of returning veterans strained the campus and its faculty and staff. As parents, the veterans raised the expectation for access to higher education for the next generation, the baby-boomers who doubled and tripled what had been the enrollment of OSU before the war.

The war also changed the character of OSU significantly. The number of foreign students and programs for international studies increased, even as the U.S. itself took a leadership role in the world after the war. Finally, OSU broadened its research enterprises as the federal government continued the support that had begun as part of the war effort.

At first, winning the war became the pressing goal of the entire campus community after the Japanese attack on Pearl Harbor on December 7, 1941. OSU's president Howard Bevis declared: "Schools take their places alongside factories and training camps as necessary agencies of preparation for war." He predicted that the war would dominate life and priorities on campus.[19]

The war did change teaching, research, and service as well as campus life in numerous ways. Enlistment and the draft significantly reduced the numbers of men

3.12 Professor Samuel Renshaw (standing and with glasses), who developed a visual recognition program in the war effort. Note CBS reporter Walter Cronkite (seated and with pipe).

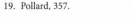

19. Pollard, 357.

3.13 *Army men in school, 1943*

as faculty, staff, and students on the campus. In 1940, student enrollment was 15,556; in 1943–44 there were only 10,225 students enrolled. Campaigns to sell war bonds and news of the war dominated campus life. Meanwhile, faculty and staff left for military service and government work in the national emergency. The pace of academic life quickened in wartime and students could take a full rotation of courses in nine months rather than twelve. Classrooms held students and professors from morning to late in the evening. Twilight School enabled many who worked in war industries during the day to attend classes in the evening.[20]

As it had in World War I, OSU hosted specialized training programs for the military and adjusted its curriculum to fit the needs created by World War II. Already in 1940 Congress had created a defense training

3.14 *OSU president Howard Bevis (left) stands in front of the marker designating status of OSU men in service.*

20. Pollard, 384.

program, which led to engineering, science, and management war training at OSU.[21] Courses in Russian, Portuguese, and Japanese appeared for the first time, as did courses in aeronautical meteorology, military geology, and the interpretation of maps for military purposes.[22]

Several programs in teaching and training achieved special prominence. Particularly noteworthy was the Navy Recognition School. Established in 1942, the program offered intensive training for sixty days in developing abilities in vision and perception to enable soldiers to quickly recognize aircraft as enemy or friendly. Professor Sam Renshaw of psychology developed the program, whose classes took place in Derby Hall.

In 1943, OSU signed a contract with the War Department for an Army Specialized Training Program. For thirteen weeks, soldiers studied engineering, languages, medicine, veterinary medicine, and dentistry. In 1943, OSU signed another contract with the War Department for the Specialized Training Assignment and Reclassification Program that tested soldiers and provided for refresher courses in mathematics, chemistry, and physics. So numerous were the soldiers on the OSU campus that the army provided a shuttle between downtown's Union Station, where the trains came in, and the Stadium Dormitories, where the cadets resided. Meanwhile, with the help of the Student War Board, a USO provided recreation and social services at Pomerene Hall.[23]

Wartime needs drove research also. As early as January 14, 1941, the trustees authorized the use of the OSU Research Foundation to enter into contracts with the War Department for research needs. In 1942, OSU received federal funding to build a War Research Laboratory on 19th Avenue. Completed in only ten months, this building still

3.15 War Research Laboratory, later renamed the Herrick Johnston Laboratory in 1970. It still stands on West 19th Avenue. Note the guard in this photograph.

21. Pollard, 362.
22. Pollard, 361.
23. James E. Pollard, *History of The Ohio State University, Vol. VIII: The Bevis Administration, 1940–1956, Part 1; The University in a World at War, 1940–1945* (Columbus: The Ohio State University, 1967), 46.

3.16 OSU Professor Herrick Johnston in the Cryogenic Laboratory, OSU's contribution to the Manhattan Project that led to the atomic bomb

3.17 Physical training exercise on the campus in wartime

3.18 Scene at a navy recruiting office

stands as mute testimony to the urgency of the time. Another and secret facility was a small laboratory north of Lane Avenue in which researchers studied and improved jet engines and rocket motors.[24] By June of 1943, OSU had fifty research projects, a majority having to do with developing weapons and with aeronautics.[25] Other research projects involved war products, health and food problems, and civilian substitutes for critical materials.

Of all the secret war-related research that OSU conducted, the most dramatic and the most secretive was its work for the atomic bomb. More than one hundred alumni and faculty participated in the laboratories of the Manhattan Project. Some of the research that led to nuclear fission took place on the OSU campus, especially in the War Research Laboratory and the Cryogenic Laboratory. Professor Herrick L. Johnston of the chemistry department headed OSU's involvement in the Manhattan Project.[26]

By the time the war ended in 1945, it had changed OSU in many ways. Some of the buildings and facilities constructed or acquired for the war effort continued. Among these were the War Research Laboratory, which was renamed the Herrick L. Johnston Building in 1970. Another was the university airport, completed in 1942 and renamed in 1943 to honor student athlete Don Scott, who was killed in Great Britain. This airport made it possible for OSU to participate in the many aeronautical projects of the war. In addition, OSU had established the Graduate Aviation Center

24. Pollard, 391
25. Pollard, 367
26. *Alumni Magazine,* October 1945, 1–3.

at Dayton (later the graduate program of Wright State University) to enable graduate students in that area to pursue advanced courses in aerodynamics, airplane structures, communication engineering, applied mechanics, theoretical physics, and more.

Probably the most important result of the war was the "Servicemen's Readjustment Act of 1944," popularly known as the "GI Bill of Rights." According to the educational provision of the law, any veteran who had served ninety days or more and had an honorable discharge was eligible. The Veterans Administration paid colleges and universities a maximum of $500 a year for each student for tuition, books, fees, and training costs and allocated for each veteran a monthly subsistence allowance. Returning veterans, supported by federal stipends, soon swelled student enrollments to unprecedented numbers. In the fall of 1944, student enrollment stood at 11,548; a year later, the number jumped to 22,169. So great was the demand for admission to OSU that the trustees authorized a preference system for admissions, giving highest priority to Ohio veterans and least to nonresidents who were not veterans.[27] As these veterans became parents as well as alumni, many expected that their own children would attend OSU.

One enduring consequence of the number of veterans and the difficulty in providing housing for them was the expansion of OSU's dormitory system. In 1948, the Ohio legislature passed a law that enabled the creation of The Ohio State University Housing Commission. It was empowered to borrow money through bonds for the purpose of constructing dormitories and other revenue-generating facilities. Rather than wait for legislative subsidies, the university could take the initiative in constructing buildings that would pay for themselves over time through fees. Seven of the OSU dormitories and related facilities memorialize OSU students or alumni who died as soldiers in World War II: Blackburn House, Halloran House, Haverfield House, Houck House, Nosker House, Raney Commons, and Scott House.

Three other buildings resulted from the expansion of enrollment after World War II. First, the increased numbers of students overwhelmed the original student union (now Enarson Hall) built in 1909. In 1947, students, many of them war veterans, petitioned the trustees for a new building more appropriate to their numbers. Ohio Union opened in 1951, largely financed from student fees. It would stand prominently on High Street until razed in 2007 to make way for a newer student union. Second was a major addition to the Main Library. The latter had been built too small when it opened in 1913; in 1951, construction added the stack tower and two "saddle bags" to the front of the Main Library. In the process, the building was renamed the William Oxley Thompson Memorial Library. About the same time, the State of Ohio anticipated the care of veterans as a pressing concern then and in the future. It therefore provided major funding for a Health Sciences Center that significantly expanded OSU hospitals, construction beginning in 1948.

After the war, research support benefitted from continuing federal as well as corporate sponsorship. Particularly noteworthy were investments and discoveries in

---

27. Pollard, 381–82.

3.19–3.21 Student housing was an adventure for returning veterans. Trailers at the state fair grounds served some married students. Other veterans found accommodations in GI village with temporary buildings on farmland west of the Olentangy River.

fields such as cryogenics, atomic energy, and antenna research. War research in recognition and perception led to the creation of the Institute for Research in Vision, which brought together biological, medical, physical, and social investigators. In 1950, OSU created an Institute of Geodesy, Photogrammetry, and Cartography, fields that OSU had developed for the war. So active was the OSU

Research Foundation in administering research grants that in 1954 OSU purchased a former Rockwell plant on Kinnear Road.[28]

Another dimension of OSU that developed greatly during World War II and expanded thereafter was an international one. As the United States became the dominant global power after the war, its major universities, including OSU, grew more international in orientation. Some foreign languages had been part of the university from its beginning; so, too, had students from other countries. In 1892, the first foreign student, a Jamaican, graduated. During the 1930s, foreign students had their own student organizations, groups such as the Cosmopolitan Club. However, after the war, the numbers of students from other countries increased substantially (from 72 in 1945 to 189 in 1948).

Furthermore, OSU faculty became more involved in international projects, including the establishment of institutions of higher education in Guam and in Korea. In 1955, OSU became one of five universities to provide agricultural education and practical expertise to India. By 1956, one speaker at OSU declared: "An essential truth is that American universities today stand preeminent in the world. This results partly from our own advance and partly from the serious impairment in recent years of European universities. But the fact is that the responsibility of leadership has come to us as once it belonged in sequence to Bologna, Paris, Oxford, and Berlin."[29]

THE STUDENT UPHEAVAL OF 1970

Student uprisings against college administrators and faculty go back as far as the medieval period, perhaps to the very beginning of the concept of university itself. Early in its history, OSU experienced incidents of mass student discontent. In 1883, following the termination of President Walter Quincy Scott, students behaved so badly toward the new president, William Henry Scott, that the faculty wrote a report to the trustees that denounced the students and defended Scott.[30] Later, issues concerning compulsory chapel, mandatory military drill, housing, and other matters agitated students from time to time. In 1961, when the Faculty Council voted not to accept an invitation to compete in the Rose Bowl, students took to the streets in mass demonstrations of protest. (See chapter 6: "Athletics at OSU.")

What made the disturbances of 1970 extraordinary were their origins, their duration, their scale, and their lasting consequences at OSU. Although directed at the university administration, especially President Novice Fawcett, the issues that

---

28. James E. Pollard, *History of The Ohio State University, Vol. VIII: The Bevis Administration, 1940–1956, Part 2: The Post-War Years and the Emergence of the Greater University, 1945–1956* (Columbus: The Ohio State University, 1972), 311–27.

29. *History of The Ohio State University, Vol. VII: Addresses and Proceedings of the Inauguration of Novice G. Fawcett; Dedication of Mershon Auditorium, April 29, 1957* (Columbus: The Ohio State University Press, 1959), 80.

30. Kinnison, 114; OSU Archives, Faculty minutes, I, 102ff.

3.22–3.23 For nearly twenty years the Speaker's Rule that required the OSU president to approve speakers from off-campus was a flashpoint of controversy between OSU administration and faculty and students.

aroused the students were national as well as local and shared by many faculty as well as students. Moreover, the protests took place during much of the 1960s and achieved a level of violence that ended classes and brought soldiers to campus. Finally, the upheaval accelerated—to say the least—patterns of change at the university that would continue for decades thereafter.

During the 1950s and early 1960s the Speaker's Rule was a flashpoint of conflict between students, faculty, and administration. Originating in 1946 and revised in 1951, the Rule required that students who wished to bring speakers to campus had to request approval from the Office of the President. The trustees who created the rule wanted to prevent OSU from hosting speakers who were perceived as Communists or subversives. Other universities with similar rules that were enacted in the early years of the Cold War also experienced protests against what appeared to be a restriction upon one of the most fundamental aspects of university life: a free exchange of differing views.

Year after year, students and faculty seethed against the Speaker's Rule and challenged it regularly by inviting controversial speakers to visit the campus. One particularly dramatic occasion occured in May 1962, when 1,500 professors attended a meeting concerning President Novice Fawcett's refusal to approve a controversial speaker. This was the largest meeting of OSU faculty. In April of 1965, when the president refused to approve another controversial speaker, students occupied the Administration Building, now Bricker Hall. Finally, in September 1965, OSU trustees changed the rule so that faculty advisors, not the president, approved invitations to speakers.[31] Nevertheless, the years of controversy made OSU's administration a target for mistrust and protest.

Conflicts over racial equality and opportunity that had spread across the nation also fired passions at OSU. Historically, African American students had had difficulty in living in OSU dormitories, although no official policy prevented them. A major incident took place in 1933 when a black student was denied permission to reside in the Home Economics house even though her academic program required her to do so. Housing and commercial establishments near campus discriminated against African Americans also. In the 1960s the Student Senate created a Human Relations Commission and a Hearing Board to act on charges of discrimination. Pressure mounted for OSU to refuse to recommend off-campus apartments owned by landlords who refused to rent to African Americans. Meanwhile, students insisted that the university hire more black faculty and create courses and programs featuring African American history and culture.

In 1968, the assassination of Dr. Martin Luther King further inflamed discontent about the progress of racial equality nationally and at OSU. In March, some one hundred black students, organized by the Black Student Union, met with university officials in Stillman Hall and charged the university with racism. On April 26, to

---

31. Francis P. Weisenburger, *History of The Ohio State University, Vol. IX: The Fawcett Years, 1956–1972* (Columbus: The Ohio State University, 1975), 158–59.

3.24 Concerns about racial discrimination on campus and in Columbus also aroused passions on campus. Shown here is a takeover of the Administration Building (now Bricker Hall) in April 1968.

protest lack of progress and an incident in which four African American students were removed from a campus bus for their behavior, approximately seventy-five members of the Black Student Union took over part of the Administration Building. For five hours, they held Gordon Carson, Vice President for Business, and two secretaries as prisoners. Legal actions against those involved followed.

As volatile as these issues were, the controversial Vietnam War polarized the campus further, especially after 1968. OSU and other land-grant institutions provided training for students to enter the military as officers. In fact, at OSU freshmen and sophomore males were required to take ROTC classes. Recruiting events and ROTC generally became targets of anti-war protestors. In December 1967, some students disrupted military recruiting that was taking place in the Ohio Union; more

3.25 *The controversial Vietnam War sparked peaceful as well as violent demonstrations. This was a peaceful one in front of the Administration Building, 1969.*

disruptions flared up in 1968 wherever recruiting by military services took place.[32] As the controversial war continued, so too did the demonstrations over war-related issues that included military research, recruiting, and compulsory ROTC.

Women students and faculty also voiced discontent. Women protested against gender-based inequities and barriers to advancement. Rules for women students were different in an era when "in loco parentis" (the university functioning in the place of parents) had prevailed. Before 1961, women had to return to dormitories by 10:30 p.m., needed written parental permission to be away overnight, and were prohibited from living in apartments. Until 1963–64, a rule had provided "Any undergraduate woman who visits a man's room or apartment without University approved chaperons will be subject to dismissal." By 1966–67, coeducational dormitories had appeared, but the pressures for more gender equality continued. The Women's Liberation Front and its supporters called for the university to investigate the status of women on campus; to establish courses in Women's Studies; to hire more female faculty and administrators; and to institute a planned parenthood center, a day-care center, and a self-defense program.[33]

Turmoil on campus—demonstrations, the circulating and posting of provoca-

---

32. Weisenburger, 166.
33. Weisenburger, 188–89.

tive leaflets, blocking access to classrooms and offices—reached its peak in 1970. In March, a group representing two hundred black students presented nineteen demands to vice president of students John Mount. On April 20, some one hundred students in the School of Social Work walked out of classes as a protest against school policies. On April 28, the Student Senate passed a resolution calling for a boycott of classes if the protestors did not prevail. Confrontation took place as students blockaded the 11th Avenue–Neil Avenue entrance to the campus and State Highway Patrol arrived to clear it. Blasts of tear gas that provoked volleys of bricks,

3.26 Women students also made their voices heard, against the Vietnam War and in support of women's studies and greater gender equality and opportunity on the OSU campus.

3.27–3.28 Two scenes on the Oval, April and May 1970, during which violence on the campus and a student strike led to occupation and then closing by the Ohio National Guard

rocks, and bottles sparked more demonstrations in a cycle of confrontation, violence, and more protests. Finally, the Ohio National Guard came to campus, but the disturbances continued.

On May 4, news that Ohio National Guardsmen had killed four students at Kent State University further inflamed the precarious situation. Efforts to shut down the OSU campus continued. Finally, the university closed on May 6 and remained closed until May 19 as an effort to cool passions and bring reason and tranquility back to campus. When classes resumed, so, too, did the student demonstrations. On May 21, militants broke the windows of business establishments and University buildings until State Highway Patrolmen, sheriff's deputies, Columbus police, and the Ohio National Guardsmen restored order. Gradually, the violence of the demonstrations diminished, and by May 29 the Ohio National Guard began to withdraw from campus. The most violent time in the history of OSU had passed.[34]

Numerous changes followed the turmoil of 1970. In that year, the OSU Faculty Council, which represented faculty only, began planning for a new governing body that would include students and administrators. This became the University Senate in 1972, which had standing committees; faculty representatives from each of the colleges; and representatives of the student organizations, undergraduate, graduate, and professional. Other changes demanded in the 1960s came to fruition in the 1970s and thereafter. The first Vice Provost for Minority Affairs was hired in October of 1970. Also in that year OSU appointed the first Director of Affirmative Action, Madison Scott. In 1975, the Committee on Women and Minorities commenced its work of reviewing the status of women and minorities and the effectiveness of OSU in fostering equal opportunity. Within the Office of Student Affairs, a Black Student Program Office began in 1974, and a Hispanic Student Program Office in 1978. From the perspective of decades, it is still unclear how much the violence of 1970 accelerated the directions toward which the university had been moving, albeit at a slower pace, in the 1950s and 1960s.

SELECTIVE (COMPETITIVE) ADMISSIONS

Although less dramatic than the events of 1970, the adoption of a selective or competitive admissions policy beginning in 1987 was no less a turning point in the history of OSU. It has the potential for changing the character, and even the basic missions and heritage of this land-grant university. In adopting selective admissions, The Ohio State University was the last among the public universities in the Big Ten to do so.

When The Ohio Agricultural and Mechanical College opened its doors in September 1873, one of the first obstacles that prospective students encountered was, in fact, an admissions test. Some people had argued that because the new college

---

34. Weisenburger, 169–72.

had a publicly funded endowment, i.e., the federal lands sold in accordance with the Morrill Act, every resident of Ohio had a right to be admitted. In defending the admissions test, President Edward Orton put to use arguments that presidents more than a century later would repeat: "It would be, in our judgment, a gross perversion of our funds to use them in any way in teaching the elementary branches. For this work public provision of the amplest kind has already been made. We want from the common [public] schools those students—and only those—who have obtained the best training that such schools can give."[35]

Applicants who failed portions of the admissions test enrolled in the preparatory department of the university. In an era when high schools were not present in all cities and even fewer in rural areas, it was common for colleges and universities to provide a remedial program to fully prepare students who needed additional help for admission. At OSU, the preparatory department admitted students as young as fourteen and continued to function until 1896.

Meanwhile, the faculty worked directly with high schools to prepare students for admission to OSU. In 1880, the trustees, at the request of the faculty, admitted graduates of high schools in cities of five thousand or more without a test, provided they had satisfactorily accomplished courses in high school that met the requirements for admission.[36] A few years later, in 1889, the OSU faculty formed a high school visitation committee to inspect schools to which they were invited to determine if graduates from the school were eligible for admission to OSU without additional testing.[37] In 1901, OSU's College of Arts, Philosophy and Science published in its bulletin the entrance requirements for beginning freshman, which included a number of units in English, social sciences, mathematics, science, and ancient and modern languages.[38]

Finally, in 1914, the State of Ohio enacted a law that "A graduate of the twelfth grade shall be entitled to admission without examination to any college or university which is supported wholly or in part by the State, but for unconditional admission may be required to complete such units not included in his high school course as may be prescribed, not less than two years prior to his entrance, by the faculty of the institution." Consequently, most graduates of public high schools in Ohio were to be admitted to OSU after application. The act also assigned the task of inspecting high schools to the State Superintendent of Public Education and rendered the high school visitation committee of OSU obsolete.[39]

This was the birth of "open admissions" but how "open" the university was to new students varied over time. The number of places for students, including classroom space, dormitories, and other elements necessary for education, always had limits; the resources of the university were never infinite. After World War II, for example, OSU

---

35. Orton, Annual Report, 1874, 674.

36. Pollard, 48; Board of Trustees, April 20, 1880.

37. Trustees, January 15, 1889.

38. *OSU Centennial History Series, Student Affairs, pt. 1, Admissions*, 4–5.

39. *OSU Centennial History Series, Student Affairs, pt. 1, Admissions*, 5.

gave priority admission to veterans over other applicants. In 1969, the State of Ohio imposed an enrollment restriction upon OSU so that, with some exceptions, there would be no admission to the university for any students in excess of 40,000.

Efforts to impose restrictions upon "open admissions" that allowed any high school student to be admitted to public colleges and universities in Ohio began as early as the 1960s, as political leaders in the Ohio House and Senate debated this issue. Defenders of the law argued that each high school graduate should have an equal chance to obtain advanced education at publicly supported institutions; no selective admissions policy could be fair to all students, especially to those whose academic aptitude did not improve until challenged by college courses.[40] On the other hand, university administrators questioned the wisdom of admitting students who required significant investment in remedial efforts. Was it ethical to admit students who had little chance of graduating? Students who paid tuition and then left for academic reasons were not likely to remain friends of the university.

In 1980, OSU president Harold Enarson, in testimony before the Ohio House Subcommittee, suggested a skills competency standard, not a high school diploma alone, as a requirement for admission to public colleges and universities.[41] In the spring of 1981, the Board of Regents and the State Board of Education agreed that state colleges and universities should require that applicants complete a college preparatory curriculum as a condition of admission.[42] When Edward Jennings succeeded Enarson as president in 1981, the efforts to restrict open admission gained new momentum. First, OSU prescribed minimum requirements for unconditional admission. Only students who in high school had fulfilled an OSU-prescribed curriculum could be admitted unconditionally to the rank of freshman at the campus in Columbus. Actual implementation took place in 1984. Students who did not meet the requirements had to attend special remedial classes at OSU, classes which did not earn credit towards graduation.[43]

Although the number of freshmen needing remedial effort rapidly declined, applications for admission continued to exceed the university's capacity. In 1986, OSU faculty and trustees approved a proposal that selective or competitive admissions would be the policy for the Columbus campus only, not the regional campuses, beginning in 1987. Factors in the admissions process would include high school class rank, grades, curricular background and test scores.[44] In addition, the admissions process would consider special talents, such as athletics, and those who by their presence would add to the cultural, racial, economic, and geographic diversity of OSU.[45] Applicants who had graduated from Ohio high schools but failed of admission to the Columbus campus could attend regional campuses of OSU, and

40. *Columbus Dispatch*, June 30, 1966.

41. *Columbus Dispatch*, March 31, 1980.

42. John B. Gabel, *History of The Ohio State University, Volume XI: The Jennings Years, 1981–1990* (Columbus: The Ohio State University, 1992), 54.

43. Gabel, 53–54.

44. OSU Press Release, Admissions OSU Archives VF, Feb. 4, 1986.

45. OSU Press Release, Admissions VF, September 24, 1987.

3.29 *Scene at Mirror Lake. Does this mean that selective or competitive admission has improved the quality of academic preparation not only of undergraduates but also of ducks?*

then enroll in Columbus after they had demonstrated sufficient academic success.

According to one account, OSU faculty applauded at a meeting where the decision for selective admission was announced.[46] Certain it is that the transition from requiring standards for admission, which had been in place at the beginning of the university, to selecting only the best qualified students from the applicant pool had significant impact upon OSU. Remedial courses diminished in number; retention rates for freshman improved. Because of the number of freshman who succeeded in becoming sophomores, the size of the freshman class began to decline, leading to more competition and a rise in academic quality among the applicants. In 1987, the first year of selective admissions, 91 percent of the freshmen were in the top half of their high school classes, up from 78 per cent in 1986. Twenty years later, 91 percent of the freshman class had graduated in the top quarter of their high school classes and 51 percent were in the top 10 percent.[47]

Subsequent to adopting selective admissions, OSU joined the ranks of the top 25 public universities, as stated in *U.S. News and World Report*.[48] Its criteria for

---

46. Gabel, 57.
47. See http://www.undergrad.osu.edu/domesticfreshman.html.
48. Baroway, 294.

ranking include peer assessment, retention of students, selectivity of admissions, financial resources, graduation rate, and alumni giving. Over the years, OSU rose steadily in the national rankings, from 21st in 2005 to 19th in 2006, and to 18th in 2009.[49]

The decision to adopt a selective or competitive policy of admissions was a momentous one. Aside from improving the academic quality of its freshman class, it brought questions that only the future could answer. Would selective admissions give an advantage to those who had graduated from wealthier school districts in Ohio? Would selective admissions be a barrier to those of talent but who lived in poor school districts? Would students who applied to OSU's regional campuses because they could not meet the standards for admission to the Columbus campus be able to compete successfully in Columbus at any time? Finally, as OSU became a more highly selective institution, would its exclusivity diminish its influence in state government and in the state legislature because there would be more taxpayers whose children were rejected by the university? Only the future will have answers.

CONCLUSION

Studying the turning points in any institution's history is useful but limiting. The narrow focus on specific events and times overlooks important people and events not directly connected to the turning points. Another limit is that when the history of the university becomes compressed to a small number of years, change appears to happen quickly. Actually, universities are places both of change and of continuity and the rhythm of campus life is the tension between the two. In the chapters that follow readers will find a broader and more comprehensive vista of OSU's past.

---

49. See OSU Press releases, August 18, 2006 and August 17, 2007.

CHAPTER FOUR

THEY DID "SOMETHING GREAT"

Twenty-Five People (Not Presidents) of The Ohio State University

Go forth and take up your stewardship, strong in the will to return to humanity, with good interest, all that humanity and nature have given to you.

—Professor Edward Orton, Jr.,
Commencement Address, March 1928

ONE MEASURE of quality of any university is how it shapes people and how they, in turn, improve the world around them. In roughly 140 years, the university has shaped the lives of more than 400,000 alumni as well as thousands of faculty and staff. Many of OSU's faculty, alumni, and staff have made a significant difference in the well-being of Ohio, our nation, and the world.

Only an encyclopedia, yet to be compiled, could thoroughly discuss the impact of OSU through its people. Instead, this chapter presents alphabetically arranged vignettes of twenty-five people of remarkable achievement. Rather than a ranked or comprehensive listing, the purpose of these stories is to show OSU's influence in many areas, from sciences to medicine and the arts, in the present as well as the past.

GEORGE BELLOWS

4.1 Bellows ca. 1903

Although George Bellows (1882–1925) lived only forty-two years, he had an extraordinary career as an artist. His paintings still attract international attention and hang in such prominent galleries as the National Gallery of Art in Washington, D.C., and the Whitney and the Museum of Modern Art in New York. The Columbus Museum of Art has a sizeable collection of his portraits and New York street scenes as well as a special exhibit of his life. Bellows's works are also prominent on the OSU campus and in the OSU Archives.

Born in Columbus, Ohio, Bellows attended Ohio State University from 1901 to 1904. At OSU, Bellows was an athletic and socially active student. He joined the baseball team and considered becoming a professional baseball player. In addition, Bellows was a member of the OSU Glee Club when it gave the first public performance of "Carmen Ohio," in 1903. Representing Beta Theta Pi fraternity, Bellows played an active role on campus and drew many illustrations for the campus yearbook, the *Makio*. As a student, Bellows studied under the distinguished portrait artist and OSU instructor Silas Martin.

Bellows left OSU before graduating and moved to New York City, where he expected to further his career as an artist. He studied at the New York School of Art under Robert Henri and became part of the Ashcan School, a group of artist who painted realistic scenes of urban life. An exhibition of these works in 1908 drew much attention to Bellows. From 1907 through 1915, Bellows painted a series of New York City winter scenes. Probably his most famous works portrayed amateur boxing matches, which captured the grit and power of the scenes as unusual works of art.

Besides painting, Bellows experimented in lithography. In 1918, he made litho-graphs that depicted atrocities committed by Germany during its invasion of Bel-gium. A year later, Bellows moved to Chicago to teach at the Chicago Art Institute. Between 1921 and 1924, he collaborated with master printer Bolton Brown to pro-duce images and illustrated many books. On January 8, 1925, Bellows died following the rupture of his appendix.

MILTON CANIFF

Many people read the comics before checking the news, advertisements, and other parts of the newspaper. One of the leading cartoonists in the history of the profes-sion was Milton Caniff, an OSU graduate of 1930. Born in Hillsboro, Ohio in 1907, Caniff began drawing cartoons at age thirteen for the Boy Scout Page of the *Dayton Journal Herald*. As a student in OSU's School of Journalism, Caniff drew cartoons for the *Lantern* and earned money by working for the *Columbus Evening News*. After

4.2 Milton Caniff, 1982

graduation, Caniff's first important career oppor-tunity occurred in 1932 when he traveled to New York and worked for the Associated Press to produce the comic strip "Dickie Dare," an action serial. In 1934, Caniff began working for the *New York Daily News* to develop a new strip, "Terry and the Pirates." This strip, and all of Caniff's later work, won much acclaim for storytelling, realism and accuracy of images, and artistic talent. When "Terry and the Pirates" ended in 1946, Caniff began a new series, "Ste-ven Canyon," an action strip that featured an airplane pilot as the cen-tral character. *Newsweek* featured Steve Canyon and Caniff on its cover on April 24, 1950. The popular series continued until Caniff died in 1988. So prominent was Steve Canyon in the popular imagination that the U.S. Air Force held a formal decommissioning ceremony for Canyon after Caniff's death.

During his lifetime, Caniff earned many honors. He was one of the founders of the National Cartoonists Society and received the Society's first Cartoonist of the Year Award in 1946. In June of 1974, Caniff was the commencement speaker at OSU. The OSU Alumni Association awarded him the Alumni Medalist Award, its highest honor, in 1987. Even after his death, the legacy of Milton Caniff continues at OSU's Cartoon Library and Museum (now the Billy Ireland Cartoon Library and Museum), which has become the foremost center for the study of cartooning in the United States. Before his death, Caniff donated his papers and cartoons to OSU.

CHARLES CSURI

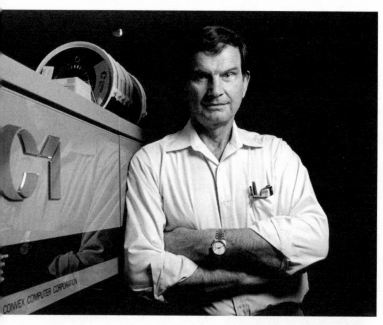

4.3 Charles Csuri in 1986

In television, movies, or video games, computer generated images are everywhere. They have enabled new modes of learning and have given us new forms of entertainment. Much credit is due to OSU's Professor Charles A. Csuri, one of the founders of computer-generated graphics.

Born in West Virginia, Csuri attended high school in Cleveland and came to OSU in 1940 to play football and to study industrial engineering. Csuri distinguished himself as an All-American tackle on football fields, but his creative talent was in the studio and in drawing. World War II interrupted his athletic and academic careers. After earning combat medals for deeds of heroism, Csuri resumed his studies in art in 1946, earned a masters degree in fine arts, and joined the OSU faculty to teach drawing and painting. As a conventional artist, Professor Csuri achieved enough prominence to have one-person shows in New York City. His early works appear in the collections of Walter P. Chrysler, and fellow artists Roy Lichtenstein and sculptor George Segal.

In the 1960s, Csuri took an interest in computer technology and began to experiment with how computers could extend art and artists beyond the limits of their hands. So pioneering was his interest that he became the first artist to receive funding from the National Science Foundation. In 1964, he created the first computer art and then produced computer animated films in 1965. Between 1971 and 1987, Csuri led the Computer Graphics Research Group and the Advanced Computing Center for Art and Design at OSU. He co-founded one of the first computer animation production companies, Cranston/Csuri Productions, one of whose accomplishments was the computer graphics for the Super Bowls of professional football. Besides movie and television productions, Csuri's work has had applications for computer technology, including in flight simulators, in computer-aided design, in magnetic resonance imaging, and even in education for the deaf.

Charles Csuri has received many honors. In February 1985 the *Smithsonian Magazine* honored him with a cover and a major article. Siggraph, the Computing Machinery's Special Interest Group on Graphics and Interactive Techniques, honored him at a special reception in 1996. A photographic portrait of Csuri hangs in the Computer Museum in Boston. At OSU, he was the commencement speaker in December 1985. In 2000, Csuri received OSU's Sullivant Medal and the Governor's Award for the Arts. Even in his eighties, Professor Csuri continued to work daily on campus and with his computers.

EDGAR DALE

How do people learn to read? In what ways can audiovisual communication improve and shape learning? These are the research questions that OSU Professor Edgar Dale explored in a career that made him a nationally respected pioneer in educational research education and studies of literacy.

Born in Minnesota in 1900, Edgar Dale taught as a rural schoolteacher in North Dakota and became a superintendent of schools even before earning bachelor's and masters degree from the University of North Dakota in 1921 and 1924, respectively. Five years later, Dale completed a Ph.D. at the University of Chicago, where he studied under Professor Werrett W. Charters.

4.4 *Edgar Dale in 1953. Note the television with big antenna.*

After graduation, Dale followed Charters to The Ohio State University and became a research associate for OSU's Bureau of Educational Research.

Dale's first interest was in the educational potential of films. Even before coming to OSU, Dale had served for one year at Eastman Kodak as a member of the editorial staff of Eastman Teaching Films in 1928. At OSU, Dale expanded his research into films and audiovisual media as educational instruments. In 1936, Dale spoke before a committee of the League of Nations because of his expertise in motion pictures. During World War II, Dale headed a division of the Bureau of Motion Pictures in the Office of War Information, and after the war he served as the Educational Film Library Associations representative to the U.S. National Commission for UNESCO. Also, Professor Dale served as president of the visual instruction department of the National Education Association, as a member of the Educational Policies Commission, and as a member of the board of directors of the National Society for the Study of Education.

Dr. Dale contributed significantly to the literature about instructional media and literacy. His books included *How to Appreciate Motion Pictures* (1935), *Teaching with Motion Pictures* (1937), *How to Read a Newspaper* (1941), and the often reprinted *Audiovisual Methods in Teaching* (1954). Near the end of his life, Dr. Dale worked on making reading materials easier to understand and developed a readability formula that assigned grade levels to reading materials.

Dale earned many distinctions. OSU appointed him a professor of education in 1939, and he received a Distinguished Teaching Award in 1963 and an honorary degree in 1980. The Educational Film Library Association honored him with an award for distinguished service in the audiovisual field in 1961. In 1968, Dale received the Eastman Kodak Gold Medal Award from the Society of Motion Picture and Television Engineers. The International Reading Association gave him its Citation of Merit in 1973. Until his death in 1985, Dale remained active as an adviser and contributor to *World Book Encyclopedia*.

MAX FISHER

Rising from humble origins, Max Fisher achieved prominence in business, philanthropy, and international diplomacy. OSU's College of Business bears his name.

Born in Salem, Ohio in 1908, Max Fisher was the son of a Russian immigrant who set up a business as a peddler and then started a clothing store. A talented athlete, Fisher enrolled at The Ohio State University with a football scholarship. Although injuries ended his football career, Fisher did graduate with a B.S. in business administration in 1930. His father had moved to Detroit where he founded Keystone Oil, which cleaned lubricating oil that had been used and sold it to industrial customers. Max Fisher joined the family company as a sales assistant. In 1932, Fisher negotiated with two Detroit businesspeople who owned Aurora Gasoline to join Keystone in building an independent refinery. Fisher chaired Aurora Gasoline,

4.5 Max Fisher, ca. 1993

one of the largest independent oil companies in the Midwest from 1932 to 1959, when Marathon Oil bought Aurora. With his profits, Fisher invested in real estate, especially in Detroit, and he played an active role in urban renewal.

Fisher also helped the Republican Party financially and persuaded others to support Republicans. A personal hero for Fisher was Richard Nixon, whom he admired for his work ethic and his rise from humble beginnings. Fisher actively supported Nixon in the presidential campaign of 1968. Later on, Fisher served as a key adviser to presidents Gerald Ford, Ronald Reagan, and George Bush. He also had close associations with political leaders in Israel and played an important, if informal, role in international relations between the United States and Israel.

Max Fisher made many gifts to philanthropic organizations. In 1993, he gave twenty million dollars to support OSU's College of Business. Besides OSU, Fisher supported other educational institutions. His generosity towards higher education won him eleven honorary degrees, including from The Ohio State University, Michigan State University, and Hebrew University of Jerusalem. In recognition of his civic leadership and his philanthropy, President Ronald Reagan awarded Fisher the Presidential Citizen Award. When Fisher died in 2005, OSU's Dean Joseph Alutto remarked "Throughout his life, Max has been a model for those who are committed to make a positive difference in the world around them."[1]

PAUL FLORY

Of the many distinguished alumni of OSU, Paul Flory achieved the distinction of being its first Nobel Prize winner. In 1974, Flory won the Nobel Prize for Chemistry for his research on synthetic and natural macromolecules.

Born in 1910 in Sterling, Illinois, Flory was the son of a clergyman-educator and a schoolteacher. Flory enrolled in Manchester College in Indiana and graduated in 1931, with a major in chemistry. One of his professors encouraged him to undertake grad-

4.6 Paul Flory

---

1. OSU News Release, March 3, 2005.

uate studies at Ohio State. Guided by OSU's Professor Herrick L. Johnston, "whose boundless zeal for scientific research made a lasting impression on his students," Flory completed a Ph.D., with a dissertation on physical chemistry.

A position with the Central Research Department of the DuPont Company kindled Flory's interest in the fundamentals of polymerization and polymeric substances when DuPont was inventing nylon and neoprene. After he left DuPont in 1938, Flory continued his research at the University of Cincinnati, at Exxon Laboratories, and then at the Research Laboratory of Goodyear. In 1948, an appointment to a lectureship and later a professorship in chemistry at Cornell University launched a distinguished academic career and more research on polymers. From 1957 to 1961, Flory was executive director of the Mellon Foundation. In 1961, he accepted a professorship in the Department of Chemistry at Stanford University.

In addition to the Nobel Prize, Flory won other accolades, including the National Medal of Science and the Priestly Award of the American Chemical Society, both in 1974. OSU awarded him its Sullivant Medal in recognition of his research on rubber in 1945, and an honorary degree in 1970. After his death in 1985, the university placed a plaque near McPherson Lab to honor Flory.[2]

4.7 William Fowler

WILLIAM FOWLER

When William A. Fowler died in 1995, the California Institute of Technology commented that he and his collaborators were "at the forefront of some of the most central issues in modern physics and cosmology: the formation of the chemical elements inside stars, the Big Bang origin of the universe; and the current dark matter debate over what most of the universe is made of."[3] A graduate of OSU, Fowler's research into the chemical elements of stars earned him a share of the Nobel Prize in Physics in 1983.

Fowler was born in Pennsylvania in 1911. His family moved to Lima, Ohio, and he enrolled at The Ohio State University, originally to study ceramic engineering. To support himself, Fowler waited tables. As a freshman, Fowler

---

2. See Nobelprize.org, Flory autobiography.
3. Caltech Media News Relations newsrelease, March 14, 1995.

heard an inspirational talk by Alpheus Smith, chair of OSU's department of physics, and decided to study engineering physics. Fowler became one of OSU's first graduates in that discipline in 1933. A graduate career at California Institute of Technology followed, with a doctorate in physics in 1936. Fowler joined the faculty in 1939 and remained at Caltech for the rest of his life.

Fowler's career in nuclear physics and nuclear astrophysics covered more than sixty years. In that time, he studied fusion reactions and how lighter chemical elements could create heavier ones. His scholarship had special importance for astronomy as well as for physics.

As a distinguished alumnus of OSU, Fowler earned many honors besides the Nobel Prize. OSU awarded him the Lamme Medal in 1952, an honorary degree in 1978, and the Joseph Sullivant Medal, awarded only every five years, in 1985. Two years later, a plaque honoring Dr. Fowler was dedicated near Smith Lab, whose namesake had so inspired him to major in physics.

THOMAS FRENCH

Famous as "the father of Ohio Stadium," Professor Thomas French had a lengthy career at OSU as a student and a faculty member. At his death in 1944, OSU Trustees praised his service to the university: "In addition to this, he found time and talent to produce textbooks and other materials in the field of engineering drawing which gave him a world-wide reputation."[4]

Born in 1871 at Mansfield, Thomas French moved with his family moved to Dayton. Even as a high school student, French had such talent for mechanical drawing that he became chief draftsman for a local firm and taught drawing at YMCA classes.

In 1891, French enrolled at OSU, where

4.8 Thomas French

he studied under Professor Stillman W. Robinson, who had also taught Benjamin Lamme, a future winner of OSU's Sullivant Medal. While French was a student, he also worked for OSU as a draftsman and part-time assistant in the drawing department. After graduating with a degree in mechanical engineering, French became an assistant professor of drawing at OSU. By 1906 he had become professor and department chair of engineering drawing.

French earned a national reputation for a series of textbooks in engineering drawing. His *A Manual of Engineering Drawing for Students and Draftsmen* was first

---

4. Trustees resolution, December 4, 1944.

published in 1911 and remained the standard text for decades. As late as 1943, the Society for the Promotion of Engineering Education called it a "truly monumental classic" which held the record as the best-selling of all textbooks in that field. In 1943, he received the Society's Lamme Medal for his leadership and contributions to engineering.[5]

A talented artist and engineer, French had an inquisitive mind that reached into many areas. He was a skilled and prolific producer of book plates and took national prizes for his art. His interest in heraldry and design inspired him to redesign the university's seal, which the trustees approved in 1940.

Today, the university's field house bears his name because of his devotion to athletics. His brother had been a talented football player for OSU, and intercollegiate athletics became his passion. Thomas French was the first to envision a stadium for OSU and was a leader in planning this monumental and award-winning building. (His importance to OSU athletics appears in the chapter 6, "Athletics at OSU.")

4.9 A. B. Graham in 1919

A. B. GRAHAM

"I pledge My Head to clearer thinking, My Heart to greater loyalty, My Hands to larger service and My Health to better living, for My Club, My Community, My Country, and My World." This pledge recited today by more than 300,000 Ohioans in 4-H clubs stems from its founder, A. B. Graham, who personified OSU's ideals of outreach and service. Before he became the first full-time head of the agricultural extension at OSU in 1905, Graham had already founded 4 H (Head, Heart, Hand, and Health) clubs for which he would become famous. These organizations educated youths by showing them and inspiring them to apply scientific knowledge to agriculture.

Born in Champaign County in 1868, Albert B. Graham attended rural and village schools and acquired a teacher's certificate in Miami County, Ohio at the age of sixteen. In 1888 he graduated from the National Normal School in Lebanon, Ohio and the following year entered OSU. In 1889, he enrolled at OSU, but stayed only one year before returning to teach. For seventeen years Graham taught in one-room schools in Champaign, Miami, Shelby, and Clark Counties. In 1900, he won election as superintendent of schools in Springfield, Ohio.

---

5. French Archives, Vertical Files; Pollard essay.

There, in 1902, Graham organized the Boys and Girls Agricultural Experiment Club in the basement of the Clark County courthouse. Its primary purpose was to inspire boys and young women to take an interest in scientific methods of farming and to learn by doing practical projects. The first club had eighty-three members who planted experimental plots of corn, vegetables, and flowers, keeping careful records of their results. They presented their products at the Clark County fair of the following year. The clubs spread quickly in Ohio and by 1904 there were sixteen clubs in ten counties. Meanwhile, Graham worked with OSU and its alumni group, the Agricultural Student Union, and the Ohio Agricultural Experiment Station at Wooster to test seed varieties and agricultural methods.

In 1905, OSU created the new position of superintendent of agricultural extension for Graham, who had already achieved statewide fame. Graham lectured throughout Ohio and published and distributed the *Agricultural Extension Bulletin* to rural teachers. So successful and influential was Graham that the state legislature required that public schools in all townships, villages, and special districts teach agriculture in 1911.

Graham left OSU in 1914 to take a similar position with the New York State School of Agriculture. In 1915, Graham moved to Washington, D.C., where he had responsibility for agricultural and home economics specialists in the U.S. Department of Agriculture until his retirement in 1938. Graham than returned to Columbus, where he lived until his death in 1960. OSU awarded him an honorary degree in 1953.

FRANK W. HALE, JR.

In the history of Ohio State, probably no one has done more to enrich the campus with cultural diversity and to provide educational uplift to people whom institutions of higher education, including OSU, had neglected than Frank Hale. Thousands of people have benefited, and more will do so in the future, from the imaginative and effective programs that Dr. Hale set up at OSU. In an oral history interview, he reminisced: "I humbly believe that God has allowed me, in collaboration with others, to establish a number of initiatives to help make the institution attractive to students and faculty of color."

Born in Kansas City, Missouri, in 1927, in a segregated hospital, Frank Hale was the son of a hardworking and entrepreneurial owner of a five-and-ten-cent store. Both parents were Seventh-Day Adventists; religion, self-discipline, self-reliance, and community involvement were prominent activities in the Hale family.[6] In 1937, the family moved to Topeka, Kansas to improve their economic opportunities. While working for a wastepaper company, the elder Hale bought discarded books

---

6 See Frank W. Hale, Jr., *Angels Watching Over Me: The Autobiography of Dr. Frank W. Hale, Jr.* (Nashville: James C. Winston Publishing Company, Inc., 1996), 5–8.

4.10 *Frank W. Hale, Jr.*

and magazines and opened a successful bookstore in Topeka.

Encouraged by his parents and blessed with good teachers, young Frank Hale succeeded in school and even won a scholarship to one of the most prominent African American educational institutions, Howard University. However, Hale and his family decided on Oakwood College in Huntsville, Alabama, which had been founded by Seventh-Day Adventists. Soon, however, Frank transferred to Union College in Lincoln, Nebraska, another institution of the Adventists that was closer to his parents. From there, he transferred again to the University of Nebraska in Lincoln and earned first a B.A. in 1950, and then an M.A. in communication in 1951.

Following graduation, Hale returned to Oakwood College as an instructor in English and speech until 1954, when he began his graduate studies at Ohio State, whose program in speech was outstanding. At OSU, he received a Ph.D. in speech and political science, and returned once more to Oakwood College as associate professor and then professor. From 1959 to 1966, Hale held the post of professor of English and speech at Ohio's Central State University. Again, Oakwood College called, this time with the presidency, an office Hale held until 1971.

4.11 *Scene at the Hale Center, with Director Larry Williamson in 1997*

In 1971, Hale accepted an offer from Ohio State, where he stayed until retirement. He became an associate dean of the graduate school and worked to raise the number of minority students in the graduate and professional colleges. One of his programs, the Graduate and Professional Schools Visitation Program, succeeded in recruiting more than a thousand students for OSU. During the 1970s and 1980s, Ohio-State graduated more minorities in its doctoral programs than any other university in the United States.[7] Promoted to Vice Provost of Minority Affairs in 1978, Hale imagined an undergraduate version of the Graduate and Professional Schools Visitation Program, and his work resulted in the pioneering Young Scholars Program in 1982. Beginning with students in middle and high schools, the program enrolled academically talented minority students, provided them with special tutoring, and for those eligible to enroll in Ohio State, offered financial support through their undergraduate years. This unique and continuing enterprise has made a great difference in the lives of many.

Hale's national influence on higher education and the challenges of recruiting and keeping minorities has been recognized in many ways. He has been a consultant on minority affairs for many institutions and agencies, including the U.S. Department of Education, the Lilly Foundation, the Mott Foundation, the U.S. Military Academy, and the Ohio Department of Education as well as many colleges and universities. His honors include honorary doctorates at several universities, the Distinguished Leadership in Graduate Education Award at Howard University.

Ohio State, too, honored Hale by awarding him its Distinguished Affirmative Action Award and by inviting him to be commencement speaker in September 1988. Probably OSU's greatest recognition of Dr. Hale occurred when in November 1988, the trustees voted to rename the Black Cultural Center, formerly in a building that had been Bradford Commons on W. 12th Avenue, as The Frank W. Hale Black Cultural Center. Open to all, it serves African American students by being a "home away from home" and offering programs such as arts events, lectures, and forums that celebrate cultural diversity.

EILEEN HECKART

In 2000, the League of American Theaters and Producers, Inc. and the American Theatre Wing presented a special Tony Award to Eileen Heckart for her work in theater. Many readers will remember her performances as a character actress with a raspy voice on television and in films as well as in theater. She was one of many OSU graduates who achieved distinction in the performing arts.

Born in 1919 in Columbus, Ohio, Eileen Heckart was the child of a broken marriage, her parents separating when she was two. Her younger brother remained with her father, but she stayed with her mother. Despite this adversity, she enrolled

---

7. Oral History of Frank Hale, Jr., OSU Archives.

4.12 Eileen Heckart in 1961

at The Ohio State University and graduated in 1942 with a determination to become an actor. In the 1940s, she worked in summer stock and then to Broadway and to television. Her first big break was as the schoolteacher in William Inge's play *Picnic*, for which she received the Outer Critic's Circle Award. On Broadway, her hits include *The Bad Seed, Invitation to a March, Barefoot in the Park,* and *Butterflies Are Free*. In films, she won Golden Globe and Oscar nominations for *The Bad Seed* and then an Academy Award for best supporting actress in *Butterflies Are Free*. As a television actor, Heckart appeared in many sitcoms, including *The Mary Tyler Moore Show,* the soap opera *One Life to Live,* and as Eleanor Roosevelt in the TV movie *FDR—The Last Year*. She continued to work until her death from cancer on December 31, 2001.

Eileen Heckart kept her ties with OSU in several ways. She flew there from London to receive a Centennial Award in 1970 and visited campus often. In 1975, she donated the documentation of her professional career to OSU's Theatre Research Institute, and received an honorary degree in 1981. Heckart spoke at her fiftieth class reunion in 1992, when she sang a duet with her husband, who was also an OSU graduate of 1942.

CHARLES F. KETTERING

Anyone who starts an automobile should thank OSU alumnus and trustee Charles Kettering. His invention of the self-starting system in automobiles liberated drivers from the always tiring and sometimes dangerous need to crank the engine. Kettering had many more inventions and contributions to science, education, and philanthropy during his lifetime. So famous was Kettering that he appeared on the cover of *Time* magazine in 1933. In 1948, the American Alumni Council, representing graduates of 1700 colleges and universities, declared that his "life and work will be honored for all time as exemplifying the college trained man at his noblest and best."

Born on a farm in Ashland County in 1876, Kettering attended local schools and graduated from Loudonville High School. He taught in a one-room school and performed a variety of manual labor, including digging holes for telephone poles, before enrolling at the University of Wooster (later renamed the College of Wooster) in 1896. Two years later, he transferred to OSU because of his interest in engineering. Problems with his sight interrupted Kettering's student career and he left school to work as a telephone lineman. Resuming his studies at OSU in 1901, Kettering worked also as a telephone trouble shooter and installer and graduated with a degree in electrical engineering in 1904. He then joined the National Cash Register Company as a member of its inventions department. One of his first accomplishments was to create the first electrical cash register.

4.13 *Charles F. Kettering*

In 1909, Kettering left the National Cash Register Company to organize, with Edward A. Deeds, the Dayton Engineering Laboratories Company (later DELCO), which was located in a barn owned by Mr. Deeds. After a friend had injured himself while cranking an automobile to start it, Kettering turned his inventiveness to developing a self-starting system. This invention helped to make automobiles easier to use for all drivers and revolutionized the automobile industry. In 1920, General Motors took over DELCO and Kettering became a leader in the company.

He continued to work for GM until 1947, when he retired as vice president and general manager of its research laboratories, although he remained active as an inventor. When Kettering's wife complained of dampness in a room, Kettering invented the first electrically operated dehumidifier. Other inventions included an electric generator for use in isolated areas, a two-cycle Diesel engine, special paints for automobiles, Freon gas, an incubator for premature infants, and a measuring instrument used by anesthetists.

Charles Kettering had a broad scope of interests and accomplishments besides his inventions. In 1925, he established the Charles F. Kettering Foundation "to sponsor and carry out scientific research for the benefit of humanity." He co-founded the Sloan-Kettering Institute for Cancer Research in New York City in 1945. His contributions to education and scientific research led to honorary degrees from about thirty colleges and universities. So important was Kettering to Dayton that one of its suburbs named itself in his honor in 1955. In 1998 General Motors' Engineering and Management Institute changed its name to Kettering University.

Kettering helped OSU as an alumnus, a donor, and a trustee. He served as a trustee from 1917 to 1925. Four years later, Kettering delivered the commencement address and received the Sullivant Medal, OSU's highest honor. In 1936, he was one of the incorporators of The Ohio State Research Foundation, which was established to encourage and facilitate research at OSU by linking faculty with private and governmental sponsors. In 1941, Kettering accepted reappointment as trustee and served until his death, the longest term of any trustee.

When Kettering died in 1958, the *New York Times* editorialized, "Charles F. Kettering was one of the benefactors of our time . . . his contributions of inventive genius, his passionate interest in research—automotive, medical and in the field of solar energy—put the world in his debt for a better, more comfortable life."

JOHN KRAUS

"We know less about the universe than Columbus knew about America in 1492," said Professor John Kraus shortly before his death in 2004. Kraus dedicated his life to studying the universe in new ways.

Born in Ann Arbor in 1910, Krause grew up with radio when it was a new invention and developed an interest in physics and electrical engineering. He earned three degrees at the University of Michigan, the last one a Ph.D. in physics in 1933. Krause remained at the University of Michigan another three years as a research physicist, then in 1937 joined the Physicists Research Company, where he worked as a private consultant and continued his research in developing antennas. Three years later, he took a position with the Naval Ordinance Laboratory in Washington, D.C., where he worked on finding new ways to protect ships from magnetic mines. His war service continued from 1943 to 1946 with the Radio Research Laboratory at Harvard University, where he worked for the National Defense Research Council.

4.14 *John Kraus*

In 1946, Professor Kraus joined the Electrical Engineering Faculty at OSU and continued a career filled with remarkable accomplishments, especially in radio astronomy. He set up the Radio Observatory in 1951 and was the only person to track accurately Sputnik I in its first orbit around the earth in 1958. Kraus invented the helical antenna and many other types of antenna. Probably his most famous was "Big Ear," a 340-foot radio telescope in Delaware, Ohio. Kraus's radio telescopes listened to detect sounds of life in the universe for more than four decades, until 1998.

Dr. Kraus received many awards for his inventions and his scholarship—including the Edison and the Hertz medals of the Institute of Electrical and Electronics Engineers. In 1960, he spoke at commencement and in 1970, accepted OSU's Joseph Sullivant Medal. Although he retired from OSU in 1960, Kraus remained active professionally until his death.

4.15 Benjamin Lamme, 1920

BENJAMIN LAMME

True to its beginnings as the Ohio Agricultural and Mechanical College, OSU has educated some extraordinary engineers, one of whom was Benjamin Garver Lamme.

Born in 1864 near Springfield, Ohio, Lamme had an unusual ability in mathematics as well as an insatiable curiosity about how machinery worked. Graduating with a degree in mechanical engineering, Lamme joined the Westinghouse Company in 1889. His research specialty was electric motors. As early as 1891, he designed a single reduction motor of unusual efficiency for Westinghouse. In a career spanning nearly four decades, Lamme designed the alternators for producing electricity at Niagara Falls and the machines that powered the Manhattan Elevated railway in New York City. He pioneered turboelectric generators in the early years of the twentieth century. Before his death in 1924, Lamme had earned more than 160 patents.

Many awards came to Lamme. In 1922, he won both the prestigious Edison Medal of the Institute of Electrical Engineers and OSU's Sullivant Award. Lamme kept close ties to OSU. He provided funding for a Lamme Mechanical Engineering Scholarship and for the Lamme Engineering Medal to honor excellence in his field.

In all likelihood, Benjamin inspired his sister, Bertha (1869–1954). Also talented in mathematics, she graduated from OSU with a degree in mechanical engineering in 1893, the first woman to graduate in engineering in areas outside of civil engineering. Like Benjamin, she joined Westinghouse and continued to work until she married her supervisor, Russell S. Feicht, who had graduated in mechanical engineering from OSU in 1890.

JEROME LAWRENCE

It has been said that every night since 1955, when their play *Inherit the Wind* opened on Broadway, some play by OSU alumni Jerome Lawrence and his collaborator Robert E. Lee has been in performance somewhere in the world.[8] Born in Cleveland, Ohio, Jerome Lawrence graduated from OSU in 1937 with honors and took up a career in dramatic writing, first for radio and then for the theater. During World War II, Lawrence was an overseas correspondent for Armed Forces Radio and later wrote for *The Railroad Hour,* the *Columbia Workshop,* and the *Hallmark Playhouse.* Apart from *Inherit the Wind,* Jerome Lawrence, together with Lee, wrote such popular plays as *The Night Thoreau Spent in Jail, Auntie Mame,* and *Jabberwalk.* He also wrote a well-received biography, *Actor: The Life and Times of Paul Muni.* As one of the nation's premier playwrights, Lawrence co-founded the American Playwrights Theatre and co-founded the Margo Jones Award, which contin-

4.16 *Jerome Lawrence (shown with Robert E. Lee at right, ca.1960s)*

ues to recognize the work of new playwrights each year.

Jerome Lawrence won many honors—Critics Poll, two Peabody Awards for distinguished achievement in broadcasting, and a Lifetime Achievement Award from the American Theatre Association. In 1990, Jerome Lawrence was named to the national Theatre Hall of Fame. OSU honored him with an honorary degree on June 7, 1963, when he was the commencement speaker, and by renaming its Theatre Research Institute "The Lawrence and Lee Theatre Research Institute." Until his death in 2004, Lawrence encouraged playwrights to donate their writings to OSU's Institute.

---

8. Friendsline, OSU Libraries, 1990.

4.17 Roy Lichtenstein, 1995

ROY LICHTENSTEIN

Great artists are often controversial because they challenge the conventional and look at their subjects and their discipline in new ways. Roy Lichtenstein achieved both fame and controversy among artists and the public. To this day, his sculpture *Brush Strokes in Flight* at the Columbus airport greets visitors and draws comments.

Born in 1923, the son of a real estate broker, Lichtenstein had an interest in drawing at an early age. At fourteen, he took watercolor classes at Parsons School of Design in Manhattan. Concerned about their son's ability to support himself, his parents advised that if he wanted a career in art, he should be prepared to teach and encouraged him to enroll at The Ohio State University, where art was part of the College of Education. Enrolling in 1940, Lichtenstein took classes from Professor Hoyt Sherman until World War II interrupted his studies. In 1946, he returned to OSU, completed his undergraduate degree, and served as an instructor in fine arts. In 1949, he completed a masters degree in Fine Arts, but OSU declined to award him tenure in 1951.

After moving to Cleveland where his wife had employment, Lichtenstein worked at various positions, including as a drawing teacher at a commercial art school, a draftsman at Republic Steel, and even as a window decorator for a department store. Whenever he could, he continued to work at his own art and traveled to New York City for exhibitions. During the 1950s and early 1960s, Lichtenstein began to incorporate images and graphic techniques from advertising and comic books in his art and became one of the pioneers and leaders in "Pop Art." In 1961, he painted "Look Mickey," when his children asked him to paint a comic strip, and with it became a celebrity. In 1962, his first one-man show of Pop Art paintings sold out before it opened.[9]

Until his death in 1997, Lichtenstein remained one of the leading figures of modern art. His works are at many prominent galleries, including the Museum of Modern Art and the Guggenheim Museum. Five institutions awarded him honorary doctorates in Fine Art, and in 1995, he received the National Medal of the Arts in Washington, D.C.

OSU also honored Lichtenstein, who periodically visited the campus to lecture. It awarded him a Centennial Award for distinguished achievement in 1970 and an honorary degree in 1988. Two years before his death, OSU's Wexner Center curated a major exhibit of his work, which included seventy-five paintings and sculptures.

RALPH MERSHON

At OSU, the name of Mershon appears prominently. Mershon Auditorium stands prominently facing High Street. In addition, the Mershon Center for International Security Studies has achieved international acclaim for its educational programs and publications.

Born in Zanesville, Ohio in 1868, Ralph Davenport Mershon dropped out of high school temporarily to work for a railroad. Since he was interested in machinery, friends encouraged him to graduate from high school and then to study mechanical engineering at OSU. Enrolling in 1886, Mershon joined the handful of students who took engineering classes.[10] Indeed, he was one of only three to earn a degree in mechanical engineering in 1890. Initially, Mershon stayed at OSU after graduation as an assistant in physics and taught a course in electricity and magnetism.

Eventually, Mershon's interest in alternating current and voltage drew him to the Westinghouse Company, which was

4.18 Ralph Mershon, 1911

---

9. *New York Times*, August 28, 1993.
10. Edith Cockins, *Ralph Davenport Mershon*, vol. 1 (Columbus: The Ohio State University Press, 1956), 10.

only beginning to develop equipment to produce electricity in high volume. Mershon remained with Westinghouse from 1891 to 1900, when he went into business himself as an electrical consultant. Mershon designed the power transmission plant at Niagara Falls and as an award-winning engineer held some ninety-three patents for commercial applications of electricity. OSU awarded him an honorary doctorate in engineering in 1936.

More than an inventor, Mershon concerned himself with human affairs as well as technology. His extensive travels for business and pleasure made him aware of cultures in Asian and Africa as well as Europe and fostered his concern for international relations and national security. He and President William Oxley Thompson, Professor Edward Orton, Jr., and Colonel George Converse were leaders in lobbying Congress to create a Reserve Officer Training Corps (ROTC) in 1916. Mershon remained keenly interested in OSU and as president of the Alumni Association reshaped the organization and even paid the salary of its first secretary. His generosity included many donations to the university, such as gifts of equipment for the engineering department and scholarships for OSU. At his death in 1952, Mershon bequeathed to OSU an estate of 11.2 million dollars. His will directed that half of the revenue of his bequest support civilian military education. This led to the beginning of the Mershon Center in 1966.

WILLIAM G. MYERS

4.19 *William G. Myers*

Is there anyone who does not know someone who has had cancer? Here, too, OSU has advanced the search for a cure, especially in the pioneering work in nuclear medicine by Professor William G. Myers.

Born in Toledo, Ohio, Myers lived his early years at an orphanage. He worked as a waiter, a photographer, and even a barber to earn money for college. Myers earned all of his degrees from OSU: a bachelor's in 1933, a masters in 1937, a Ph.D. in 1939, and finally an M.D. in 1941.

While studying for his doctorate, Myers made use of the cyclotron (which speeds up charged particles with a high frequency, alternating current) that OSU trustee Julius Stone had bought for the university in 1938. In 1945, Myers received the Stone fellowship for research in applications of the cyclotron in medicine. In 1953, he became OSU's Stone research professor of medical biophysics. He was the first to use Cobalt-60 and during his three-decade career at OSU, Myers created ten radio nuclides to trace and treat cancers. One of his medical colleagues said that Dr. Myers "has done more than any single physician to broaden the uses of radioisotopes in medicine, the source of radioisotopes for medicine, and the availability of radioisotopes for the medical profession."[11] Besides undertaking research, Myers founded the Society of Nuclear Medicine in 1954 and the Education and Research Foundation of The Society of Nuclear Medicine. Although he retired in 1979, Myers continued to do research and lecture until his death in 1988.

RICHARD OLSEN

Anyone who has owned a pet can testify to its importance and can also agree that the death of one's dog or cat is like losing a member of the family. In 1980, Professor Richard Olsen of OSU's College of Veterinary Medicine discovered a vaccine to prevent the onset of feline leukemia that had afflicted more than a million of the 50 million cats in the United States.[12]

Born in Missouri, Professor Olsen did his undergraduate work at the University of Missouri, his masters at Atlanta University, and Ph.D. at SUNY Buffalo. He taught in a high school and a junior college in Missouri before joining the faculty

4.20 Richard Olsen

11. Newsreleases, VF, 1973.
12. *Quest,* Spring 1986.

of microbiology at the university in 1969. From then until 1980, Olsen experimented with traditional ways of developing vaccines for feline leukemia. Finally, he discovered a way of creating a vaccine based on two protein molecules, one protecting against the virus and another preventing tumors. Thus, Olsen's work has had importance not only in feline leukemia but in finding new processes for producing vaccines.

JESSE OWENS

OSU honored its former student, Jesse Owens, considered by many sportswriters to have been one of the greatest athletes of the twentieth tentury, with a sculpture and a stadium. Also, OSU has the papers documenting his career in athletics, in his years of promoting recreational and developmental activites for young people and the Olympics. The collection includes four medals from the Olympic Games in Berlin in 1936.

Born in poverty in rural Alabama in 1913, Jesse Owens was the last of ten children. One of his sisters had moved to Cleveland, Ohio, found work, and recommended the whole family join her. Thus in the 1920s, Jesse's family, like many African Americans, moved north to Cleveland for jobs and other opportunities not available in the rural South. In an elementary school in Cleveland, one of the teachers misunderstood Jesse's southern drawl and called James Cleveland "Jesse." Interested in sports, Jesse joined the track team at East Technical High School and became a superstar. His graceful and efficient style of running won him 75 of 79 races in his senior year in 1933. At the National Interscholastic Championship, Owens won the long jump, set a world record in the 220-yard dash, and tied a world record in the 100-yard dash.

Recruited by many universities, Owens came to OSU in the fall of 1933. Under the coaching of Larry Snyder, Owens quickly became a standout on the track team. In one day of 1935, at the Big Ten Finals in Ann Arbor, he set world records in the 220-yard dash, the 220-yard low hurdles, and the long jump. At the Olympic Games in Berlin the next year, Owens won four gold medals, the first to do so in the history of the modern Olympics.

That accomplishment changed his life forever. A disagreement with the U.S. Olympic committee, which wanted the homesick and exhausted Owens to continue touring Europe, ended his amateur career. At the same time, Owens had so many academic difficulties because of inadequate preparation, the demands of athletics, and the distractions of public appearances, that he became academically ineligible at OSU. Meanwhile, Owens had a wife and a daughter to take care of and decided to try to earn money from the many offers that followed his Olympic fame. These included running before baseball games, competing against the fastest athletics in town, even running against horses, and appearing at public events for a fee. To be

4.21 Jesse Owens, 1935

more with his family, Owens opened a dry cleaning service in 1938, but this failed a year later. During World War II Owens traveled in promoting physical fitness among African Americans. After the war, with the revival of the Olympics, Owens traveled around the world, representing the United States and the Olympics. During the 1950s, the State Department sent him to Asia as a goodwill ambassador for the United States. In 1971, President Richard Nixon sent him to the Ivory Coast in West Africa.

When not engaged with the Olympics or in his role as a diplomatic ambassador, Owens was much in demand as a public speaker throughout his life, until his death in 1978. He was active with organizations such as the Boy Scouts of America and for the Atlantic Richfield Company, which sponsored the Atlantic Richfield Games.

Many honors came to Jesse Owens. In 1972, OSU honored him with an honorary doctorate of athletics. President Gerald Ford gave him the Medal of Freedom, the highest national honor a citizen can receive. After Owens's death, OSU dedicated the sculpture in front of Ohio Stadium in his honor in 1983, and a new stadium for track was named for him in 1999. His papers, including medals and many of his awards, are at the OSU Archives. Annually since 1983, the Jesse Owens Games have taken place at OSU.

While the accomplishments of Jesse Owens command attention and respect, there is one aspect of his relationship to OSU that is a continuing mystery. At the Berlin games in 1936, Owens and other athletes received English Oak seedlings. Owens declared that he would plant one of his seedlings on the OSU campus. There is, in fact, an English Oak on the south side of the Thompson library that some people claim is the Owens tree. However, it bears no sign because there is no record—not even a newspaper article or press release—that reports Owens planting a tree in 1936. In the absence of decisive evidence, the mystery continues.

4.22 *Lonnie Thompson and Ellen Mosley-Thompson*

LONNIE THOMPSON AND ELLEN MOSLEY-THOMPSON

Global warming is a topic that concerns many. If the earth is warming, glaciers will melt, oceans will rise, and flooding and significant biological and economic damage will be everywhere. Modernization and the burning of fossil and hydrocarbon fuels could be important reasons for global warming. OSU's Lonnie Thompson and Ellen Mosley-Thompson are two scientists widely acknowledged as leading experts in the subject of world climate change.

Born in West Virginia, Lonnie Thompson grew up on a farm. Since many farmers were constantly concerned about the weather, weather forecasting for Thompson became an interest and a hobby. While in high school, he built a weather station and used it to make forecasts for his schoolmates. Following graduation, he enrolled at Marshall University, majored in physics first as a path toward meteorology, but switched to geology as a potential career. At a geology department party, Thompson met Ellen Mosley, a physics major, and they married. In 1972, Thompson entered OSU to pursue a degree in geology, while Ellen-Mosley Thompson worked as a secretary in Columbus. While in his first year of studies, Thompson received a research assistantship at OSU's Institute of Polar Studies (now the Byrd Polar Research Center) to perform analyses on dust in ice cores from Antarctica.[13]

That experience launched Thompson's career. The ice cores, like the rings of a tree, serve as an archive of not only snowfall but atmospheric and meteorological conditions over centuries. As a scientist, Thompson ventured across the globe into tropical as well as polar areas to find ice cores in mountain glaciers in such distant and remote places as Peru and China. These provide a more complete record of the earth's climate than Polar regions alone.

In 1973, Ellen joined Lonnie in the lab and completed her Ph.D. Together, the two have led teams to extract ice cores and to analyze them for evidence—gases, pollen, dust, and so forth—that point to climate change and the influence of humans in developing industrialized societies. Both are award-winning scientists who are full professors (in geology and in geography, respectively) at OSU. In 2001, *Time* magazine named Lonnie Thompson one of America's Best Scientists. Since then, he and Ellen have won Distinguished OSU Research Professor awards, among many other accolades, national and international.

JAMES THURBER

James Thurber is perhaps the greatest American humorist since Mark Twain. His cartoons and writings are a valued and much-used collection in the OSU libraries.

Born in 1894, James Thurber grew up in Columbus, Ohio. His mother was known for her sense of humor and may have been an inspiration to young James. When Thurber was a child, his brother shot him with an arrow that blinded him in one eye. Eventually, Thurber would lose most of his eyesight.

Thurber began writing in high school and as a student at OSU developed his talent further. A professor in the English department, Billy Graves, read one of his stories in class and praised the work. At OSU, Thurber became news editor of the *Lantern* and editor-in-chief of the *Sundial,* the campus humor magazine. Failing eyesight forced him to withdraw from OSU in 1918. From late 1918 to March 1920, he worked at the U.S. Embassy in Paris as a code clerk. In March 1920, he returned to Columbus as a reporter for the *Columbus Dispatch*. In the 1920s Thurber wrote several stories and even a novel but failed to impress publishers. In 1926, Thurber moved to New York City, where he found a position with the *New York Post,* but

---

13. See Mark Bowen, *Thin Ice: Unlocking the Secrets of Climate in the World's Highest Mountains* (New York: Henry Holt, 2005), 38–41.

4.23 *James Thurber*

continued to write his own stories. Finally, the *New Yorker* magazine, which had rejected several of Thurber's stories, published one about a man caught in a revolving door. The *New Yorker* then hired Thurber and his career began to flourish. In 1933, he left the *New Yorker* staff to become a freelance writer. His quirky cartoons, which had begun as doodles in the office, became a feature of the magazine.

Until his death in 1961, Thurber wrote books, short stories, and plays (including *The Male Animal* co-written with Elliot Nugent in 1940). His first book, *Is Sex Necessary* (1929) was written jointly with fellow *New Yorker* writer E. B. White. His book *My World and Welcome to It* (1942) includes the famous story "The Secret Life of Walter Mitty," which became a movie in 1947. During the 1950s, Thurber wrote fairy tales for children, including *The 13 Clocks* (1950) and the

Wonderful O. His experiences as a student at OSU appear in his book *My Life and Hard Times* (1933).

LES WEXNER

"Your college experience and mine are part of a continuing life experience. . . . That simple thought nearly evaded me. That continuing process, that seed of the idea, began here at Ohio State. . . . I firmly believe that if we stop learning, we stop growing, and if we stop growing, we begin to die." So spoke Leslie H. Wexner, nationally prominent business leader, philanthropist, and OSU alumnus at OSU's graduation in 1986.

Born in Dayton, Ohio, in 1937, Leslie H. Wexner was the son of Russian immigrants who began a clothing business. In 1951, they opened a clothing store, Leslie's, in downtown Columbus. Les Wexner worked in the store, enrolled at The Ohio State University, and completed a degree in business administration in 1959. He dropped out of law school to work in the family business. Seeing that sportswear sold well, Wexner had the entrepreneurial idea of creating a store that specialized in women's sportswear. Borrowing $5,000, he opened The Limited, which is limited to a line of clothing, at the Kingsdale Shopping Center in a suburb of Columbus in 1963. Attention to detail and skills in marketing and design brought success. So successful was the store that by 1969, there were six of them. Wexner then made The Limited a public corporation, offered stock, and used the

4.24 *Les Wexner*

earnings to expand into malls. In the process, he also expanded the Limited into more apparel and invested in other businesses, such as Galyan's Trading Company, Victoria's Secret, and Bath & Body works.[14] In 2003, *Fortune* magazine named Limited Brands the World's Most Admired Company.

---

14. http:www.referenceforbusiness.com/bibliography/s-z/Wexner-LeslieH-1937.html

Les Wexner has given many millions of dollars to nonprofit causes. He established the Wexner Arts Fund at the Columbus Foundation to support innovation in the arts. He has been a prominent leader of the United Jewish Appeal. At OSU, Wexner was a founder of The Ohio State University Foundation; his many gifts to the university have included 25 million dollars to building the Wexner Center for the Arts and in 2011 an extraordinary donation of 100 million dollars, which will primarily support OSU's Medical Center, its Arthur G. James Cancer Hospital, the Richard J. Solove Research Institute, and the Wexner Center for the Arts. As Wexner put it, "I love Ohio State, and all the good it does." Additionally, Wexner has served his alma mater as a member of the OSU board of trustees.[15]

ROBERT ZOLLINGER

Known as the "Big Z" by colleagues and former students, Dr. Robert M. Zollinger was a commanding figure in medicine, a world-famous surgeon at OSU's College of Medicine and University Hospitals, and a leader in civic life.[16]

Born on a farm in Millersport, Ohio, Zollinger received a bachelor of science degree from OSU in 1925. Two years later, he earned his M.D. and did his surgical training in Cleveland and at Harvard University. In

4.25 *Robert Zollinger*

1939, he became an assistant professor of surgery at Harvard. During World War II, Zollinger headed the Harvard Medical School Unit and served as senior consultant on general surgery for the European Theater of Operations. His distinguished services, especially in improving care at field hospitals, earned him the U.S. Army's Legion of Merit and from the French the title of Chevalier of the Légion d'honneur.

Following the war, Zollinger returned to OSU as professor and chair of the department of surgery and director of surgical services at University Hospitals. Despite his considerable administrative, teaching, and surgical responsibilities, Zollinger had an extraordinary career in medical research and scholarship. He contributed to or shared in the authorship of more than four hundred publications, including an *Atlas of Surgical Operations* and a *Textbook of Surgery,* and was editor-in-chief of *The American Journal of Surgery* from 1958 to 1986. With Edwin

---

15. See http://www.osu.edu/features/2011/butforohiostate.

16. George W. Paulson, *The Ohio State University College of Medicine* (Blanchester, OH: Brown Publishing Company, 1998), 243.

H. Ellison, Zollinger diagnosed a rare disorder of the pancreas and duodenum that became known as "Zollinger-Ellison Syndrome."

Zollinger's research and teaching won him many honors. He was president of the American College of Surgeons, president of the American Surgical Association, and chair of the American Board of Surgery. In 1963, OSU set up the Robert M. Zollinger Chair of Surgery, one of the university's first endowed chairs. Two years later, OSU awarded Zollinger the Sullivant Award for distinguished service. When Zollinger retired from OSU in 1974, he continued to teach, do research, and practice medicine. Of special interest to Zollinger were gourds and roses. He was president of the American Rose Society. Zollinger remained active until his death in 1992. His professional papers are now a prominent feature of OSU's Medical Heritage Center.

OSU ALUMNI ASSOCIATION

Aside from talent, creativity, and energy, nearly all of these twenty-five individuals shared something more: the OSU Alumni Association. In 1879, graduates of the class of 1878, the first graduating class, reassembled at OSU the next year during commencement and formed an alumni association. Although practically all colleges and universities have alumni associations, OSU's is both unusual and important. Unlike other associations, the OSU Alumni Association has always been a private organization, independent of the university. In its history, the Association has helped

4.26 Alumni reunion in 1935

4.27 The Longaberger Alumni House is the headquarters of The Ohio State University Alumni Association. Located on Olentangy River Road, across from the Fawcett Center for Tomorrow, it is an impressive building that provides attractive rooms for receptions and meetings, as well as up-to-date news about the university and its alumni.

the university in many ways. During the Great Depression, for example, it helped OSU to raise scholarships and financial support for research. Additionally in the Great Depression, the Association rallied members in Ohio to petition in behalf of OSU when Governor Davies refused to approve budget allocations. Today, the Association, through its many clubs in Ohio and other states, visits high schools and encourages students to apply to OSU. Many OSU students benefit from scholarships created by clubs and the generous members of the Alumni Association.

CHAPTER FIVE

STUDENT LIFE AT OSU

A Historical Review

Student life is not as might be supposed by the outsider looker-on a mere routine of reading, recitation and physical evaluation, of study in the rich old fields of the world, and of research into the mysteries of nature, but with this, there comes the reactionary desire for sports, joviality and general good times.

Because a man works hard in college, is no reason why he should ignore college sports; because he is tired at the end of the week, does not justify him in shirking the duties of a literary society. You cannot afford to neglect them; they are as much part and parcel of your college life as your books and laboratories. All the knowledge of the world gained from books is but a small fraction, and will avail you but little compared with the experience of life. Aside from that, you leave out a large factor in your enjoyment here.

(*Makio* [OSU Student yearbook], 1880)

ANNUALLY in September, a day or two before the school year begins, the Student Involvement Fair takes place on the Oval. Students set up hundreds of tables and displays and entice new or returning students to join their organizations. The campus has a staggering number of organizations—more than eight hundred—that students can join. Many are recreational clubs, and others are fraternities and sororities, political parties, and groups devoted to religious and cultural exchange. Large or small, they offer friendship and diversion to all and opportunities for leadership to some.

Student life at OSU takes place within an institutional setting that includes administrators, faculty, and students. Even the Alumni Association has a Student Alumni Council. OSU's Vice President for Student Life presides over an administrative structure dedicated to monitoring and improving student life outside classrooms. Departments focus on such topics as campus events, student organizations, housing and residence education, and student counseling programs. The Council on Student Affairs, a standing unit of OSU's University Senate, reviews and allocates funding for student organizations and serves as the official forum of students, administration, and faculty for the purpose of exchanging ideas about nurturing the student environment outside the classroom.

This chapter will discuss student life as it has changed at OSU. Even as the physical environment of OSU has developed in time, so, too, has the world of students outside the classroom changed. Student life began spontaneously and without

5.1 Welcome Week, the first week of classes in the fall quarter, is an opportunity for students to find organizations to join. The Involvement Fair, which is often held on the Oval, typically includes refreshments, entertainment, and displays and sign-up sheets for student organizations.

official encouragement. Gradually OSU developed the managerial tools that both regulated and nurtured the student experience outside classes. Always, student life has had a diversity and scale that stretched beyond official control and sponsorship.

THE EARLY YEARS, 1873–1900

The first students arrived in small numbers and came chiefly from Columbus and surrounding communities. Only twenty-four students enrolled on the first day of class on September 17, 1873. Yearly, however, students increased their numbers. As they did, students formed their own organizations within which they could socialize, express students' points of view, and pursue common interests.

Literary societies were the first student organizations on campus. Members shared books because OSU's library in its early years contained relatively few books, apart from what was related to subjects of instruction. As early as 1874, the faculty approved the Deshler Society, a student literary society that honored John Deshler, who donated books to the university. At Deshler's request, students renamed the organization the Alcyone Society, in honor of a character in Greek mythology. For its part, OSU's faculty allowed the Society to use a room in University Hall, provided President Orton serve as an ex officio member. In 1875, OSU's trustees approved that two literary societies could use rooms in University Hall. Here, students could read and discuss books that might not be available in the small library. Women students joined these groups and enjoyed the discussions, but had no opportunities for leadership. In 1882, they organized their own literary society, which they named the Browning Literary Society in honor of poet Elizabeth Barrett Browning.[1]

Social organizations dedicated to fellowship developed early and quickly at OSU. In 1878 fraternities began on campus and proved so popular that by 1880 they had published the first college yearbook, the *Makio,* and in 1881 a newspaper, the *Lantern,* publications that continue still. In 1882, the YMCA opened at The Ohio State University and then the YWCA in 1887. By 1888, the two hundred students and 150 preparatory students at OSU had formed six fraternities, three literary societies, a YMCA, a YWCA, and a missionary society. In addition, each class—freshmen, sophomores, juniors, and seniors—had an organization, as did boardinghouses away from campus.[2]

At first, OSU's president and faculty viewed the students and their organizations with some suspicion. As graduates of private colleges and universities, the first faculty knew the sometimes rebellious behavior of undergraduates at other institutions, especially in the East. The land-grant college, they believed, was a new undertaking in higher education, one that was less frivolous and more closely

---

1. Pouneh Mouhadam Alcott, "Women at the Ohio State University in the first four decades 1873–1912" (OSU Ph.D. dissertation, 1979), 42–44.

2. William A. Kinnison, *Building Sullivant's Pyramid: An Administrative History of The Ohio State University, 1870–1907* (Columbus: The Ohio State University Press), 125.

5.2 *The first student organizations were literary societies that enabled students to share books and discuss them. This is the Horton Literary Society in 1894. The group took its name in honor of Valentine B. Horton, who was the first president of the board of trustees.*

5.3 *Some women students formed their own organizations, such as the Philomathean Literary Society (shown here in 1903).*

5.4 Students, most of whom lived near campus, formed organizations in boarding clubs. Above is Mollie Murry's Boarding Club in 1892.

5.5 A student room in 1897

connected to the public than the private colleges. From this perspective, students should be exemplary models of conduct and should abstain from the rowdiness and endless socializing that characterized student life at older institutions. Another reason for faculty and administrators to worry was that so many students lived in boardinghouses, away from campus and out of sight of adults. Finally, the nearness of the legislature and OSU's efforts to win financial support from state government caused both administrators and faculty to fear that students who misbehaved and attracted public disapproval harmed the university's appeals to the legislature.

Under the presidency of Edward Orton (1873–1878), relations between the small number of students and faculty appeared harmonious. After five years of experience as president, Orton commented in his annual report for 1878 that "We have been happily free during our short history from the relics of that barbarism that still survives in so many colleges in the shape of hazing and the reckless destruction of property."[3] A year later, Orton noted, "We have been happily spared, so far, those unfortunate collisions between faculty and students that, wherever they occur, interrupt college work and embitter college life."[4]

Harmony proved short-lived, for the 1880s were difficult years in student relations, especially during the presidency of William Henry Scott (1883–1895). Early in the decade, conflict between the board of trustees and the faculty over compelling students to attend chapel services led to the nonrenewal of presidential term of Walter Quincy Scott (1881–1883), an event that stirred the students. So unhappy were some students that they published a poem in their yearbook that described OSU's faculty and students at the mercy of the trustees:

And thus their whim becomes a law,
One more august you never saw
Which to repeal we strive in vain
For we must pray though it does pain
But this we write to send above
To show how well we freedom love.[5]

Many students took a dislike to the new president, William Henry Scott, who was older, more reserved in his manner, and more willing to enforce the wishes of the trustees. One flashpoint was dancing. In deference to Scott, who was a Methodist minister, the faculty prohibited students from holding dances in university rooms. Of course, this angered the students, for whom dances featured prominently in social life.

Other issues stirred the students also. OSU seemed tardy in developing a set of

---

3. Quoted in James E. Pollard, *History of The Ohio State University: The Story of its First Seventy-Five Years, 1873–1948* (Columbus: The Ohio State University Press, 1952), 62.

4. Pollard, 62.

5. Kinnison, 112.

5.6 *The Makio, OSU's student yearbook, began as the work of fraternities. Shown here is the staff of 1887.*

5.7 *Staff of OSU's student newspaper, the* Lantern, *which began as a monthly publication. Here is the staff of 1893.*

electives in 1886 from which students could choose some of their courses.[6] Compulsory attendance at daily chapel, which some professors themselves opposed, became enforced under the second Scott and was a constant source of friction. In 1889, for example, faculty tried to recruit the senior class to take attendance at chapel; when the senior class demanded a holiday in exchange for their cooperation, negotiations failed.[7]

Students complained about demerits. The demerit system, which had been imposed by the faculty to govern behavior, was temporarily suspended in 1881, but enforced again in 1883. Students who failed to attend classes or missed chapel received demerits; excessive demerits led to letters to parents and even dismissal from the university. Meanwhile, faculty warned students that rooms approved for meetings of literary societies were not available for general socializing. As an example, they denied an application to hold a reunion of alumni in rooms earmarked for the literary societies.[8]

Finally, students chafed when faculty forbade them from holding orations and giving out publications to college visitors without permission. Sometimes, students distributed leaflets that were critical of university administration and the trustees. Particularly troubling to trustees and administration was the practice of giving such leaflets to state legislators who had been invited to visit the campus.

At events presided over by President William Scott, students resorted to distractions and rudeness to express their disrespect. By 1884, there had been so many instances of disrespect that faculty addressed a letter to the trustees that expressed confidence in William Henry Scott and regretted that students appeared to have undertaken " . . . a more or less organized effort to embarrass and annoy the president of the university and to disparage his efficiency, and his fitness for the high position which he holds."[9] As late as 1891, eight years after the administration of President William Scott began, students still held a grudge. The senior class held a meeting at which they declared the university could never achieve greatness unless OSU had a new president. OSU's faculty forced the students to withdraw this resolution by threatening to withhold their degrees at commencement.[10]

Meanwhile, students continued to join fraternities, form new clubs, and develop a life outside class. In 1890, the *Lantern* editorialized, "Those who come here and attend only the curriculum of studies make a grave mistake. They lost that part of college which is like the life of the big world about us." In contrast, President Scott warned that some students were immature and did not use time wisely: "It must be accounted an evil, however, that so much attention is given to extraneous things; not only the ball and tennis clubs, but class and fraternity meetings, political clubs,

---

6. Kinnison, 120.
7. OSU Faculty minutes, October 9, 1889.
8. OSU Faculty minutes, May 6, 1885.
9. Quoted in Pollard, 93
10. Pollard, 93.

5.8–5.9 Then and now, educational societies drew students of similar interests together. Shown here are the Townshend Society in agricultural education (5.8) in 1908 and (5.9) the Chemical Society in 1892.

5.10 Sphinx in 1919

5.11 Chimes, 1936

5.10–5.12 Honor Societies promote and reward scholarship and serve as opportunities for friendship. Sphinx and Bucket and Dipper began in 1907, Mortar Board in 1914 and Chimes in 1918.

5.12 Bucket and Dipper, 1931

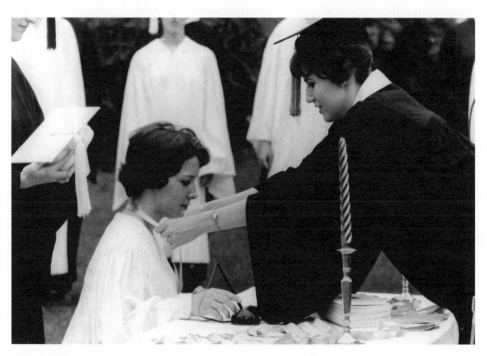

5.13 Mortar Board, 1965

attendance at parties, banquets, legislative sessions and other forms of distraction, are liable to make great and sometimes disastrous inroads on the student's time."[11]

President James Canfield (1895–1899), who succeeded Scott, had a more modern outlook and achieved much better relations with students. For example, he and the faculty approved petitions to hold student dances. Canfield and the faculty took significant steps to impose rules on student activities, without discouraging the students from organizing and socializing. As an example, in 1897 the faculty addressed abuses in all student organizations, but especially in athletic associations. They required that anyone representing OSU in an intercollegiate game or off-campus event must be a student in good standing. Furthermore all "entertainments, events and inter-collegiate games" that involved absence from the city or interference with college work must be approved in advance by the faculty. In addition, all student organizations that received moneys from nonmembers (e.g., selling tickets to events) had to be audited twice yearly by a committee that included a member of the faculty.[12]

Still, Canfield could not avoid entirely conflict with students. In 1895, the cane rush in which freshmen and sophomores fought one another to move a cane across a goal line was so violent that Canfield forbade the event the next year. In 1896, however, the sophomores defied Canfield by disrupting a meeting of the freshman class, attacking them with arms and backs broken from chairs and challenging them to a cane rush that soon took place. Later, the sophomores apologized to Canfield and declared that they had intended no disrespect. Canfield accepted the apology, but warned that if students did not behave as adults, then a closer supervision of them, more like that of a small college, would follow.[13]

BUILDING THE OFFICIAL FOUNDATION OF STUDENT LIFE, 1900–1960

At the beginning of the twentieth century, a new administrative attitude toward student life dawned. In 1900, Charles Thwing, president of Western Reserve University, published *College Administration,* which claimed to be the first to study the college presidency as a management position akin to the chief executive of a corporation. In a later work, *The College President,* Thwing presented his views of how a president should manage relations with students: "The life of the college is a highly organized and complex life. Its organization numbers hundreds of clubs and societies. . . . To all such societies, the president holds relations." In other words, students and their organizations were among the many constituencies—along with alumni,

---

11. Kinnison, 124–25; President Annual Report for 1891, 36.

12. James A. Pollard, *Ohio State Athletics* (Columbus: Ohio State University Athletics Department, 1959), 15; OSU Faculty minutes, vol. 2, February 27, 1897.

13. OSU Faculty minutes, November 1, 1896.

5.14 Service is another theme that brings students together in organizations. Ohio Staters, shown here in a campus cleanup project in 1984, had begun in 1933 and was chartered in 1935. It has accomplished much, including an OSU historical museum in University Hall.

5.15 Cheering for OSU's teams led to the organization of Block O in 1938, although card-cheering began as early as 1919. Today it is the largest of student organizations. Note the Brutus Buckeye of 1974.

faculty, and trustees—that deserved presidential attention. Their activities were not threats to institutional order and educational mission, but part of the educational life of any college or university.[14]

The change in management philosophy and strategy also reflected a contemporary change in social awareness. At the beginning of the twentieth century, as more young people lengthened their years of schooling and delayed entering the workforce, psychologists and sociologists defined adolescence as a distinct stage in the life cycle. From this perspective, the arena of nonacademic activities by adolescents was actually a place of learning in which the young learned the lessons of leadership, competition, and cooperation that would prepare them for life after graduation. (Of course, this is what students had said for decades.) The challenge of the modern administrator was to foster an extra curriculum that helped students grow as citizens and as potential leaders.[15]

Theories of management aside, the fact was that student life outside the classroom had become more than any professor could oversee in addition to teaching classes and writing for publication. In 1900, the OSU campus had 1,465 students, of whom 242 were women. These students had organized five literary societies, fifteen fraternities, and four sororities, and developed teams in football, tennis, track, and basketball. In addition, students had five musical groups (Orchestra, Glee Club, Mandolin and Guitar Club, and even a Banjo Club), a weekly student newspaper,

5.16 The Cosmopolitan Club, an organization of international students, in 1918
5.16–5.18 From its beginning to the present, OSU's students have been diverse. Women enrolled in the first year of classes in 1873. International students and African Americans soon followed. Some joined other OSU student organizations while others formed their own clubs.

14. Franklin Thwing, *The College President* (New York: MacMillan, 1926), 69–70.

15. Joseph F. Kett, *Rites of Passage: Adolescence in America, 1790 to the Present* (New York: Basic Books, 1977), 148–52.

5.17 *Omega Psi Phi in 1930*

5.18 *Alpha Kappa Alpha in 1929*

and military units. Also, there were clubs centered on common academic interests, such as law, political science, and engineering. Not included in these numbers were the clubs formed at boardinghouses and the class officers elected each year by the freshmen, sophomores, juniors, and seniors. Whether OSU presidents approved or not, the students were social beings, enjoyed each other's company, mimicked student groups at other colleges and universities, and organized themselves.[16]

Gradually, OSU embraced student life as part of the official university experience and developed an administrative architecture to foster and regulate it. The University YMCA that had set up a chapter in 1883 continued to be a source for basic student services. It found housing, made short-term loans, and helped place

16. Based on *Makio,* 1900.

students in jobs. Until 1910 the YMCA even published the university's student handbooks and directories.[17]

The turn of the twentieth century was a time for both improvement in facilities for student life and for new opportunities in student leadership and self-governance. In 1907, students, upon the approval of faculty, created a Student Council composed of members of the freshman, sophomore, junior, and senior classes. The Student Council, later renamed Men's Student Council, had a liaison role with the OSU administration and had responsibility for voicing student concerns to the president and faculty. In addition, the Council had responsibility for all school and class elections and interclass contests as well as student athletic associations. Finally, the Council had a court that reviewed minor student violations of university rules.[18] A year later, in 1908, OSU's trustees approved plans for the Ohio Union. Renamed Enarson Hall in 1986, the building was a gathering place for students, largely male, and their organizations.

5.19 Dr. Caroline Breyfogle, first Dean of Women at OSU, taken from a photograph in the OSU Alumni Magazine, October 1912

Women students also took initiatives and had success, even when male students excluded them from organizations. In the same year that men students gained a student union, women students had their first dormitory, Oxley Hall. In 1909, women students organized the Women's Student Council (renamed Women's Student Government Association in 1927) composed of members of each of the undergraduate classes and with similar responsibilities to that of the men. Two years later, the Women's Student Council petitioned OSU for " . . . the appointment in the immediate future of the Dean of Women, who shall have the much-needed supervision, now entirely lacking, over our cultural as well as our general welfare, and over the various activities of our student body."[19] That petition led OSU to appoint Dr. Caroline Breyfogle, a Ph.D. from the University of Chicago, as the first dean of women, a position that continued until 1967.

The Women's Student Council and the Dean of Women petitioned for a wom-

---

17. *OSU Centennial History*, "History of Student Affairs," 1.

18. Thomas C. Mendenhall, *History of The Ohio State University, Vol. II: Continuation of the Narrative from 1910 to 1925* (Columbus: The Ohio State University Press, 1926), 177.

19. "History of Student Affairs," 133

en's student union, which became a reality with Pomerene Hall in 1922. A pressing problem for many years was that women students had little support or supervision, a significant concern in an era when many believed that females needed special supervision and protection. President William Henry Scott (1883–1895) once remarked that because of the absence of dormitories for women on the campus, he made his own office available to those female students who needed a place to rest.[20] As a place for women students to meet, there was a room in University Hall called "the gab room." More than a place to visit, Pomerene sponsored not only cultural, social, and educational programs but also a counseling service for young women to orient them to the university and help them take part in the social environment.[21]

5.20 Joseph Park, first Dean of Men, appearing with the symbols of the Bucket and Dipper Club.

During the 1920s and 1930s, OSU largely completed the establishment of administrative offices for fostering and managing student life. In 1923, OSU created a Council on Student Affairs, consisting of faculty and students that superseded and included previous committees that had regulated student life outside the classroom.[22] In 1924, OSU appointed a director of residence halls. In 1927, a Student Counselor for Men appeared, renamed Dean of Men in 1929. Also in 1927, President George Rightmire encouraged OSU to take responsibility for student orientation and created Junior Deans for advising freshmen and sophomores in each of the colleges.

During the Great Depression, previous programs for students to find employment, which were the responsibilities first of the University YMCA, and then the Men's Employment Bureau of the Ohio Union, proved inadequate for the scale of the financial crisis. OSU took responsibility for the financial aid of students through the Student Employment Office, the predecessor of the modern Office of Student Financial Aid, to direct students to employment opportunities that had federal, university, and private funding.[23]

---

20. "History of Student Affairs," 1.
21. "History of Student Affairs," 68
22. "History of Student Affairs," 70.
23. "History of Student Affairs," 113.

5.21 Some aspects of student life are practically timeless, although fashions do change.

5.22–5.24 Having fun, from attending concerts to participating in campus recreation, has been a constant part of student life.

World War II and the years following changed much of campus in many ways. One was that the campus had more international diversity. Even in its early years, however, OSU had students from foreign countries. In fact, the first international student, from Jamaica, graduated in 1896. As their numbers increased, foreign students formed their own organizations, such as the Cosmopolitan Club in 1907, which included many nationalities, or single nationality clubs, such as the Chinese Students Club.

After the war, when the United States became the world's leading nation in research and in education, its universities attracted more and more students from other countries. When the war ended in 1945, there were only 72 international students at OSU. Ten years later, they numbered 334 and grew to 679 in 1965. Government programs in the United States and in other countries encouraged and promoted student exchanges. OSU and other universities developed programs to welcome international visitors and to arrange for studies abroad.

Federal and state support for graduate and professional studies available after World War II also led to a steady increase in the number of graduate and professional students at OSU. In autumn 1946, there were 2,127 graduate students. Five years later, they numbered 3,269, and by 1955, they had reached 3,679. By 1960, there were 3,842 graduate students and another 2,309 in the professional colleges of dentistry, law, medicine, nursing, optometry, pharmacy, and veterinary medicine. As their numbers grew, graduate and professional students formed their own organizations to serve their interests and to communicate in an official way with the university. The Council of Graduate Students began in 1955, and in 1970 professional students outside the Graduate School formed the Inter-Professional Council. Both organizations continue to participate in university governance and have seats on the University Senate.

Of course, official nurturing of student life did not end conflict between students and administration. Student discontent surfaced periodically during the 1920s and later, despite the efforts of deans and other administrators responsible for student relations. In 1925–26 and in 1931, investigations of alcohol consumption and Communist influence among students and faculty that were mandated by the state legislature stirred unrest on the campus. During the 1930s, the impending war in Europe renewed complaints of some students against compulsory ROTC, concerns that had begun as early as the 1880s. In 1931, students formed an Optional Drill League and urged a student strike against compulsory drill. Although dissident students and supporting faculty led Faculty Council to approve a student petition to end compulsory military drill, the Council later reversed itself when state legislators threatened to take punitive actions against the university.[24]

During the 1950s, issues that aroused students included limits on speech, discrimination against minorities, and panty raids. In May of 1950, campus police used tear gas for the first time to quell male students who raided Neil, Baker, and Canfield Halls in search of female undergarments. Another set of raids in 1953 involved both a women's dormitory and a sorority house off campus, which halted buses and broke windows and streetlights.[25] The Speaker's Rule that tried to regulate invitations by student organizations to off-campus speakers sparked controversy among students who valued a free exchange of information and ideology Another event involving freedom of speech had taken place earlier, in 1944. The student humor magazine, the *Sundial*, featured on its cover caricatures of a buxom woman and a gawking young man. President Howard Bevis objected so much that he stopped its sale, without consulting the Student Publications Committee.

A seasonal source of friction between OSU officials and students were excesses of enthusiasm during and after football games. During the Ohio State–Penn State game of 1912, which OSU hosted and was losing badly, an OSU freshman climbed a goal post that displayed Penn State's colors and set them ablaze. President Thompson had to apologize to Penn State's president, who was attending. In 1954, a victory over Michigan stirred the jubilant crowd not only to charge the goal posts but also to attack the Michigan band, seizing hats and damaging instruments. Almost regularly, the OSU campus prepares for the excesses that sometimes go with the game against Michigan, excesses caused both by youthful enthusiasm and the consumption of alcohol. Too often, property damage and unauthorized bonfires have followed the game. In recent years, blood drives and other programs have directed youthful energies into more positive activities during "Michigan Week."

24. Pollard, 300.

25. James E. Pollard, *History of The Ohio State University, Vol. VIII: The Bevis Administration, 1940–1956; Part 2: The Post-War Years and the Emergence of the Greater University, 1945–1956* (Columbus: The Ohio State University, 1972), 119–20.

5.25–5.26 *Protests erupted when OSU decided not to accept an invitation to play football in the Rose Bowl of January 1, 1962.*

THE TURBULENT 1960S AND 1970S

From time-to-time, the pressures of student life have become more than any university can manage. During the 1960s and before, one source of difficulty was generational because university administrators served in the role of parents for students. Known as "in loco parentis," the philosophy reflected a view that students were not adults until they reached the age of twenty-one. In 1971, the 26th Amendment to the U.S. Constitution fixed the age of eighteen for citizens to vote. This largely ended the era of "in loco parentis" on campus, because students had the rights of citizens and insisted on those rights.

Another source of conflict has been the pace of change at colleges and universities. Students often demand quick action, but institutions of higher education respond to social changes slowly. Typically, universities look to committees and task forces to study controversial issues and recommend actions only after lengthy deliberation. Sometimes, students make demands the university cannot grant because it does not have the power or there are contractual and legal obligations. Ending the war in Vietnam and abrogating contracts that supported the war were examples of issues that the university could not address because it lacked the power to do so.

During the 1960s, issues of racial integration and concerns for civil rights prompted many student demonstrations nationally and on the OSU campus. The university had always admitted students regardless of gender or race. The first students admitted to the Ohio Agricultural and Mechanical College included two daughters of Professor Norton Townshend. As early as 1884, the university had an African American trustee, and by 1888 had admitted the first African American student, Sherman Guss, who graduated in 1892. While a student, Guss had joined the Alcyone Literary Society and served as its sergeant-at-arms.[26] The Ohio Union and Pomerene Hall made their facilities available to students regardless of race.[27] By 1920, African American students had organized two fraternities and two sororities.[28] Nevertheless, African Americans on the OSU campus experienced significant hardship and unofficial segregation. The university prevented them from living in the few dormitories on campus until the early 1940s, a circumstance common at other universities in the North also.[29] Off campus, African American students experienced even more segregation as white landlords refused to rent to them. On campus, these students formed their own organizations because many student organizations did not allow them to join. As an example, the OSU alumni magazine of 1915 noted, "The colored students have their own glee club. They have

---

26. Pamela Pritchard, "The Negro experience at the Ohio State University in the first sixty-five years, 1873–1938: with special emphasis on Negroes in the College of Education" (OSU Ph.D. dissertation, 1982), 33.

27. Pritchard, 67.

28. Pritchard, 73–75.

29. *Centennial History of Student Affairs*, p. 99; Francis P. Weisenburger, *History of The Ohio State University, Vol. IX: The Fawcett Years* (Columbus: The Ohio State University, 1975), 161

5.27 Student scene in 1964

been practicing all winter and will probably assist the University Glee Club at the spring sings and other University events."[30]

In 1930, the University YMCA reported as unusual that "Two Negro students have been included in the Sophomore Council, and one has been added to the Cabinet to take chairmanship of a new committee."[31] Nevertheless, the general climate at OSU and in Columbus was unfriendly to African American students. In 1933, the Ohio Supreme Court ruled that OSU had acted legally when it prevented an African American student from living in a house for students in Home Economics, even though her academic major required her to do so. This occurred at the same time that Cleveland track star Jesse Owens decided to enter OSU. Owens received letters advising him against the racial intolerance in Columbus and at OSU.[32]

During the 1950s and early 1960s, discriminatory housing and racial exclusion stirred students on the OSU campus. In 1955, the Student Senate had a student–faculty committee that developed a study of race, creed, color, religion, and national origins in human relations that prompted much discussion. In 1959 and 1960, OSU brought pressure on fraternities and sororities to remove discriminatory clauses in their constitutions by 1961. In the 1960s, a Human Relations Com-

30. *OSU Monthly* (March 1915), 19.
31. Quoted in *Centennial History of Student Affairs,* 99.
32. William J. Baker, *Jesse Owens: An American Life* (New York: Free Press, 1986), 34–35

mission and a Hearing Board acted on discrimination and places found guilty of racial discrimination fell from the list of recommended housing.[33]

Social pressures on the OSU administration, exerted in ways not previously imagined and largely by students themselves, shaped the institutional environment that managed student life. Increasingly in the 1960s, students added to their

representation on university committees, including on Faculty Council (the predecessor of the University Senate). Separate programs for men and for women became increasingly unpopular in the 1960s even as civil rights groups challenged "separate but equal." In 1967, the retirements of both the Dean of Men and the Dean of Women brought these offices together. Eight years later, the Women's Student Government Association came to an end as a separate student government for women.

5.28 Student demonstration scene, February 1969

5.29 Student demonstration, May 1970

---

33. Weisenberger, 161–64

CHAPTER FIVE

The 1960s and 1970s were a time of much social conflict. Many students, as well as faculty, spoke against and took part in demonstrations opposing the Vietnam War, compulsory ROTC, the Speaker's rule, limits on women, opportunities for minority students, as well as parking and "red tape." (See chapter 3, "Five Turning Points.") Among the continuing legacies of that era of conflict have been the Office of Minority Affairs, Women's Studies, and university-sponsored child care for students as well as faculty and staff. In addition, the University Senate that began in 1972 included representatives of student organizations as full and voting members. In the 1970s, the pace of changed cultural representation on the campus continued, but without much of the drama of the 1960s. Thus, OSU established the Office of Black Student Programs in 1974, the Office of Hispanic Student Programs in 1978, the Asian-American Student Programs in 1988, and the Office of Gay, Lesbian and Bisexual Student Services in 1990.

One issue during the 1970s and 1980s was the divestiture of OSU's ownership of stocks in companies that invested in South Africa and its racially segregated society. Because of student pressure and administrative support, OSU joined other universities and nonprofit institutions in disassociating itself from segregation and discrimination.

During the 1990s, students, faculty, and staff began discussions about creating a multicultural center that would complement the Frank Hale Cultural Center set up for African American students in 1989. Years of sometimes heated deliberation and planning finally culminated in the Multicultural Center, whose goal is "to provide intellectual and cultural enrichment, programs and services, and to create a community environment that recognizes cultural differences, respects cultural uniqueness, and facilitates cross-cultural interaction, learning and appreciation."[34] The Center opened in 2001.

BUILDING THE PRESENT AND THE FUTURE

The most important and most comprehensive review of student life at OSU was the work of the Committee on the Undergraduate Experience in 1994. Inspired by a national report of the Kellogg Foundation that expressed concerns about the quality of the undergraduate environment in the United States, OSU undertook its own assessment of the campus. A large committee of twenty-three students, and twenty-three faculty and staff members, spent over a year "examining the academic, social, and service components of the university as they affect undergraduates."[35] To gather information and identify problems, the committee undertook a telephone survey of 300 undergraduates, interviewed key individuals, and gave out some 1,800 questionnaires.

---

34. See Student Affairs website, Multi-Cultural Center http://multiculturalcenter.osu.edu/.
35. Press Release of Committee on Undergraduate Experience, June 12, 1995, OSU Archives, Vertical File.

In 1995, the final report pointed to goals of improving the sense of community among OSU's diverse population and enabling more students to end their undergraduate experiences with an academic degree. As recommendations for action, the report pointed to needs for improving safety and security (including support for Campus Partners in redeveloping the neighborhood east of High Street and more emergency telephones), better transportation and parking, and increasing the number and variety of activities for students on campus. Finally, it addressed the problem of students who abused alcohol by recommending more events on campus as alternatives to the bars nearby and more counseling about the consumption of alcohol.

To improve the academic experience, the report proposed some new ideas. It called for restructuring orientation, Welcome Week and survey courses and for creating a special First Year Experience program. Qualified students, the report argued, should be able to enter their college directly rather than pass through a preparatory program. In addition, the report encouraged OSU to experiment with cre-

ating communities of students who had similar majors and could take the same classes together. (One of the outcomes of this recommendation was residential scholars programs and living communities where students of similar academic interest shared residential environments.)

5.30–5.31 Student life has always had its informal moments, from chatting with friends to quiet and solitary reading and contemplation.

5.32–5.33 Fashions and
fads have always been part
of student life.

The Committee on the Undergraduate Experience also pointed to a need for OSU to ease frustrations students felt in engaging OSU's official bureaucracy. It recommended a Student Advocacy Center to provide a central place for students to find help, get information, and obtain support. In addition, it called for integrated financial services to centralize and simplify transactions with Student Financial Aid, Fees and Deposits, Student Loans Services, and all university offices involved with financial transactions.

Fundamentally, the committee set the stage for actions that followed in the future. The Student Advocacy Center, opened in 1995, replaced the more broadly focused University Ombudservices. The Scholars Program provided for students of similar academic interests to live together. As the final report stated: "We often said we wanted to plant some annuals, some perennials, and a few oak trees as well."[36] Today, the report of the committee is still a useful point of reference in setting goals and programs to nurture and guide student life.

36. Press Release of Committee on Undergraduate Experience, June 12, 1995, OSU Archives.

CONCLUSION

OSU's commitment to enriching the student experience is more than a set of offices and programs. It also appears in the official representation of the university itself. In 1938, OSU adopted a new coat of arms designed by Professor Thomas French, a professor of Engineering Drawing. It includes a motto in Latin, "Disciplina in Civitatem," or "Education for Citizenship," that continues to the present. Those words embody the philosophy that OSU does more than use classrooms to communicate and create knowledge. It engages students both intellectually and socially and builds a social as well as physical environment that educates its students to become good citizens. Developing citizens who care about others and the social and physical environment remains a fundamental goal of The Ohio State University and the programs it develops to enhance the student experience.

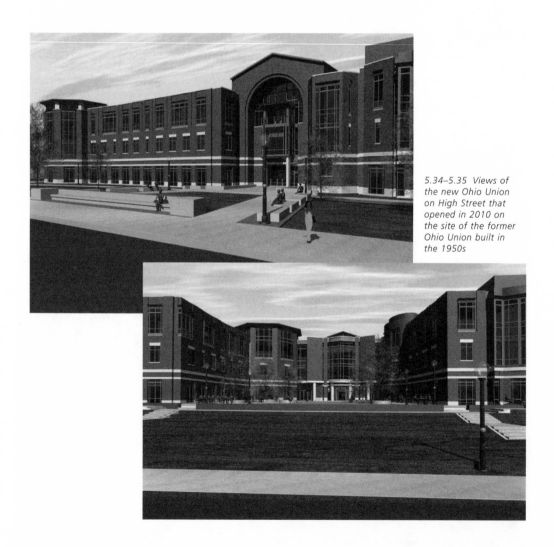

5.34–5.35 Views of the new Ohio Union on High Street that opened in 2010 on the site of the former Ohio Union built in the 1950s

CHAPTER SIX

OSU AND ATHLETICS

Another evil that attends the present system of athletics is its interference with university work. This is especially true of intercollegiate athletics.
　　　—OSU President William Henry Scott, 1890

Our intercollegiate athletic programs will routinely rank among the elite few.
　　　—Vision Statement of The Ohio State University, 2001

I N MARCH of 2007, *Sports Illustrated* featured OSU's athletic program on its cover and commented that in the new Gilded Age of college sports, Ohio State was "the standard against which all other schools are judged." With thirty-six varsity sports, OSU has the largest—and one of the most successful—athletic program in the nation. It is one of a handful that not only earn enough money to pay salaries, scholarships, and more, but also contribute financially to their universities. In 2006, as one example, OSU Athletics committed 5 million dollars (and an additional 4 million in 2008) to renovating the Thompson Library. No truly informative history of OSU can neglect this important and distinctive part of the university.

Many books, especially about OSU football and basketball, present great teams, inspirational coaches, and stellar athletes. A greater story, however, is how athletics grew to become part of the vision as well as the program of the university. Essentially, this panoramic history of intercollegiate athletics at OSU has three parts. First is a review of the growth of athletics, from humble beginnings to national giant, with special attention to people, pressures, and the rhetoric that supported the expansion. A second part presents athletics for women because, until recently, women's athletics had a different direction and philosophy. A final section concerns itself with controversies and questions about the compatibility of large-scale intercollegiate athletics with the academic mission of the university, a debate that has accompanied the athletic program nearly from its beginning.

6.1 *Pole vault in 1893*

THE EARLY YEARS, 1873–1898

According to the first historian of OSU, James Pollard, athletics evolved through several stages in its development.[1] During the 1870s and early 1880s, sports at OSU were

---

1. James E. Pollard, *Ohio State Athletics, 1879–1959* (Columbus: Ohio State University Athletic Department, 1959), 4.

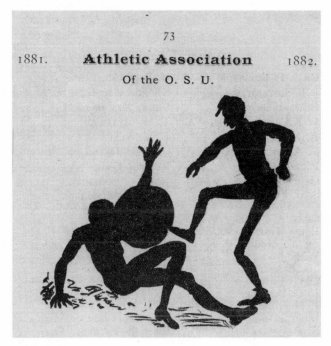

6.2–6.3 Two images from the OSU yearbook, Makio, 1880s

largely spontaneous and loosely organized. In the 1880s, students had contests with teams off campus, not all of which were collegiate. Ten years later, much had changed: there now was an organized schedules of games, a group of Ohio colleges that competed against one another, and professional coaches, especially in football. In the 1890s, football emerged as the sport that inspired the most enthusiasm and attention.

Joseph Bradford, who was a student from 1877 to 1883 and later became a professor and the first university architect, recalled that the earliest athletic contest was in the spring of 1877 or 1878 and it consisted only of footraces. The track was a gravel road from High Street to University Hall and then to Neil Avenue. Faculty members served as officials and students watched from the steps of University Hall.[2]

Probably the first efforts to move athletics from play to organized sports were in 1879. A Baseball Association organized a team and two years later the *Lantern,* in only its third issue, pleaded for more sports and an athletic association to organize them: "An Athletic Association is what is needed, one that will install a regular series of games, offer prizes, and get the members awake to the sport. Surely amongst two hundred and fifty men there ought to be some who can make good records in the various sports common to colleges."[3]

Whether inspired or chastised, students formed an Athletic Association and organized the first Field Day on April 2, 1881. Field Days included track events and baseball and drew on faculty as judges. The *Makio* of 1882 reported not only the

2. Joseph N. Bradford, *OSU Alumni Magazine* (Feb. 1920), 21.
3. Pollard, *Athletics,* 4–5.

Athletic Association but also five baseball teams (a college nine and one team for each class) and a Cricket Club that included J. F. Firestone, who said "Don't play on warm days." Besides a Field Day, Class Day was another occasion for track and field events to take place.

Gradually, interest in sports led to contests between colleges and universities in Ohio. Nationally, intercollegiate sports began in the United States when Harvard and Yale competed in crew in 1852. In 1859, Amherst and Williams colleges played baseball against each other. Ten years later, Rutgers and Princeton had the first game of intercollegiate football.[4] Student newspapers at OSU and other campuses reported news from other campuses, especially athletic contests of colleges and universities in the East. In fact, it is fair to speculate that students saw the growth of athletics not only as entertainment but also as a way of being like other colleges and universities

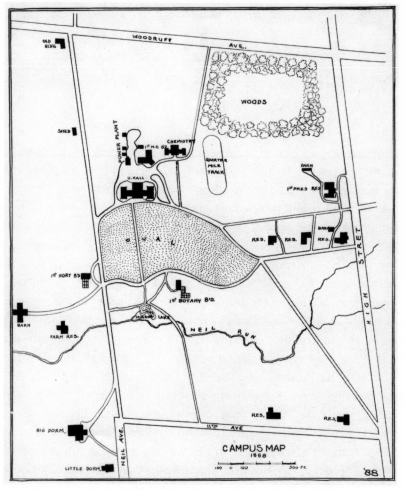

6.4 Campus map from 1888. Note Quarter Mile track northeast of Oval.

4. Joana Davenport, " From Crew to Commercialism—The Paradox of Sport in Higher Education," in Donald Chu, Jeffrey O Segrave, and Beverly U. Becker, eds., *Sport and Higher Education* (Champaign, IL: Human Kinetics Publishers, Inc, 1985), 6–7.

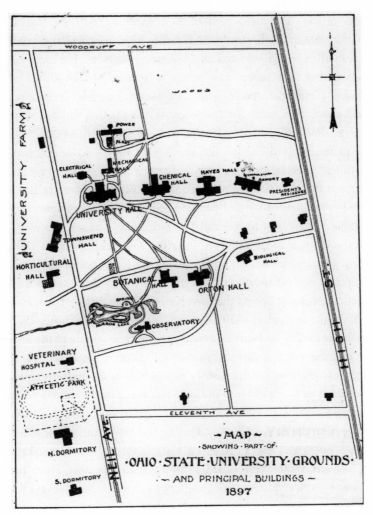

6.5 Campus map from 1897

that loomed larger in reputation. By 1882, interest in the state led to an Ohio Inter-collegiate Athletic Association that both fostered and tried to oversee intercollegiate competition within Ohio.

During the 1870s and 1880s, OSU lacked the facilities—the athletic fields and gymnasiums—that other institutions had. The first athletic events took place on the north side of campus, about where Derby and Hayes Halls now stand. Professor Bradford recalled a well-built quarter-mile track and spectators stood during events, the most exciting of which were the bicycle races on the old "high wheel" (the first all-metal bicycle invented about 1870, which had a tall wheel in front). Footraces, hurdle races, and potato and egg races took place there. Between events spectators sat on the grass.[5]

After 1886, when academic buildings began to populate the area, cam-

5. Bradford, 21.

pus athletics moved to a field west of Neil Avenue, north of North dorm and opposite where Oxley Hall now stands. This site followed the contour of the land and sloped downhill toward the Olentangy River.[6] Baseball games had a comical aspect because there was nearly a seventeen-foot difference in level between home plate and center fields. Professor Thomas French remembered, " . . . a good many flies went for hits because the visiting fielders were not good mountaineers." Partially fenced on the east, north, and south sides, the field included a primitive stadium on the south side that held about two hundred.[7]

While student publications such as the *Lantern* and the *Makio* embraced athletics as a virtue, official support developed slowly. Some professors saw athletics as harmless and even useful play and participated as judges of athletic contests; some even contributed financially to the athletic association. Others, however, feared that athletics would distract from and even interfere with academics. In 1890, President William Henry Scott, for one, acknowledged the importance of cheerful and hearty physical exercises, such as in lawn tennis, but had doubts about football and intercollegiate athletics generally. Sports that involved practices during the school week and caused participants to neglect their academic studies were harmful. "We have great confidence in the loyalty and earnestness of our students. Some of the most loyal and earnest are members of the various teams, and others are zealous friends and supporters of the association. Yet the history of athletics in the Eastern colleges and the manifest tendency of those of Ohio indicate that some limits should be prescribed."[8]

Nevertheless, enthusiasm for athletics spread across campuses in Ohio, even as it had sprung from the East originally. During the 1880s and 1890s, OSU competed against such schools as Western Reserve, Case Institute, Wooster, Akron, Oberlin, Otterbein, Kenyon, Ohio Wesleyan, Cincinnati, and Denison. From time to time, presidents voiced concerns about sporting events that involved players who were not students and about profanity, betting, and payments for performance. To regulate competition and to assure propriety, presidents organized the Intercollegiate Athletic Association of Ohio. However, students resisted rules imposed by presidents and faculty. In fact, an editorial in OSU's *Lantern* declared that it was "hideous in the extreme" that faculty should think they could grant or deny participation in athletics as a privilege to students.[9]

1898–1912: SETTING THE STAGE FOR BIG-TIME ATHLETICS

Until 1898, faculty and administrative supervision of athletics on campus had been slight. Students had formed athletic associations, organized teams, and sponsored

---

6. Pollard, *Athletics,* 23.
7. Bradford, 21.
8. Pollard, *Athletics,* 12.
9. Pollard, *Athletics,* 20.

6.6 *First football team, 1890*

6.7 *First basketball team, 1897–98*

events with the support of the Student Athletic Association. Increasingly, faculty and administrators grew concerned that athletic competition and its financing would embarrass the University some day. There was good reason for concern. In February of 1898, the Student Athletic Association had only two cents in its treasury but debts of more than $1400. OSU faculty passed a resolution " . . . that the good name of the University has been used by those representing college athletics to incur a large indebtedness involving the credit of the University. . . . " Thus they refused to receive any petitions concerning the use of university property for athletics until students formed a new and more responsible association that could present a plan to pay the debts. Not only could the Student Athletic Association not pay its debts,[10] but a search for its constitution proved in vain. In short, athletics as a program run by students had reached a standstill in which the fans and financial transactions overwhelmed the managerial structure for college athletics.

From the collapse of the Student Athletic Association came two new organizations. One was the Athletic Association of the Ohio State University, founded in March of 1898 at a meeting that OSU President James Canfield attended. Its purpose "was to create an association under such a constitution as would insure its financial stability."[11] Open to students, faculty, alumni and the public, the association collected membership subscriptions to build its treasury and pay debts. Concerts and other special events helped also to pay the amassed debt, as did other student societies and fraternities.

To govern the Athletic Association an Athletic Board was established. It consisted of three faculty, selected by the OSU faculty, three resident alumni, and the student managers of the football, baseball, and track teams, plus a secretary who was also a student. This board was to " . . . have absolute control over all matters pertaining to athletics in the University provided that their action shall not conflict with the rules established by the University faculty."

Founding the Athletic Association and its Athletic Board of The Ohio State University was a landmark in the history of athletics on campus. From that point, athletics took its place as part of the official life as well as culture of the university. The Athletic Board, in which professors held a leadership role, was the official instrument for regulating and managing athletics, subject to the board of trustees. Faculty governance of athletics became a legacy that continues today.

Another milestone in developing athletics was when the Armory and Gymnasium, on the site of what is now the Wexner Center, opened in January 1898. The university needed a building in which military training could take place, as expected of a land-grant university, and where all students could have physical education classes. The Armory had a large main floor with a running track around the entire room. On that floor, OSU's intercollegiate basketball program began with a game against North High School in 1898. The basement had two parts, one for men and one for women. Each con-

---

10. Pollard, *Athletics*, 55–56.
11. Pollard, *Athletics*, 6.

6.8 *The Armory in 1902*

6.9 *The gymnasium in the Armory*

tained bathtubs, showers, swimming pool, toilets, locker rooms, and a bicycle room.[12]

The Armory heralded physical education at OSU. In January 1898, Dr. Christopher P. Linhard began as director of the gymnasium and as instructor in hygiene and physical training. To help him, Miss Stella Elliott supervised the women's program. At first, students engaged voluntarily in physical education classes. In 1900, with the support of President William Oxley Thompson, physical education and drill became required of all freshman and sophomore males. Women took hygiene classes and physical training in place of cadet activities.[13]

Of course, students in physical training did not necessarily become stars or even participants in intercollegiate athletics, but the Armory could serve this purpose. As early as 1900, two years after the Armory opened, OSU's student newspaper connected physical education and intercollegiate athletics: "OSU can never have a body of well trained athletes and gymnasts until the elements of athletic practice are thoroughly mastered, which will never be the case under the present conditions. The only way to mend this matter is to make class work in the gymnasium compulsory and to hold the student responsible for so many hours of gymnasium work, just as is done in Latin or Greek."[14] In fact, the director of physical education (Dr. H. Shindle Wingert) had charge of the athletic program from 1906 to 1912. After that, physical education and athletics became and remained administratively separate as the former focused on nonathletic training and the preparing of teachers of physical education.

Even as the Armory and Gymnasium provided for athletic and physical education programs on the campus, the new building led to a reconsideration of where athletic fields should be on the campus. It seemed sensible to have an athletic field nearby. In May 1898, OSU trustees adopted a report of its farm committee that " . . . the best and really the only suitable grounds are at the south end of the long pasture which lies north of the president's house. These grounds require no general grading, while other grounds require much; their use will interfere with farm operations little, while the use of their proposed grounds interfere much; they are near the gymnasium and near the most effective street railway, which is a considerable advantage."[15] The old athletic fields that bordered Neil Avenue became farm land again.

All expenses—preparing the new field, skinning a baseball diamond, laying a running track, erecting a grandstand, and more—were the responsibility of the Athletic Board, not the university. The board had to accept the debt and pay it by various means—dances, membership subscriptions, and donations. That separation of finances for intercollegiate athletics from the budget for teaching and research would become a continuing characteristic of OSU.

The site for an athletic field near the Armory had humble beginnings in 1898.

---

12. Ralph Joseph Sabock, "A History of Physical Eduation at The Ohio State University—Men and Women's Divisions, 1898–1969" (MA thesis, The Ohio State University, 1969), 13.

13. Sabock , 17–18; OSU Faculty minutes, March 31, 1900.

14. Sabock, 17; quoted in OSU *Lantern*, January 24, 1900.

15. Minutes of OSU Board of Trustees, May 5, 1898, 331.

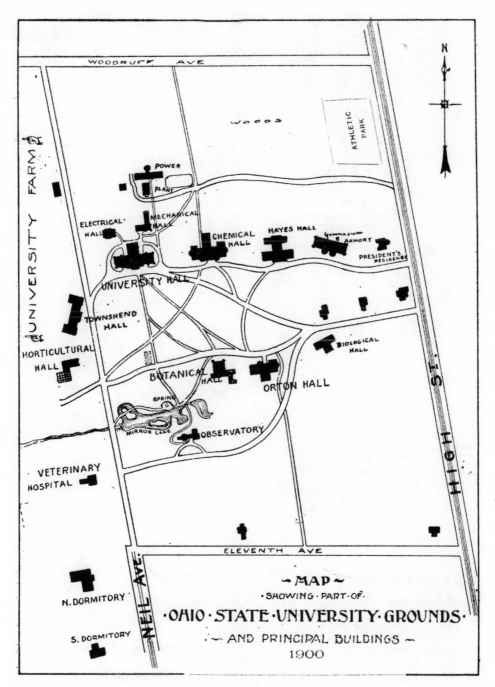

6.10 Campus map, 1900. Note the Athletic Park in the northeast corner, the site of Ohio Field.

At first, a good-sized lot stood between it and Woodruff Avenue, where Professor George Knight's cow occupied the pasture. In 1903, the trustees decided to extend the athletic field to Woodruff Avenue but away from High Street. According to one account, "A strong argument in favor of the removal to the site west of the woods was that its location on High Street was offensive to those living oppo-

6.11 Ohio Field in 1915.

site to it on that street, that it depressed the value of real estate, and retarded the development of that part of the city immediately east of it."[16]

When the trustees allowed, the Athletic Board gradually extended and improved "University Field." In 1908, major improvements—a grandstand and bleachers— led to a rededication and renaming ceremony. Mrs. Estelle Clark Thompson, wife of President Thompson, christened the field with water from Neil Run and renamed it "Ohio Field." A report to the OSU Alumni Association, remarked, "The alumni will please take notice that not one cent of this sum has been paid by either the University or the State."[17] More improvements in the following summer included a permanent iron fence, with gates and ticket offices that were completed on the south side of the field.[18]

6.12 *Professor Thomas E. French in 1902 yearbook*

At its greatest expansion, with bleachers on both east and west sides, Ohio Field could seat roughly twelve thousand. The 1909 student yearbook waxed enthusiastically: "The completion of 'Ohio Field' at the beginning of the present school year marked a new epoch in Varsity athletics. With equipment second to none and with an abundance of material to represent it in every branch of sport, Ohio State has now taken a position in athletics among the leading universities of the land."[19]

Already in 1909, Professor Thomas French, who would become first among the faculty in his support of athletics, envisaged that more improvements were just ahead: "It is hoped that this is only the beginning of the final Ohio Field. The fence will be continued around the entire enclosure, with perhaps behind the bleachers a concrete wall paneled for bronze tablets to be left by future classes; and with the continued splendid financial management and the support of the alumni the dream of a magnificent concrete stadium in horse shoe shape may be realized sooner than anyone would expect."[20] French, whose brother Edwin had been a star athlete, would serve on the Athletic Board from 1912 to 1944, thus becoming known as the "father of Ohio Stadium."

Another faculty advocate for expanding athletics was George Rightmire. As a student at OSU, Rightmire had been active in athletics. He played football and ran track before graduating in 1895. Thereafter, Rightmire served as graduate manager of athletics, and had responsibility for scheduling as well as general support of athletic events. In 1902, Rightmire joined the OSU faculty as an instructor in law, but continued to work in support of athletics. So popular was the young professor among the undergraduate students that they devoted the 1911 student yearbook to him.

16. Alexis Cope, *History of The Ohio State University, Vol I: 1870–1910* (Columbus: The Ohio State University Press, 1920), 367.

17. *OSU Alumni Magazine* (October 1909), 32.

18. Thomas C. Mendenhall, ed., *History of The Ohio State University, Vol. II: Continuation of the Narrative from 1910 to 1925* (Columbus: The Ohio State University Press, 1926), 168.

19. Pollard, *Athletics,* 65–66.

20. Pollard, *Athletics,* 65.

Rightmire became president of the Athletic Board and also chaired a special committee of five faculty members who investigated how other universities governed athletics. In fact, the governance of intercollegiate athletics—and football especially—had become a topic of national interest.

In 1905, U.S. President Theodore Roosevelt called upon colleges to either reform or to abolish football, which had reached a shocking level of violence and scandals, academic and financial. The resulting organization, which had begun as the Intercollegiate Athletic Association of the United States, attempted to establish rules of conduct for intercollegiate athletics. In 1910, it renamed itself the National Collegiate Athletic Association (NCAA).

Rightmire's committee sent questionnaires to the twenty-five largest universities in the East and the Midwest. In addition, they interviewed faculty representatives of the Western Athletic Conference, the University of Michigan, Oberlin, and Case School of Technology. Finally, in February of 1912, Rightmire and the committee "... came to the conclusion

6.13 George Rightmire as a young professor at OSU, ca. 1911

that the Western [i.e., Western Conference] method of faculty control of athletics is best suited to conditions at Ohio State."[21]

Founded in 1896, even before the NCAA, the Intercollegiate Conference of Faculty Representatives (or Western Conference and later the Big Ten) consisted originally of the University of Chicago, the University of Illinois, the University of Minnesota, Northwestern University, Purdue University, the University of Michigan, and the University of Wisconsin. In 1899, Indiana and Iowa joined. As Rightmire put it, "In that conference, athletic competition will, generally, be on a higher plane than Ohio State has hitherto been able to reach, and the effect upon us should be a stimulating one, and no enduring reason appears why we should not at a very early day be the athletic peer of any of these universities."[22]

At least three concerns confronted Rightmire and the advocates for joining the Western Conference. First, competing against a new set of rivals would be costly, because of travel to other states and because of the need for more training to compete successfully. Confidence in OSU athletics was high, but a greater concern was that OSU could not play against the University of Michigan, which had left the Western Conference because of a disagreement with at least one of the rules in 1907. Beginning in 1897 and taking place annually since 1900, the football competition between the University of Michigan and OSU has drawn huge numbers of fans. Nevertheless, many at OSU, including George Rightmire, believed Michigan would

---

21. OSU Faculty minutes, February 14, 1912, 114–115.
22. Pollard, *Athletics*, 110.

6.14 Lynn W. St. John, 1914

return to the Western Conference. (Michigan did in fact return in 1917; the teams played each other again in 1918.) In January 1912, the Athletic Board petitioned the Conference for admission.

Shortly after the application, the Athletic Board and OSU faculty and trustees addressed the third obstacle: governance of athletics. As the "Intercollegiate Conference of Faculty Representatives," the organization required its members to have a professor represent each campus and to empower faculty to have full authority over athletics. This requirement continues today, as faculty representatives from each of the Big Ten universities have responsibility for the welfare of student athletes, the protection of academic integrity, and the general supervision of their athletic departments. For OSU, membership in the Conference led to a major change in the Athletic Board. In February 1912, with the support of the Athletic Board, OSU faculty and trustees created a new Athletic Board of Control to regulate athletics. Membership of faculty members increased to five while representatives of alumni and students fell to two each. President Thompson appointed the five faculty members, one of whom was George Rightmire, who became president of the Board of Control. This Board of Control had the power to appoint an athletic director, who was separate from the Director of Physical Education, and who was to have charge of both intercollegiate and intramural athletics. Also, full-time coaches for major teams, such as football, basketball, and baseball, were to be members of the faculty with rank and tenure and ". . . should be identified with the life of the University."[23] In May of 1912, the board recommended John R. Richards as athletic director and head coach of football and track. In addition, it put forward L. W. St. John as

23. Pollard, *Athletics*, 108.

6.15 *Chic Harley as a runner, kicker, and passer brought crowds to Ohio Field to witness his heroic and winning performances, 1916, 1917, and 1919.*

manager of athletics, head coach of baseball and basketball, and assistant coach of football.

OSU ATHLETICS BECOMES A NATIONAL POWER, 1912–1947

The Western Athletic Conference approved OSU's application for membership in April of 1912. Rightmire's optimism aside, there was no certainty that OSU would become a major power even within the Conference, let alone the nation. Credit for this achievement belongs to many: an outspoken and well-respected athletic director; OSU presidents who encouraged the intercollegiate athletic program and helped its expansion in the number of sports and facilities; and a faculty athletic representative who encouraged others to work to improve OSU's competitive position. Meanwhile, OSU's star athletes, such as Chic Harley in football (1916–1919) and Jesse Owens in track (1933–1936), drew national attention as reporters in newspapers and on radio fed the insatiable appetite of the general public for news of athletic heroics on campuses.

Lynn W. St. John presided as Director of Athletics for thirty-five years, the longest tenure of any director at OSU. St. John provided stability of leadership and a

6.16 *The perfect play, in which Harley swept around Northwestern's end, had every OSU player make a block in this game from 1916.*

program of continuous growth. Soon after graduating high school, he turned to teaching in Barberton, Ohio. Besides his classroom duties, St. John organized YMCA gymnasium classes. In 1900, he enrolled at OSU and joined the football team, where he played halfback. However, a death in the family forced him to seek employment, this time at Fostoria High School, where he taught in classrooms and coached sports for a year. He resumed his student career at Wooster College where he also coached, and graduated in 1906. Following graduation, he became an assistant in Wooster's biology department while continuing to coach and teach physical education.

In 1909, St. John transferred to Ohio Wesleyan as athletics director and coach. While at Ohio Wesleyan he traveled to Columbus in the mornings to study medicine at Starling-Ohio Medical College. An offer from Ohio State to become business manager of athletics, head baseball and basketball coach, and football line coach enabled him to be even closer to his medical studies in Columbus. That St. John could expect to study medicine as well as coach illustrates not only his boundless energy but the scale of OSU's athletics program at the time. In 1912; when St. John came to OSU, the university had six varsity sports.[24]

The following year, 1913, changed his career forever. John R. Richards, the new athletic director and head coach of football and track, resigned suddenly and

24. OSU *Makio,* 1913.

6.17 Radio broadcast of OSU football, ca. 1935

accepted a position as recreation director for the City of Chicago.[25] Quickly the Athletic Board of Control named St. John at age twenty-five head of football as well as Director of Athletics. In the next thirty-four years, until 1947, St. John led OSU to national stature in athletics and presided over the building of new facilities for athletics. As one of the leading athletics directors in the United States, St. John had a record of service that included membership in the National Collegiate Athletic Association Executive Committee and its basketball rules committee, and the American Olympic Executive Committee, to name only a few of his honors.[26]

During almost all of the many years of his career, St. John had the support of one of the chief leaders of the faculty members of the Athletic Board. Professor Thomas French served on the board from 1912 to 1944 and for most of those years was OSU's faculty representative to the Western Conference. One of the national leaders in engineering drawing (see chapter 4), French's brother Edwin had been a star athlete at OSU. In 1929, President Rightmire praised the leadership of French on the Athletic Board: "For seventeen years you have been a moving spirit in the development of athletics, both intercollegiate and intramurals here; during this time the Ohio State University has become distinguished in Western Conference

25. Pollard, *Athletics*, 114.
26. St. John Bio file, Pollard essay, OSU Archives.

circles . . . large plans for the development of sports have been laid and in a great part achieved. . . . Your contribution in this field of University activity has been most notable and leaves a indelible impression upon the history of the University during the period 1912–1929."[27] French would continue on the board for another fifteen years, ending his service in 1944, three years before St. John retired.

Ohio Stadium was one of many new stadiums at colleges and universities. As one historian put it, "Intersectional football games and the dedication of a sparkling new stadium became a symbolic rite of passage for an ambitious university claiming newfound stature.[28] This enthusiasm included basketball, track and field, crew, and swimming as mass media such as newspapers, magazines, and news films popularized athletic heroes, winning teams, and prominent athletic programs expanded the audience well beyond students, alumni, and neighboring communities. In the 1930s OSU began broadcasting football and basketball games, first by campus radio and then in a networked arrangement with other radio stations. Radio broadcasts of football games and other contests added to the excitement and brought revenues from commercial sponsors to the athletic programs.[29]

Another force in expanding OSU athletics was presidential leadership. William Oxley Thompson and George Rightmire were presidents of OSU during most of St. John's tenure as director and proved steadfast in their enthusiasm for intercollegiate athletics. More than any other president before him, Thompson took an active interest in athletics during his lengthy tenure of twenty-six years.[30] In 1905, he devoted a substantial section of his annual report to athletics and explained: "In the modern college, athletics assume so large a place that it seems appropriate to offer a few remarks upon that subject in a formal report of the University. . . . A wide-spread interest has developed among the students in base ball, football, track, basketball, and in the various other forms of athletics. "[31] Thompson called on the faculty of OSU to take leadership in guiding athletics along ethical principles.

Years later, around 1913, Thompson commented more about athletics and education. In "The Educational Idea in Athletics," Thompson observed that athletics provided for boys a positive outlet for an instinctive craving for action, opened a field of achievement, promoted good habits and self-discipline among participants, and created a sense of community and companionship among students. Intercollegiate athletics served to break down provincialism by bringing students into contact with other colleges and from other regions. "Athletics are, then, assuming proper administration, the most normal, healthful and hopeful form of expression of the adolescent tendency found anywhere in the world." He ended by saying that because athletics were so important to the education and well-being of students, it followed that " . . . the University should support an athletic plant for physical education on

---

27. *OSU Alumni Quarterly* (November 1929), 60–61.
28. John R. Thelin, *A History of American Higher Education* (Baltimore: Johns Hopkins University Press, 2004), 208.
29. Pollard, *Athletics*, 252.
30. Pollard, *Athletics*, 61.
31. OSU Annual Report for 1905, 30–31.

6.18–6.19 Stadium Drive parade in downtown Columbus. The billboard promises that the proposed stadium "will draw the rest of the world to Columbus." A year later, in 1921, Ohio Stadium was taking shape (6.19).

the principle of large opportunities for all students physically fit to participate."[32]

Ohio Stadium embodied the interest and enthusiasm of President Thompson in promoting OSU and in expanding its athletic prominence. It represented also the university's first organized efforts to draw financial donations to OSU. Supporters of the stadium conducted the first major fund-raising campaign for the university. and Thompson wrote letters to alumni. Some of the letters that Thompson received in reply questioned why the stadium should be so large and recommended that the energy expended on it and athletics generally should be on meeting academic needs instead. To one critic, Thompson replied at length that the monumental size of the building was appropriate because it served more than a single sport. Besides track and field events, the stadium would enable the university to host large events including mass exercises in physical education, reunions of veterans of World War I, and any occasion that would draw a large audience. To the criticism that the university had become too well known for its athletics, Thompson responded: "I do not, however, believe that there is as much truth in the statement as we are sometimes disposed to assume. I find that in the circles where real service is demanded the question of athletic attainments have very little to do with the issue."[33]

Thompson took an active role in the campaign for the stadium. The final report of the Ohio Stadium Campaign paid tribute to him: "All through the stress and strain of the campaign, President Thompson did whatever service that could come properly from him. . . . . In fact, whenever a big man was needed the President was called upon and met all the requirements; whenever a difficulty appeared, he straightened it out; whenever a word from him would be helpful he applied it."[34]

George W. Rightmire, who succeeded Thompson as president of OSU, was no less encouraging of OSU's athletic program as valuable to the educational mission of the university. As a student and as a faculty member he had been a leader in speaking for intercollegiate athletics. Rightmire's enthusiasm for education echoed Thompson's opinion that athletic competition could be beneficial to students. In 1914, as one example, Professor Rightmire reported in the *OSU Monthly* that he had conducted a study of more than one hundred alumni of OSU who had taken part in competitive athletics. The survey confirmed the favorable effects of intercollegiate athletics. Respondents cited benefits in health, self-discipline, and moral development. Nearly half mentioned that the demands of training and competition had interfered with their scholastic standing. Some noted, however, that their scholarship had been poor even before becoming an athlete; others pointed out that " . . . by rigorously confining the attention outside of studies to athletics there need be no lowering of standards."[35] Thus, Rightmire felt as comfortable as Thompson in presiding over the expansion of the athletic program during the era of Lynn St. John.

---

32. "The Educational Idea in Athletics," William Oxley Thompson Papers, OSU Archives.
33. Thompson to C. C. Hayden, March 28, 1921, Thompson papers, box 35, f. 5.
34. Campaign for Ohio Stadium, 34–35, OSU Archives.
35. *OSU Alumni Monthly,* December 1914–Jan. 1915, 21–24.

6.20 Even in the worst of financial times, some people had money to attend football games. Note the uniform of the Stadium Pilot, who directed people to their seats in this photo from 1930.

6.21 This photo shows the dormitory that was created within the stadium to house students who had good grades but could not afford to live in other dormitories.

As it did with the academic programs, the Great Depression caused hardship for athletics. Between 1928–29 and 1933–34, revenues fell by more than two-thirds. Dwindled receipts from football and basketball, which produced the most revenue, led to a closer scrutiny of expenses, especially the scheduling of intercollegiate games. As an example, in January 1933 and for the next six months, all sports except baseball and track were on an intramural basis only. There were fewer events for track. Another effect was on salaries. Even though Athletics ran largely on its own funding, some staff received salaries from OSU for their work in physical education. During the Depression the State of Ohio reduced its support for high education and caused three cuts in salary. Staff members in athletics whose salaries were partly paid by OSU also suffered proportionately from the decreases.[36]

Another of OSU's difficulties in the Depression was Ohio Governor Martin L. Davey. In 1935–36, the governor's unwillingness to support more appropriations for OSU included opposition to its athletic program. He charged that members of the 1935 football team had received state-subsidized jobs. An investigation by the Western Athletic Conference followed. Its report noted that four football players worked as pages in the legislature and another six had part-time jobs in the public works department. However, other students, who were not athletes, also worked in those departments. The report closed by saying that it found no favoritism or influence exerted in behalf of the athletes by OSU and the State of Ohio. As a matter of fact, employing OSU athletes did not differ substantially from the practices of other members of the Western Athletic Conference.[37]

Financial difficulties aside, OSU grew in buildings and grounds for sport. When the Great Depression began in October 1929, the Athletic Board had already approved the purchase of nine parcels of land, almost three hundred acres, for use as a new golf course, and had hired Dr. Alister MacKenzie, a renowned golf architect, to lay it out. The Works Progress Administration, a federal program to create jobs in the Depression by sponsoring construction projects, provided the necessary financial support.[38] In 1931, OSU opened a new Natatorium that was built with athletic revenues. It had three pools and launched swimming as a varsity sport at OSU, one that it dominated nationally under the coaching of Mike Peppe (who directed his teams to 12 Big Ten Crowns, 11 NCAA championships and 10 A.A.U titles until his retirement in 1963). Attached to it, but built with state appropriations, was a men's gymnasium that also opened in 1931.

Even as the university itself had a "belt-tightening" but still achieved overall stability of enrollment and academic programs, so too did athletics. At the end of the Depression, OSU sponsored thirteen intercollegiate sports and had an active intramural program for men, with 21 sports and 10,182 participants, and for women 14 sports and 1,076 participants.[39]

---

36. Pollard, *Athletics*, 240–43.
37. Pollard, *Athletics*, 242–43.
38. Pollard, *Athletics*, 218.
39. Pollard, *Athletics*, 246.

6.22 *The Men's Physical Education Building and Natatorium in 1932*

6.23 *A scene at the Natatorium in 1935*

6.24 Don Scott in 1938

The outbreak of World War II challenged OSU athletics in different ways. Schedules for intercollegiate competitions were shortened, especially because wartime rations on gasoline affected transport. Rationing of construction materials and the high cost of labor ended the expansion of athletic facilities. OSU students and athletes, men such as football stars Charles Csuri and Don Scott, left campus for military service. Scott lost his life and OSU honored him by naming its airport in his honor in 1943. Freshmen, who had been banned from taking part in Varsity sports, were allowed to play during the war because so many student athletes were in military service. By the spring of 1944, seven members of OSU's varsity coaches, including Paul Brown in football, were in the armed forces. Revenues from football receipts helped to support relief funds for the Army and Navy Relief Fund. At war's end, the athletic program remained strong and ready for another era.

OSU ATHLETICS IN THE MODERN ERA, 1945 TO THE PRESENT

In 1947, Lynn St. John retired, but the athletic directors who succeeded him continued to expand OSU's athletic program. Nationally, several factors influenced developments on the OSU campus. Students returned to campus from military service and many had financial support of a GI Bill that paid tuition and provided a living allowance. The postwar boom in student enrollment helped boost attendance at college athletic events. In 1949, the University of Michigan enlarged its stadium from 72,000 seats to 97,239, while Purdue raised its football seating from 13,500 to 51,000.[40] Ohio State added to Ohio Stadium's seating capacity by reducing the width of seats from 20 to 17 inches.[41] A public, eager to enjoy life after the sacrifices of war, flocked to collegiate games.

The postwar economic boon and the new medium of television helped to fuel a steady growth in intercollegiate athletics, especially football. Discussions of broadcasting football games began as early as 1948. OSU's Athletic Board agreed to the telecasting of two games by the university's own station, provided there was no commercial sponsor.[42] At first, the Western Athletic Conference opposed commercial, large-scale, live-broadcasting of games for fear that attendance, and thus ticket revenue, would decline. By 1950, the board allowed broadcasting of out-of-town games, selected games of the week, and sold-out games " . . . provided there is adequate protection of the sports program."[43] In 1951, the Conference did sign a three-year contract with the National Broadcasting Company for the radio and television rights to the Rose Bowl. This contract earned $1,510,000, money that was shared with the Western Conference and the Pac 10 and the participating teams. By 1961, the NCAA had accepted the concept that television contracts could both publicize games as well as raise money, and the organization became an active negotiator of well-paid contracts for its conferences. It had decided that rather than overwhelming the audience with too many athletic events, televised games increased the market and added to the revenue of athletic programs.[44] So important was television to athletics that the Big Ten inaugurated its own television network in 2007.

In the years following World War II, the university, through its Athletic Board, added and improved athletic buildings. In 1947 and 1949, Ohio Stadium, the program's chief revenue producer, expanded its press box to include two camera booths. In 1957, OSU completed St. John Arena, which enabled varsity basketball to return to campus from the State Fair Coliseum. That year French Field House opened for

---

40. John R. Thelin, *Games Colleges Play: Scandal and Reform in Intercollegiate Athletics* (Baltimore: The Johns Hopkins University Press, 1994), 98.

41. Pollard, *Athletics*, 230.

42. Pollard, *Athletics*, 253.

43. Pollard, *Athletics*, 254.

44. Thelin, *Games Colleges Play*, 156.

indoor track events. Expansion continued throughout the 1960s as the university added an ice rink in 1961, a football practice field and baseball diamonds, and in 1967, Athletic Facility North that contained dressing rooms, lockers, and training equipment. The university added hockey in 1964, pistol in 1967, and volleyball in 1968, raising the number of varsity sports to eighteen.[45]

Another major change of the period was scholarships for student athletes. The prevailing practice of providing student athletes with part-time jobs was fraught with problems. Apart from the accusations that Governor Davey launched against OSU's football players in the 1930s, the practice gave off-campus boosters, who could employ students, significant influence in recruiting and keeping student athletes. There was little supervision to make certain the student-athlete was working. From a coach's view, a student athlete's dependence on a part-time job had the potential of interfering with the hours needed for physical development and practice.

As early as 1939, the Western Athletic Conference permitted members to host scholarships for athletes in financial need.[46] In 1948, the NCAA adopted "Principles for the Conduct of Intercollegiate Athletics," which forbade athletic scholarships, limited a student-athlete's aid to tuition and fees, and required that awards be based on financial need rather than athletic merit.[47] However, these strictures lasted only two years. By 1957, scholarships for student-athletes based on athletic talent rather than financial need became common in the NCAA and at The Ohio State University.

At OSU, the grants-in-aid program developed by the Western Athletic Conference provoked discussion. President Fawcett objected that its cost was unrealistic and OSU had other financial needs caused by the dramatic growth in the numbers of students and faculty. Philosophically, Fawcett believed that financial reward at an academic institution should arise from intellectual achievement, not athletic skills. Nevertheless, if OSU was to remain competitive, the university had to follow what the Conference decided, because it would be difficult to compete against universities that had developed programs of athletic scholarships based on talent rather than financial need.[48]

In 1957, OSU offered eighty-nine scholarships to high school athletes under the new program. This was the start of an upward trend that fed on itself and appeared to have no limit. Even as television added to the revenues of the athletic program and expanded the audience and the market for tickets, the cost of athletic scholarships added significantly to the financial requirements of competitive athletics. Losing teams, especially in the chief revenue-producing sports of football and basketball, could undermine the entire athletic program. To remain competitive, however, demanded ever-growing investments in physical plants, training facilities, and effective coaches. Athletic scholarships added to the growing list of expenses, but

45. Francis P. Weisenberger, *History of The Ohio State University, Vol. IX: The Fawcett Years, 1956–1972* (Columbus: The Ohio State University, 1975), 219.

46. Thelin, *Games Colleges Play*, 57–58.

47. Thelin, *Games Colleges Play*, 101–102.

48. Pollard, *Athletics*, 267.

unless OSU had talented student athletes and was able to offer the best scholarships, it could not compete with other institutions. If that happened, its other investments in the athletic programs would be less valuable. In 1969, one administrator in athletics warned, "If expenses get too burdensome, some varsity sports may have to return to an intramural basis."[49]

During the economic slump of the 1970s and 1980s, OSU's presidents worried about the financial well-being of the athletic enterprise. President Harold Enarson reflected on how much the athletic programs depended on winning in football or basketball and commented: "Today, the financial crunch is here and it is bound to worsen. Travel costs are staggering. Laundry bills for cleaning uniforms are skyrocketing. And Title IX imposes new cost burdens, the measures of past neglect of women's sports. . . . I cannot emphasize enough—there must be a de-escalation of spending on intercollegiate sports."[50]

6.25 Andy Geiger with model of the renovated Ohio Stadium in 1997

President Edward Jennings, who succeeded President Enarson, learned the Department of Athletics was facing a financial shortfall of $793,000 in 1984 and charged his new athletic director, Rick Bay, to take cost-cutting actions. In his first year, Bay managed to reduce the shortage to $86,000 and then proposed to reduce the number of varsity sports from 31 to 23. By downgrading eight sports (synchronized swimming, pistol, rifle, men's and women's fencing, and men's soccer, lacrosse, and volleyball) to nonvarsity status, the Athletic Department expected to save more than $400,000 each year in travel costs and in scholarships. In the end, however, students and alumni raised an outcry and the number of varsity sports remained the same.[51]

President E. Gordon Gee took a different view from his predeces-

49. *Centennial History of OSU: Athletics*, 40.

50. Paul Underwood, *History of The Ohio State University, Vol. X: The Enarson Years, 1972–1981* (Columbus: the Ohio State University, 1985), 153–54.

51. John B. Gabel, *History of The Ohio State University, Vol. XI: The Jennings Years, 1981–1990* (Columbus: The Ohio State University, 1992), 144–47.

6.26 *Schottenstein Center under construction, 1998*

sor. He saw athletics as opportunities to shine a public spotlight on the university's academics; thus during the 1990s athletics grew even more in prominence and diversity. Brunches before football games and public service announcements during athletic contests, to cite two examples, became elaborate events at which President Gee and others talked about the accomplishments of OSU in teaching, research, and service.[52] At each pregame brunch, Gee typically had students with academic scholarships make presentations about why they selected Ohio State and how much they valued the university.[53] A history of Gee's first presidency notes that the president was so enthusiastic about athletics that he even telephoned potential student athletes, urging them to attend OSU.[54]

Probably the greatest partnership between an OSU president and an athletic director since the era of Lynn St. John began when President Gee hired Andy Geiger from the University of Maryland to become athletic director in 1994. Gee and Geiger shared enthusiasm for linking scholarship and intercollegiate sports. Geiger was a popular and articulate speaker who talked about the educational value of sports. In addition, he earned respect in the university for his broad interests, especially in jazz. Although he realized that football and basketball "paid the bills," Geiger worked to strengthen the entire athletic program rather than concentrate only on the revenue sports. His competitive goal for OSU's athletic department was the Director's Cup, an award of the National Association of Collegiate Directors of Athletics that "honors institutions maintaining a broad-based program, achieving

52. Malcolm S. Baroway, *History of The Ohio State University, Vol. XII: The Gee Years, 1990–1997* (Columbus: The Ohio State University, 2002), 151.

53. Baroway, 151.

54. Baroway, 150–51.

success in many sports, both men's and women's."[55] From 1994 to 2006, when Geiger retired, the number of varsity sports at OSU increased from 31 to 36.

Most spectacular was the increasing investment and value of athletic facilities during the Gee and Geiger years. At least one newspaper referred to the expanded and renovated athletic grounds as "Andyland."[56] One project was renovating the largest athletic building, Ohio Stadium. Now nearly seventy-five years old, the stadium was showing its age in many ways. Cracks appeared in its lowest deck. There were so many building code violations—insufficient toilets for women and the disabled to name only two—that even minimal improvements would cost $50 million.

In the spirit of the ambitious generation that had founded the stadium, the university undertook a monumental renovation. To add seats that would bring in more revenue and help to pay for improvements, OSU lowered the playing field to create another deck, and partially enclosed the south end. Completed in 2000, the renovation increased seating capacity to 101,568 at a cost of $194 million.[57] About eighty percent of the money for the renovation came from the sale of leases on suites and club seats, while donations and naming rights for portions of Ohio Stadium helped to pay for the rest. Because the renovation removed the Jesse Owens track from the Stadium, OSU built a separate Jesse Owens Stadium, which opened in 2001 and seats 10,000.

6.27 Bill Davis Stadium, 1997

55. Baroway, 188. See http://nacda.cstv.com/directorscup/nacda-directorscup.html.

56. Chris Perry, *History of The Ohio State University, Vol. XIII: The Kirwan Years, 1998–2002* (Columbus: The Ohio State University Press, 2006), 189.

57. See http://en.wikipedia.org/wiki/Ohio_stadium.

With Geiger's leadership and Gee's support, OSU built a new athletic arena for both basketball and ice hockey and a new stadium for baseball. By the 1990s, St. John Arena had grown too small for the crowds that wanted to see basketball and was inadequate for major concerts. Also, the ice rink next to St. John Arena was among the smallest in Big Ten competition. Major gifts from the Jerome Schottenstein family and Value City led to the Jerome Schottenstein Center for basketball and hockey, which opened in 1998 and had 19,200 seats. As in the renovation of Ohio Stadium, seat licenses, luxury boxes, and donations covered most of the cost of $118,000,000. The Bill Davis Stadium for baseball came about as a gift from Dorothy Wells Davis, an alumna and philanthropist, who had also supported OSU Hospitals and the College of Medicine. Named after her stepson, William H. Davis, who died in 1991, the new stadium opened in 1997 and can accommodate some 4,450 fans.

Before stepping down as director in 2005 and retiring in 2006, Andrew Geiger significantly improved support for other sports that produced relatively little revenue. As examples, the Steelwood Center that opened in 2002 was a new practice building for wrestling, fencing, and men's and women's gymnastics. The Bill and Mae McCorkle Aquatics Pavilion helped the swimming, diving, and synchronized swimming teams. Perhaps the most important building, the one that symbolized the unity of the athletic and academic missions of OSU, was the Younkin Success Center, which opened in 2000. Here, the university provided tutoring and academic support services for athletes as well as other students.

WOMEN'S ATHLETICS

For many years, women had fewer opportunities in athletics, especially in intercollegiate competition, than men. While men's athletics ranged from physical education and intramurals to varsity sports that had specialized equipment, buildings, and coaches, women's athletics consisted largely of intramurals and physical education. Play and participation, not competition, were dominant themes for women at OSU and nationally. As one educator stated, "The predominating role in women's sports should always be the joy and exhilaration and fun of playing, not the grim determination to win at any cost. Social features should be retained as a part of these sports, lest they become too business-like."[58] Widely held cultural concerns about the harmful impact of competitive athletics on women remained until the 1960s, when many conventional points of view fell to scrutiny and challenge.

In 1898, when OSU's Armory opened, it provided opportunities for women as well as men. In the gymnasium of the Armory, basketball was a popular sport for women. The *Lantern* of January 1899 reported, "The young ladies played an inter-

---

58. Quoted in Mary A. Daniels, "The Historical Transition of Women's Sports at The Ohio State University, 1888–1975 and Its Impact on the National Women's Intercollegiate Setting During that Period" (Ph.D. dissertation, The Ohio State University, 1977), 16; Frances A. Kellor, "Ethhical Value of Sports for Women," *American Physical Education Review,* XI (September 1906), 161–62.

6.28 *Women's physical education in the Armory, 1908*

6.29 *Girls championship basketball team in the Armory, 1919*

esting and exciting game of basketball last Friday morning at 9 o'clock. The teams were taken from the advanced gymnasium classes." In the next month, a women's team of OSU students participated in a city-wide basketball competition, but fell to a YWCA team.[59] A few years later, in 1904, an OSU women's basketball team played against Otterbein and then later against Miami University.[60] However, in 1907 OSU's Physical Education banned women's intercollegiate basketball to travel to other campuses, owing to " . . . the belief that such games are detrimental to women, both physically and morally. . . . " Financial considerations also led to that decision.[61]

Even as President Thompson championed men's athletics, he spoke in favor of physical education for women. An increasing number of women had enrolled at OSU and periodically, they complained to the president about the inadequacy of the Armory for women.[62] Also, OSU lacked a building to serve organizations of women students and to be a base to support them administratively and academically. The new College of Education would draw even more women students, who aspired to become teachers, to the campus. Therefore, a special building for women became a priority: "But now that the number of young women is increasing and will rapidly increase in the event that a Teachers College is organized, the need for such a building cannot be overlooked. Such a building should provide suitable quarters for physical culture and rooms at the disposal of the young women for study, rest and such social life as would be incident to college life on campus."[63]

6.30 Physical education volleyball class in Pomerene Hall, 1932

59. Daniels, 555–56; OSU *Lantern,* Jan. 18, 1899.
60. Daniels, 65
61. Daniels, 70; *OSU Lantern,* November 27.
62. Sabock, 36.
63. Sabock, 17.

6.31 *Women's Physical Education Field Day, 1929*

The years 1916 and 1917 were especially eventful for women at OSU. An annual report of the women's division in physical education noted that students had organized the women's athletic association and conducted tournaments in field hockey, basketball, volleyball, swimming, baseball, and tennis.[64] Set up in 1916, the Women's Athletic Association and the women's division of Physical Education continued to work together in creating opportunities for women athletes. In 1920, the student yearbook commented: "In spite of cramped conditions and inadequate equipment, athletic activities of the women of Ohio State University are increasing in enthusiasm and spirit and are improving in quality of work and competition each year." Women held an interclass basketball tournament and classes of women competed in baseball and tennis. Also in 1920, women faculty in Physical Education organized OSU's first track meet for women students at Ohio Field.[65] At last, in 1922, a separate building for women opened on the campus, Pomerene Hall. Besides offices and meeting rooms, the building had a gymnasium and later a swimming pool. In 1928, OSU added a women's field house, with golf cages, lockers, and showers and fields nearby.[66]

---

64. Sabock, 71–72.
65. Daniels, 84.
66. Sabock, 161.

In the 1920s, many people argued that modern women should be both intellectually and athletically active. At a banquet sponsored by OSU's Women's Athletic Association, Dean of Women Elizabeth Conrad said: "To be a modern and all-round girl, one must be interested in athletics and should participate in all athletic events possible, in order that she may develop the good-sportsmanship attitude toward everyone in all her work."[67] In 1923, OSU's social sororities petitioned for a basketball tournament and the physical education division and the Women's Athletic Association agreed.[68] The success of the inter-sorority basketball tournament led to expanding women's intramurals for all women's organizations.[69] In fact, OSU developed a nationally prominent program of women's intramural athletics. One unintended outcome of expanding intramurals was the dissolution of the Women's Athletic Association in 1930, because intramurals had become an institutional program that did not need leadership from students.

Sports clubs, for women, rather than varsity sports, also provided opportunities for women to learn sports and to engage in limited competition.[70] By 1937, women had clubs for hockey, fencing, tennis, archery, swimming, badminton, and table tennis, to name a few. The student activity fee supported them financially while the Women's Recreation Association helped to coordinate their events and orga-

6.32 Gladys Palmer

nizations.[71] However, a defining characteristic of women's sports at OSU up to the 1950s was that they did not award trophies or prizes for winners because the governing emphasis was on participation, not competition.[72]

During the 1940s, a broader view of women's athletics arose on the OSU campus. Professor Gladys Palmer served as chair of the Women's Division in Physical Education from 1933 to 1951. As a leader, she worked tirelessly to bring about more opportunities for women to compete in intercollegiate athletics. In 1941, she and OSU took a major step in that direction as OSU's Physical Education Division for

67. Daniels, 96; *OSU Lantern,* March 16, 1923.
68. Daniels, 111.
69. Daniels, 96–98.
70. Daniels, 122; *OSU lantern,* October 13, 1930.
71. OSU Football program (November 13, 1937), 62–63.
72. Daniels, 172.

6.33 Phyllis Bailey

Women sponsored the first Women's National Collegiate Golf Tournament on the OSU Golf Course in 1941. As one of her colleagues, Mary Yost, put it, "We at Ohio State were among the minority who believed that competitive sports, when properly organized and directed, had a contribution to make to the education of college women and therefore [it] was as much our responsibility as our required teacher education, and intramural programs. As a result, we decided to act upon our convictions."[73] In 1949, OSU had its first schedule of intercollegiate competitive seasons for women. Intercollegiate competitions took place in basketball, tennis, field hockey, and golf. Most of the opponents came from other colleges in Ohio, such as Bowling Green, Denison, and Miami.[74]

Some OSU faculty and students continued to speak in favor of intercollegiate athletics for women. In 1958, the women's division of the Department of Physical Education adopted a statement of intercollegiate policies that read, in part: "As a basic philosophy on competition the staff of physical education has accepted the following as beliefs: The majority of life experiences are of a competitive nature—with one's self, with another individual, and with groups. An individual should be educated for the world in which he lives, and the school has an important responsibility in educating individuals for competition. . . . "[75]

In the 1950s, Phyllis Bailey became a leader for women in athletics on the OSU campus and a force for women nationally. Bailey arrived at OSU as an associate professor of physical education in 1956. In 1959, following a tragic car accident that led to the death of Dorothy Wirthheim, Ms. Bailey assumed Wirthheim's responsibilities as coordinator for women's intramural and intercollegiate sports. From 1966 to 1970, she was OSU's first women's basketball coach.

Several factors played a part in changing women's athletics from mainly intramurals to include significant intercollegiate competition. The 1960s and 1970s at OSU and nationally were a time for challenging social conventions, especially gen-

---

73. Sabock, 202–203.
74. Daniels, 189–90.
75. Sabock, 244.

der roles. Students and nonstudents alike spoke for more opportunities for women and for equality of treatment, regardless of gender. Special curfews for women fell, as did barriers to women taking part in student organizations like the OSU Marching Band. So, too, did the conventional attitude that women should not join in the intercollegiate athletics that men did.

A major event was Title IX of the Education Amendments Act of 1972, which became effective in 1975. Essentially, it outlawed discrimination in higher education because of gender and had a great influence on intercollegiate athletics for women. Already in 1975 planning began to provide locker space for women athletes in St. John Arena and in French Field House, places where only men had had lockers. Also, in 1975, the women's intercollegiate athletic program, which had eleven sports, became part of the Athletic Department; the women's intramural program separated from women's intercollegiate athletics and joined the University Department of Recreation and Intramural Sports. Thus, women athletes began to have more access to training facilities and the medical support necessary for intercollegiate competition.In the same year, Phyllis Bailey became the first woman to become an Associate Athletic Director at OSU, a position of leadership she kept until her retirement in 1994. In 1976–1977, women athletes received the first grants in aid, which male athletes had been receiving for two decades. By 1981–82, women's sports became part of the Big Ten Conference.[76]

As important as the federal law was, it would be unfair and inaccurate to say that Title IX alone developed athletic opportunities for women. That had already been the direction during the 1950s and 1960s. As President Harold Enarson recalled, "I am inclined to think that the key contribution of Title IX has not been what it may have seemed to have forced in terms of additional dollars for support of women's athletics. I think it dramatized the problem, and once dramatized, we and other universities have moved into the breach."[77] Phyllis Bailey herself credited others, such as Gladys Palmer, and generations of women and supportive men: "I've said many times, girls had fathers, girls had desires, the rules had been changed and the nation was beginning to accept, slightly, girls participating as respectable activities. Title IX came along and was just the engine that pulled it down the track much more rapidly than would have ever come otherwise."[78]

CONCERNS ABOUT ATHLETICS AND ACADEMICS

As athletics at OSU rose to regional and national prominence, athletes and coaches became prominent public figures. Their actions—good and bad—draw attention

76. Gabel, 140–43.
77. Underwood, 119.
78. Interview of Phyllis Bailey Interview, OSU Knowledge Bank, See https://kb.osu.edu/dspace/handle/1811/29293 P. 39.

and sometimes cast a shadow over the reputation of the university itself. So prominent nationally was football coach Woody Hayes that President Gerald Ford once remarked that the university was "sometimes known as the Land of the Free and the Home of Woody Hayes."[79] From time to time, athletes and coaches have made errors in judgment that became national news, more so than honors achieved by faculty and talented students. Other issues, such as whether those in intercollegiate sports are athletes first and students second, equity in gender and race, the high cost of intercollegiate athletics and its funding, are continuing matters of attention, locally and nationally.

Athletics at OSU grew up in tandem with concerns about the place of athletics in the academic enterprise and about whether athletes were, in fact, students first and foremost. In 1890, OSU President William Henry Scott worried that enthusiasm for athletics threatened to distract from the academic mission. A few years later, President Thompson, himself a prominent supporter of intercollegiate athletics, also voiced concerns that competitive athletics threatened to have a corrupting influence: "An absorbing interest of the public, of alumni, and of students has created an atmosphere not always the purest."[80]

Other OSU presidents also worried about athletics. President Jennings once joked that his version of hell included a university with two athletics programs.[81] President Kirwan pointed out that the buildings for athletics were better than many academic ones, notably the Thompson Library, and commented. "There is an upside and a downside to it. The upside is that it builds tremendous school spirit, rallying friends and alumni. And it is a spectacle. But the community and statewide fixation on football pushes the real purpose of the university into the background."[82] Kirwan also fretted, as did presidents at other universities, about graduation rates for athletes and charged Geiger to work toward improving that, even as the NCAA developed new requirements. Finally, Karen

6.34 *James Fullington*

79. President Gerald Ford, OSU Commencement Address, August 1974.
80. Pollard, *Athletics,* 62–63.
81. Gabel, 136.
82. Perry, 189.

Holbrook, who followed Kirwan, sought to improve fan behavior during and after athletic events. Her administration worked to eliminate the drinking of alcohol near Ohio Stadium and joined with students to make fans of visiting teams feel welcome.

In the history of OSU, two events sparked intense scrutiny and fierce debate about athletics. In 1955, the Western Athletic Conference investigated OSU for improper conduct. Specifically, one accusation was that Woody Hayes had made personal loans to players, a violation of Conference rules that Hayes admitted and defended. Another was that some athletes who had part-time jobs received payments before working, which OSU also admitted. The result was that the Conference placed OSU football on probation. At the same time, OSU Faculty Council charged a special committee of faculty, headed by Professor James Fullington, to review intercollegiate athletics at OSU and make recommendations.

In 1957, after thirty months, the longest and most extensive review of OSU and athletics, the Fullington Committee issued its report.[83] Among its twenty-one recommendations were that "[a]t no time shall the unique advantage of football be considered license for expenditures out of balance with other sports" and that "as long as coaches hold rank on the faculty they should take part in academic life. . . ." Another declaration was that athletic buildings and grounds should be available for the use of all students, and that student athletes must have academic advisers and follow standard procedures in registering for courses. Athletes should have tutors from academic departments directly.[84] In addition, the report charged that "the control of athletics, at least on vital matters, has been largely removed from the hands of the Athletic Director, the Athletic board, and the Faculty Council to the administration of the University." It called for replacing the Athletic Board, to which the president appointed faculty members, with an Athletic Council whose faculty members received appointments from Faculty Council and who reported to Faculty Council.

Much of the report concerned itself with students as amateur athletes. It recommended that coaches and university officials lessen their demands on students in public appearances. Also, it called for abolishing the job program for athletes and if that was not possible, then the University Student Employment Services should run the program. The report also expressed disappointment that students alone, rather than coaches and employers, suffered penalties for improper loans and payments.

Most importantly, the Fullington Committee called for recognizing that the traditional ideal of the amateur athlete in intercollegiate competition was out of date: " . . . it is foolish to expect the program can continue at that level [2 million dollars a year] without letting the athlete in for some portion of the gain either as an inducement for him to come or as aid to him as a resident student. We have been facing the new day rather poorly and it is high time we faced it fully and with

83. Pollard, *Athletics*, 263.
84. *OSU Alumni Monthly,* December 1957, 5–6.

6.35 Coach Woody Hayes in 1963

intelligence."[85] The committee recommended that the Athletic Department and the Athletic Council develop a workable plan for financial aid to athletes and that athletic grants-in-aid be separate from the university scholarship program.

In February 1958, Faculty Council approved the recommendations reaffirming and bolstering faculty control of athletic policies. A new Athletic Council of six faculty, two students, and two alumni replaced what had been the Athletic Board. Faculty members would be named by the president but approved by Faculty Council. In addition, the Council approved "in principle" thirteen other committee recommendations. In the end, the Fullington Committee strengthened faculty control over intercollegiate athletics and accepted that intercollegiate athletics would continue to be prominent part of OSU.

Three years later, in 1961, the principle of faculty control over athletics faced a challenge. Ohio State and other members of the Western Conference disliked the contract with the Pacific Coast Conference that governed the Rose Bowl. Issues of concern included the number of tickets awarded to Western Conference teams

---

85. *OSU Alumni Monthly,* December 1957, 12.

and dividing revenues between the two conferences. In 1959, the unhappiness caused OSU and other Conference members to vote not to renew the contract for the Rose Bowl.

In 1961, OSU's football team became the undisputed champion of the Big Team and earned an invitation from the Rose Bowl committee. The team voted to play in the Bowl, as did the Athletic Council. However, by a majority of three votes, Faculty Council rejected the invitation because the contract for the Rose Bowl had not been renewed. In the heated debate in Faculty Council, some faculty and administrators complained about how much the Rose Bowl cost OSU and how participation disrupted the academic schedule. Others talked about how rejecting the invitation would highlight that academics, not athletic competition, were priorities for the university. One stated, "If we refuse, we will win prestige in academic circles—and may not be known as an appendage to a football stadium."[86]

The decision provoked an outcry and demonstrations on campus and elsewhere. Thousands of students marched, hung effigies of Jack Fullen, the head of the OSU Alumni Association, whom Coach Hayes had accused of influencing the decision, and called for Faculty Council to reconsider the vote. Many hoped the trustees would overrule the Faculty Council. However, the trustees chose not to interfere with the decision and in doing so, reaffirmed that athletics was part of, and subordinate to, the faculty and the academic mission of the university. A significant reason was the realization by the trustees and OSU administration that their interference could threaten OSU's membership in the Western Athletic Conference, for whom faculty governance of athletics was a cardinal principle.[87]

6.36 John B. Fullen in 1969

Today, faculty governance of intercollegiate athletics remains a continuing challenge. Nationally, critics have argued that athletic programs have become too large and too complex for faculty to review. Some faculty have been reluctant to take time away from research and teaching to serve on the committees supervising athletic programs. A continuing problem is that most universities reward faculty for scholarship first, teaching second, and service—such as participation on committees—hardly at all. As membership on committee changes, it is difficult to develop and retain the expertise needed to evaluate athletics.[88]

86. *OSU Alumni Monthly,* December 1961, 23.
87. Weisenberger, 213.
88. John R. Thelin, *Games People Play,* 187–88.

These difficulties aside, faculty remain well positioned to balance athletics with academics and to protect the student athlete. Professors have an appreciation first and foremost of the academic mission of their university and the importance of students in the learning enterprise. To develop the expertise needed to oversee modern intercollegiate athletic programs, faculty athletic representatives have an organization, the National Association of Faculty Athletic Representatives, which conducts workshops and seminars. Ultimately, the protection of tenure enables professors to make decisions that may be unpopular among presidents, trustees, students, alumni, and the general public. Over the years, the principle of faculty governance of athletics has served OSU well and has withstood crises.

In 2005, the NCAA developed an Academic Progress Rate (APR) that may have a significant impact upon maintaining the academic balance within inter-collegiate sports. Essentially, APR shifted academic scrutiny of student athletics from grade point average to progress towards graduation. No longer could students select courses and change majors simply to maintain a grade point average necessary for eligibility to compete in athletics. A mathematical formula sets academic performance standards for each sport. Teams that fail to show a sufficient number of students maintaining progress towards a degree or that have students leave colleges and universities when they have not maintained progress towards a degree fall below the standard for the sport. In doing so, athletic programs risk losing scholarships that are so important in recruiting athletes from high schools.

Although the rule is recent, some Faculty Athletic Representatives consider APR the most significant action by the NCAA in decades.[89] In fact, student athletes face greater academic pressures than nonathletes. For example, while many nonathletes change majors in the course of their studies, athletes do so at the risk of jeopardizing their eligibility and their teams' Academic Progress Rate. Concerns about APR should lead to more selective recruiting of students who are both athletically talented and academically prepared. Similarly, such concerns will prompt even more attention to providing academic support to student athletes. Time will tell.

Probably the most timeless advice for all in the governance of athletics came from President William Oxley Thompson. In 1905, he stated: "It is a manifest waste of energy . . . to spend time in denouncing athletics; what is needed is efficient leadership by men to whom principle is dearer than anything else. If university faculties are set for the education of youth, it is little more than a corollary to add that they can not ignore the ethical conditions existing in college sports. . . . We shall never reform athletics simply by rules; we shall reform it only when we have inspired young men to cling to high ideals and to be governed by sound ethics. . . . "[90] A reader today should add "women" to Thompson's words and then say "Amen."

---

89. Based on comments to author by Dr. John Bruno, OSU Faculty Athletic Representative, May 21, 2008.
90. Pollard, 63.

CHAPTER SEVEN

TRADITIONS

Every tradition grows ever more venerable.
The more remote is its origin, the more
confused that origin is. The reverence due
to it increases from generation to genera-
tion. The tradition finally becomes holy and
inspires awe.

—Friedrich Wilhelm Nietzsche

EOPLE have disagreed about the value of campus traditions. David Starr Jordan, as president of Stanford University, called them "the greatest instruments of culture in college." However, Woodrow Wilson, as president of Princeton University, is said to have remarked, "these sideshows have ruined the business of the big tent."[1] In 1929, OSU's *Lantern* expressed regret that the university was losing one of its oldest traditions, the cane rush: "We are sorry indeed to see another of Ohio State's old and memorable traditions go into oblivion, as have many others which were strictly observed."[2] A few days later, the *Lantern* published a letter from a student who challenged the value of traditions: "We represent an age that is done with the sentimental customs of the past. Why should we continue on the Ohio State campus the more or less silly ideas of our predecessors?"[3] Nevertheless, traditions are part of campus life and anyone who has seen commencement and the robes and hoods of many colors will agree that they add significantly to the color and pageantry of campus life.

A comprehensive encyclopedia of OSU's traditions, past and present, may not be possible. Too many traditions have little or no documentation; others appear for a few years but do not take hold. A case in point is the relatively recent (ca. 1990) tradition of jumping into Mirror Lake one evening before the football game against the University of Michigan in order to "awaken the spirit of Woody Hayes." In late November, this bone-chilling spectacle draws thousands of students as well as medical personnel but may disappear because of the physical discomfort to participants.[4] Thus, what follows is a selective list of major traditions, both continuing and obsolete.

7.1 Brutus Buckeye in 1965. Note how big the head was and how awkward it was to move

TRADITIONS OF THE PRESENT

Brutus Buckeye

Enthusiasm for athletics inspired Ray Bouhis, an art major, to create a mascot for athletic teams in 1965. Ray proposed the idea to Ohio Staters and with their help put together a model built with pieces of Styrofoam, aluminum, and glue. Although fans liked it, the model was so heavy and so large that it was difficult to wear and blocked the views of too many fans. A

---

1. Quoted in *OSU Alumni Monthly*, April 1935.
2. OSU *Lantern*, October 13, 1929.
3. OSU *Lantern*, October 23, 1929.
4. OSU *Lantern*, November 17, 2005.

7.2 *A leaner and more mobile Brutus Buckeye in 2001*

fiberglass model appeared the following year. "Brutus" as a first name resulted from a campus-wide contest to name the mascot, which Kerry Read, a student from West Virginia, won. As the photographs show, Brutus has changed in appearance over the years.[5]

Buckeye (All-American) Grove

President Harold Enarson once remarked that football was Columbus's peculiar religion. Although Enarson may have been speaking "tongue in cheek," football has

---

5. *OSU Alumni Monthly,* December 1965, 22.

7.3 Members of the first football team of 1890 plant Buckeye Grove near Ohio Stadium in 1931

7.4 Another buckeye tree is planted in Buckeye Grove in 1949.

been a source of many traditions, among which is Buckeye Grove. Yearly, a Buckeye tree is planted in the grove for each OSU football player who has attracted national acclaim by becoming an All-American.

The history of Buckeye Grove is uncertain. Originally, the grove honored the first football team of 1890, with its first eleven trees gathered in a huddle. However, it is unlikely the grove began in 1890 because it has always been near Ohio Stadium which opened in 1922, far from where games took place in 1890. More likely is that Scarlet Key, an organization of athletic team managers, began the grove, possibly in 1929. The latter date seems reasonable for two reasons. The earliest photographs of Buckeye Grove in the OSU Archives begin in 1931. Second, a volume of OSU history published in 1926 discusses many traditions but not Buckeye Grove.

Change is part of many traditions, including Buckeye Grove. The student organization Ohio Staters took responsibility for it in 1963. Since then, OSU has renovated the grove and changed its location. In 1997, the grove was moved from a space between the southeast corner of the Stadium and the McCracken Power Plant to stretch north to south on the east hillside near Morrill Tower, where new trees have been planted.[6]

"Carmen Ohio"

OSU's traditions can be controversial as well as colorful. Such is the case with OSU's school song, "Carmen Ohio." By 1902, students and alumni sang numerous songs, the most popular of which was "Wahoo" sung to the tune of "Roll Jordan Roll."[7] Others were "We hail from OSU," "The Scarlet and Gray Forever," "Vive La O.S.U." Nothing became memorable and popular until "Carmen Ohio."[8]

Fred Cornell, a student, not only wrote the song but later stoked a controversy about its origins. According to the most dramatic version, written in 1961, Cornell was on the football team that on October 25, 1902 lost to the University of Michigan by the humiliating score of 86–0: "When we battered players returned for the second 35 minute half at Ann Arbor, October 1902, Michigan students stood in old Ferry

7.5 Fred Cornell

Field singing 'Maize and Blue.' Unhappily I wished we had a similar song for comfort in losing and, some better day, calm praise in winning."[9] Cornell began thinking

---

6. Based on vertical file information at the OSU Archives.
7. Fred Cornell, "The Writing of 'Carmen Ohio,'" *OSU Alumni Monthly*, Feb. 1915, 26.
8. See "Songs of OSU" 1900 (OSU Archives).
9. Fred Cornell to Bennie Kline, February 28, 1961, OSU Archives, vertical file.

7.6 "Carmen Ohio"

of words for the song while on the sideline and continued to find more words on the train from Ann Arbor to Columbus. He took the music from a popular hymn, "Spanish Chant." According to Cornell, students first sang "Carmen Ohio" at convocation in 1903, but it did not take hold immediately. During the football season of 1906, the song had a revival and has remained popular since then.

However, Cornell wrote this account late in his life and many years after the event itself. The historical facts, as supported by evidence, are different and not so dramatic. Writing in 1915 to help the author of an OSU history, Cornell confessed that he could not remember where he was or on what days he composed the text, but: "Carmen Ohio was first sung in public by the University Glee Club of 1903–1904. The verses were written late in 1903 [not 1902 at the Michigan game] while I was a sophomore. Early in 1904 we sang it at a Chapel Convocation. . . ."[10] In 1906 a football rally drew more attention to the song, which the *Lantern* had printed for the occasion.

Evidence supports this second account. The *Lantern* of December 9, 1903 announced that the Glee Club would perform in the chapel of University Hall on December 11 and commented: "Several new Ohio State songs have recently been written and will be sung for the first time at the concert."[11] At the time, the *Lantern* appeared weekly and the issue of December 16 reported the concert had been a great success: "Two compositions written for this concert found place on the program, 'A Hymn to Ohio,' used as the opening number, and 'Carmen Ohio,' with words and music by F. A. Cornell, '06, the closing song." So impressed was the reporter by Cornell's work that he recommended that, "[t]his last song might well be made a part of every glee club program, as it has all the elements of a good college chorus, easily sung and easily remembered words, and a simple, catching air. We have too few songs to call our own."[12] Clearly, the request of the Glee Club had inspired the song that became OSU's inspirational tradition.

Cornell had more to say about the origins and meaning of "Carmen Ohio." As a member of the choir of Trinity Episcopal Church, Cornell had often sung "Spanish Hymn" which he remembered as so easy to sing that "Even the Glee Club could try so easy a tune."[13] His thought behind the words was "that the University goes on, unshaken by incidental considerations." Cornell believed that OSU endured because it was more important than any of its parts: "And so, if you, while singing the song, feel that the University is finer, fuller, more fundamental than any of its functions, I am happy to have recorded an enduring ideal in 'Carmen Ohio.'"[14]

10. Thomas C. Mendenhall, *History of The Ohio State University, Vol. II: Continuation of the Narrative From 1910 to 1925* (Columbus, Ohio: The Ohio State University Press, 1926), 251.

11. *OSU Lantern*, December 9, 1903.

12. *OSU Lantern*, December 16, 1903.

13. Cornell, "The Writing of 'Carmen Ohio,'" 26.

14. Mendenhall, 252–53.

7.7 *The chimes ready to be installed in Orton Hall in 1915*

7.8 *The chimes in 1975*

Chimes

So important has the tradition of ringing the bells in Orton Hall become to the timing of university life that it is hard to imagine OSU without those sounds. Credit for the chimes belongs to the graduating class of 1906, who thought a gift of bells to OSU would be a memorable and remarkable donation. However, collecting enough money proved too challenging for one set of seniors. Another seven classes (1907, 1908, 1909, 1910, 1911, 1913, and 1914) also contributed. Finally, on February 20, 1915, as part of the revival of the University Day tradition, the bells rang for the first time and played "Oxford Changes." In reporting the ringing of the chimes, a student wrote: "It is expected that the advent of the chimes will create a new interest in college music at the Ohio State University, and will bring out original compositions of the collection of 'Alma Mater' songs which students and Alumni have so long desired."[15]

The tradition of the chimes has changed over the years. The classes of 1919 and 1920 added electric strikers. In 1923, the university began playing chimes daily for ten minutes at 11:50 and 4:30.[16] Renovations in 1986 and 1987 provided a turning of the bells to change the locations of the striking and a Westminster chime to mark the hour and quarter hours.[17] Finally, in 2003 the university added two more bells to the original twelve to allow a greater range of music.

Commencement

This is the oldest of OSU's traditions and has continued from 1878. So important has commencement been that the university even developed its identifying colors because of this tradition. In 1878, the first graduating class of students wanted ribbons with which to wrap their diplomas. A committee of four students compared ribbons of different colors and decided they liked orange and black. When they learned that Princeton University used these colors, the committee gathered again at the Lazarus department store and decided on scarlet and gray ribbons for the diplomas.[18]

In the more than one hundred and twenty-five years of the tradition, there have been more than three hundred and sixty commencements at OSU because the quarter system that began in 1923 resulted in four commencements each year. Although commencements have always involved awarding degrees, the tradition has undergone many changes, especially of place. Between 1878 and 1908, commencements took place in the University Hall chapel, later called an auditorium. After that, OSU experimented with new locations: a tent on the Oval (1909 and 1918), a tent in Mir-

---

15. *OSU Alumni Magazine,* March 1915, 39.
16. *OSU Alumni Magazine,* July 1950, 22.
17. *OSU Alumni Magazine,* October 1990, 36.
18. Mendenhall, 247; a set of original ribbons is at The Ohio State University Archives.

7.9 *Commencement parade on the Oval in 1907. Degrees were awarded in University Chapel, which was in University Hall.*

7.10 *Commencement beneath a tent on the Oval in 1918*

7.11 Commencement at the State Fair Coliseum in 1923

7.12 *Commencement at Ohio Stadium, June 1978*

ror Lake Hollow (1910), and the Armory (1911–1921). As graduating classes of OSU grew in number, no single building on campus could hold all the graduates and their families. So, from 1922 to 1927 commencement moved off campus to the Coliseum of the Ohio State Fair. When Ohio Stadium became available, the first commencement took place there in 1928. Other locations have been the men's gymnasium, St. John Arena, and the Schottenstein Center. Regardless of location, weather has been remarkably constant for the spring commencements. Only in 1941 and 1997 did rain curtail the graduation exercises.

Rituals for commencements have also changed. The first commencement included the reading of senior theses, a class oration by graduate Ferdinand Howald ("The Nineteenth Century"), and an address by President Orton. Eventually, the festivities became more complex. In 1882, commencement took four days. It began with a baccalaureate sermon and address by President Walter Q. Scott on Sunday, followed by a meeting of the faculty with examination results. Other events included lectures, a parade, commencement exercises, and a closing reception at the home of the president. The commencement of 1899, too, was a multi-day festivity that featured sunrise ivy planting and an accompanying address.

The Great Depression cast a pall over commencement festivities, which became one-day events in 1932. Change, however, continued. "Pomp and Circumstance" which was played for the first time in 1928 but as a recessional, began to be played as a processional in 1931. In 1949, WOSU televised the commencement.[19]

Distinguished speakers have always been part of the commencement ritual but the types of speakers have become more diverse in the professions they represented. In the first fifteen years of the university, all the speakers were presidents of universities, professors, or ministers. Academic figures still dominate the growing list of OSU's commencement speakers. In 1895, Governor William McKinley became the first political leader to give a commencement address at OSU, followed by other governors of Ohio in later years. United States Senator John Bricker appeared in 1956 as did John Glenn in 1984. Vice President Spiro Agnew took President Richard Nixon's place as commencement speaker in 1969; other vice presidents who spoke were Walter Mondale in 1979 and George H. W. Bush in 1983. The first U.S. president to speak at an OSU commencement was Gerald Ford in August of 1974, followed by George W. Bush in 2002.

Among the unusual speakers were Branch Rickey of the Brooklyn Dodgers in 1950, television journalist Walter Cronkite in 1968, astronaut Neil Armstrong in 1971, cartoonist and alumnus Milton Caniff in 1974, and author Alex Haley in 1976. Memorable and now much requested from the Archives was the commencement address by football coach Woody Hayes in 1986.

Honorary degrees have been a feature of many commencements but not all. OSU awarded honorary doctorates at its first commencement in 1878 to Thomas C. Mendenhall and to John B. Peaslee. However, honorary degrees were not a regular feature of the commencement tradition. Three years transpired before OSU awarded more honorary degrees, this time to Edward Orton and Joseph Millikin. Faculty criticized awarding honorary degrees, and OSU did not award any between 1897 and 1928. In 1929, OSU resumed the practice. Recipients have included the poet Robert Frost, airplane inventor Orville Wright, Olympic medalist Jesse Owens, and Dorothy Canfield Fisher, novelist and daughter of former OSU President James Canfield.

Commencement Grove, also known as "The Five Brothers"

To celebrate Arbor Day in 1890, the class of 1891 planted an English elm in the center of the Oval. Next year, the graduating class added six more trees, but lightning destroyed two of them. The remaining five trees or "The Five Brothers" stood as a campus landmark for many years.

Dutch elm disease destroyed many of the elm trees on campus. Eventually, it claimed the Five Brothers, with the last being cut down in 1972. Fifteen years later,

---

19. See vertical file "Commencement" at OSU Archives.

7.13 *The Five Brothers, elm trees, as they appeared on the Oval in 1951*

as OSU celebrated its 300th commencement, the university restored the landmark by replanting Commencement Grove with five Eastern Red Oaks.[20]

Convocation

In the last fifty years or so, convocation has been the tradition that begins the academic year. Freshman and returning students gather to hear the president make inspirational remarks to start the academic year. Historically, however, convocation began much differently. It developed from the compulsory and daily chapel exercises that some students and faculty had opposed as inappropriate for a publicly funded university.

In 1899, during the first year of his presidency, William Oxley Thompson inaugurated the first convocation as a substitute for daily chapel exercises. Thompson

20. Based on *Commencement Grove Dedication Ceremony* brochure, 1987 (OSU Archives).

7.14 *The Chapel as it appeared in 1913 in University Hall, the site of the convocation tradition that evolved from compulsory chapel services*

presided over a weekly convocation ceremony at 11:00 each Wednesday morning.[21] Typically the exercises included a reading of the Scriptures, prayer, and remarks by Thompson or by a distinguished visitor. Faculty and students attended voluntarily. In 1925, when Thompson retired, weekly convocation ended temporarily. When Freshman Week began in 1927, convocation soon became part of the annual festivities. After that, convocation occurred only once each year.[22]

Homecoming

At first, Homecoming—alumni returning to campus—was part of commencement week. Commencement programs had time set aside for alumni gatherings. In fact, Alumni Day began as early as the 1880s. Members of the Alumni Association used the event to hear reports, to elect officers, and to listen to university leaders.[23]

Homecoming as it is known now began as an idea of professor and former OSU student George Rightmire in 1912. He organized an "Ohio State Day" for alumni as an event before a home football game. Previously, the Franklin County Alumni had been holding reunions in association with football games as early as 1901, but participants did not refer to them as "Homecoming." Nor did these reunions have the

21. James E. Pollard, *William Oxley Thompson: "Evangel of Education"* (Columbus: The Ohio State University, 1955), 66; Mendenhall, 248.

22. Mendenhall, 248.

23. Pollard, "Traditions at Ohio State," *Campus Review* (November 1965), 8

7.15 Homecoming with "Queen Maudine," 1926

rituals later associated with the modern tradition. In 1912, students first decorated houses and dormitories for the occasion; beginning in 1914, official themes helped to organize homecoming events and festivities. The Homecoming of 1918 added a pep rally and bonfire to the tradition. A Homecoming Dance was added in 1920. Parades with floats were organized, in some years but not others, as early as 1920 and have been a continuing tradition since 1965. Until 1953, Homecoming was a game late in the football season but repeatedly poor weather moved the tradition to earlier in the season.[24]

Another change in the tradition was creation of a Homecoming court that included first a queen and then a king. In 1922, Eloise Fromme became the "Stadium Girl" and "Stadium Queen" and had the honor of raising the flag to dedicate Ohio Stadium on October 21, 1922. The first to bear the title "Homecoming Queen" was Helen McDermott in 1923, an honor announced at the Homecoming Dance. In 1960, Marlene Owens, a daughter of Jesse and Ruth Owens, became OSU's first African American Homecoming Queen. The first Homecoming King was Alex Lambrinides in 1976.

Probably the most memorable of the many Homecoming celebrations occurred in 1926. Students had vigorously campaigned in the election for queen. Maudine

---

24. Homecoming history, compiled by Bertha Ihnat, OSU Archives, vertical file "Homecoming."

Ormsby was the candidate of students in the College of Agriculture, who promoted her candidacy against rivals from the sororities. When contest officials discovered there was no "Maudine Ormsby" in the student directory and that she was a Holstein cow owned by the College of Agriculture, judges dropped her from the competition. However, there were so many irregularities in the election—more votes counted than OSU had students—that the judges decided to award the contest to the cow anyway. The resulting publicity spread nationally. To those who complained about the election and the media, one student declared: "The publicity is telling the world at large that the students at Ohio State University are merely fun loving, human, boys and girls hoping to have a jolly good time at one of the season's biggest events: Homecoming. No more than that. And a good time will be had if someone doesn't crab [*sic*] the party."[25]

Marching Band

The band has been the source of several traditions unique to The Ohio State University. Like OSU itself, the band grew from modest, even humble, beginnings to

7.16 The band in 1886

25. "In Defense of Maudine," The Homecoming Heifer, Archives vertical file "Homecoming."

7.17 The OSU Marching Band in 1979

become "The Best Damned Band in the Land." As early as 1878 a drum corps—three fifes, eight snare drums, and a bass drum—accompanied students who marched for military training. Edward Orton, Jr., student and son of the president, recruited more players, increased the size of the band to eighteen members, and increased the number of performances besides those for military drill. The Marching Band had its first public performance at a reception in the home of President Edward Orton, following the commencement of 1879. The military style uniforms that members continue to wear link the Marching Band with its origins as a military band.

Having played now for more than one hundred years, the band has been a tradition that has also included change. The distinctive ramp entrance into Ohio Stadium began in 1928. In 1934, conductor Eugene Weigel (for whom Weigel Hall is named) changed the band, which had included woodwinds, into an all brass and percussion band. Beginning in 1965, the playing of "Hang on Sloopy" has become a crowd-pleasing favorite. The Alumni Marching Band appeared in 1966. In 1973, five women joined what had been an all-male group; in 1981, Shelley Graf became the first female drum major. The first drum major or leader was Joseph Bradford in 1878; Bradford later became a professor and the first University Architect at OSU.[26]

Military Traditions

From the beginning, military training has been part of university life. The Cannon Act, which established OSU, required a department of military science. For most of the university's history (until 1969), able-bodied males undertook some military training. By the time the requirement for males ended, the ROTC program was so large that OSU commissioned more officers than any institution except West Point.[27] Up to this point, military drills, contests, and reviews of the cadets by representatives of the professional military or by the president of OSU had been a large part of university life. In the 1960s and early 1970s, the controversial conflict in Vietnam forced administrators to move military reviews and exercises from the Oval to a fenced area near Converse Hall, which served as the ROTC building. The end of the requirement for military training significantly lessened the prominence of military traditions on the OSU campus, although the university has continued to

7.18 Taps ceremony, 1937, when campus life stopped to commemorate the veterans of World War I

26. All of this information is from *Script Ohio: 110 Years of The Ohio State University Marching Band, 1878–1988–89* (Columbus: The Ohio State University Marching Band, 1989).

27. Francis P. Weisenberger, *History of The Ohio State University, Vol. IX: The Fawcett Years, 1956–1972* (Columbus: The Ohio State University, 1975), 190.

7.19 Review of ROTC students on the Oval, 1955

be a leader in the national ROTC program as evidenced by the numbers of commissioned officers for the air force, army, navy, and marines that it graduates.

One of the most emotional and impressive of military traditions was the taps ceremony. Begun during World War I, in November of 1918, taps was played from the chimes in Orton Hall to honor those who had lost their lives in the conflict. The tradition took a new form after the war when a bugle at the center of the Oval sounded each Wednesday morning. All pedestrians on campus stopped for moments of reflection. The tradition continued as a weekly event until it became monthly in 1963. Eventually, the tradition of taps became part of the "Rock Ceremony," near a boulder facing Bricker Hall. This boulder or rock bears a plaque dedicated to those from Ohio State who gave their lives in World War I. This has become an annual event, with wreath-laying and speeches, as part of the Veterans Day celebrations in November.

Orientation/Welcome Week

For many years, the university did not have a campus-wide program to orient new students. Welcome Week began in 1927, some fifty years after the opening of campus. In the early days, student organizations greeted new students and introduced them to student life—and to their status as newcomers. The class of 1910 claimed to have originated a rule requiring all freshmen to wear distinctive, if not always flattering, caps known as "beanies." Another rule forbade freshmen to walk on the

7.20 Freshman Week, 1927

7.21 Picnic during Freshman Week in 1973. To the left and seated is President Harold Enarson.

Long Walk in the center of the Oval. Other dictates, as recorded in 1919, included a requirement to attend varsity football games but keep to the freshmen bleachers, and not sit on the steps or ledges of University Hall. New students had to recite or sing three OSU songs before the second football game.

By 1925, with the increasing number of new students every year, OSU's administrators and faculty concluded that the university should develop a formal program of orientation. President George Rightmire and a faculty committee called for a set of activities that would make students feel welcome and better prepare them for the adjustments and expectations of university life. As Rightmire put it: "The Freshman needs a friend; he ought to find a cordial welcome at the school from the teachers and older students, and he should form an early acquaintance with the buildings and places and environment of the University . . . the new student should get the 'at home' feeling at once."[28]

Following the recommendations of a faculty committee, OSU inaugurated the first Freshman Week in 1927, extending from September 21 through September 26. Activities included a get acquainted night, physical examinations, lectures on health and university history and traditions, placement and intelligence tests, tours, rallies, and library lectures. As the week ended, students gathered on the Oval, faced the Library, and sang "Carmen Ohio."[29] President Rightmire forbade older students from hazing freshmen generally and specifically from dunking them into Mirror Lake.[30]

Freshman Week and Orientation have changed only slightly. In 1958, the testing took place in the summer and students oriented themselves to campus two days before classes. In 1968, parents became part of the orientation programs. Currently, orientation takes place during most of the summer quarter.

President's Scholarship Dinner

Established in 1948, this event honors scholastic achievements by undergraduate students. For some time, it bore the name "Honors Day Convocation."[31]

7.22 The President's Scholarship dinner in 1962

28. *OSU Alumni Magazine,* June 1927.
29. *OSU Alumni Magazine,* November 1927, 57.
30. James E. Pollard, "Traditions at Ohio State," 11.
31. Pollard, "Traditions," 21.

7.23 Practicing the new formation in 1936

Script Ohio

Excluding the ramp entrance, the most memorable of OSU traditions associated with the Marching Band is its "Script Ohio" formation, which presents "OHIO" in script rather than block lettering. Band director Eugene Weigel had wanted to make the marching formations more and impressive and more complex. To that end, he required members of the band to memorize the music so that they could concentrate on the maneuvers. In all likelihood, evidence suggests that the "Script Ohio" first appeared at the Pittsburgh game on October 10, 1936. Although OSU lost the game, the OSU *Alumni Magazine* reported that a crowd of 71,714 watched the contest and that "Ohio's matchless band reached a new high with a sensational 'Ohio' formation in script." A trumpet player dotted the "i"; four games later a tuba player did so with more dramatic—and lasting—effect. The first double "Script Ohio" with the Marching Band appeared in 1966.

Apparently, no good tradition is without controversy. Some people claim that Weigel may have been inspired by seeing "Ohio" written in script on the marquee of the Ohio Theater in downtown Columbus.[32] However, another inspiration could have been that in October 15, 1932 the University of Michigan marching band performed an Ohio formation in script diagonally across the field at Ohio Stadium.[33] If Weigel sought to improve on what Michigan had done or whatever its origins,

---

32. *Script Ohio.* 43.
33. *Script Ohio,* 190.

7.24 The formation in 1998

7.25 *Victory Bell in 1954*

"Script Ohio" is a colorful and complex formation that has become one of OSU's most cherished and inspirational traditions.

Victory Bell

Another tradition associated with football is the ringing of the Victory Bell in Ohio Stadium for about fifteen minutes after each victory. The graduating classes of 1943, 1944, and 1955 gave the bell as their senior gift to OSU. It first sounded after a victory over the University of Southern California on October 2, 1954. The bell itself weighs 2,420 pounds. Since its first sounding in 1954, members of Alpha Phi Omega have had the honor of ringing the bell.[34]

---

34. Based on vertical file information at OSU Archives.

FIVE DEAD TRADITIONS

Cane Rush

Imagine two mobs of students who rush at each other. One mob tackles, rips clothing, and does anything necessary to seize and then search the bodies of the other to find a walking cane. Meanwhile, the other mob blocks, knocks down, and tries to move the hidden cane forward and across a goal line. The winning mob is the one that has come closest to moving the cane toward the opponent's goal. This was the cane rush at OSU.

The first cane rush took place as early as 1880 or 1881 and began as a rivalry between student classes. This was a time when students admitted in the same year elected officers for their class, chose distinctive colors, and selected a historian to chronicle the deeds of the class. One recollection of the first cane rush, which is otherwise undocumented, is that seniors decided as a class to carry walking canes during the spring of their academic year. On the first day, the seniors carried their canes during compulsory attendance at chapel exercises. At close of services, the juniors tried to extract the canes from the swaggering seniors and break them. The struggle continued fiercely until President Edward Orton (1873–1881) appeared on the scene and said sternly, "Gentlemen cease this disturbance and pass to your places."

Until the arrival of President Thompson in 1899, the cane rush had no schedule and almost no rules. The one in 1889 was said to have lasted one and a half hours. In the fray itself, the combatants sometimes crossed the ill-defined boundary separating youthful enthusiasm from brutality. In 1890, the *Lantern* described the cane rush: "Fierce as the struggle had been, in spite of sprained ankles, torn clothes, mashed noses, broken heads, scratches and bruises, not the slightest ill-feeling was manifested by anybody." However, the one in 1894 was so violent that the *Lantern* complained: "If our young men are to do that for which in the ordinary walks of life they would have to answer to the law of the land, it is high time that the iron hand of discipline be imposed. University history should not be blotted by the record of many such affairs as occurred last Thursday."

In 1899, William Oxley Thompson became president of The Ohio State University and a new era for the cane rush began. During his first months as president, Thompson took charge of the cane rush. Rather than wait for the rush to begin spontaneously as the result of some provocation, Thompson orchestrated the event himself. He ordered the sophomores to prepare for a rush and challenged the freshmen to participate. Thompson told the participants that he had no objection to the annual rushes if they were conducted in an orderly manner. In 1900, representatives of the sophomore class approached Dr. Thompson and announced that they were challenging the freshman class to a rush. President Thompson encouraged the freshmen to take up the challenge but ended the event himself by tossing his hat in

7.26–7.27 Cane rush at Ohio Field, 1919. In these photographs from 1919, freshmen have tackled a sopho-more and are searching him for a cane. Note that it was common for one class to paint their faces to identify team members.

the air after twelve minutes, as a signal to end the contest. The student newspaper waxed enthusiastic about the new president and announced, "A new epoch has certainly been reached in college life and class spirit which we firmly believe is largely due to the wise policy of our beloved president."

In the years that followed, President Thompson worked with student organizations and transformed the cane rush into an official and regulated tradition. Under his supervision, the event had official rules, a time, and a place. Typically, the cane rush began in September or early October, at the beginning of the academic year. A common site was the athletic field, away from the Oval and classrooms. In October 1903, for example, the president read to the freshmen and sophomores the rules for the rush, chose the goals across which the cane had to be carried by the sophomores, and set a time limit of twenty minutes. So closely identified with the cane rush was Thompson that in 1904 the event stalled for some minutes until the students could find the president.

With the sponsorship of Thompson and assisting student organizations, the cane rush reached a peak of popularity in participation, during and after the event. In one year there were so many spectators that the student organizations responsible for organizing the rush charged a fee for admission. The rush of 1908 drew about 10,000 spectators. In a field roped by the student council to keep spectators from entering, some 350 freshmen with faces painted fought 250 sophomores, seized the sophomore cane, and carried it across the goal line. Typically, the victorious class celebrated with bonfires in the evening and paraded in their "nightshirts."

At the height of its popularity in the early 1920s, the cane rush already contained elements that would lead to its decline. The number of freshmen so far exceeded the sophomores that the contests became very one-sided. Another problem was that the retirement of President Thompson in 1925 had removed one of its leading advocates and supporters. One could also argue that the cane rush, which grew from rivalry between freshman and sophomore classes, declined as year of class mattered less as a central factor in student organizational life, far less than fraternities, sororities, and other social and professional clubs.

Whatever the reasons, the cane rush continued to fall in popularity. In 1932, no cane rush took place at Ohio State, as the *Lantern* reported, "for the simple reason that no one cared to be bothered." Efforts to revive the tradition throughout the 1930s failed to raise enough enthusiasm. By 1940 the cane rush was only a memory. It reappeared briefly in May of 1948 as part of "traditions week," a nostalgic celebration of all traditions as a festival of spring.

Christmas ("White Christmas") Program

Although OSU has always been nondenominational, the university celebrated Christmas officially for years. As early as the 1880s, a walnut tree standing near University Hall became the Christmas tree for OSU. By 1916, a tree near the Long

7.28 OSU official Christmas tree on the Oval in 1918

Walk on the Oval served that purpose. Beginning in 1928 and until World War II, the university chorus and orchestra held an annual White Christmas program that centered on a production of Handel's *Messiah*. In the 1941 program came the announcement that Pearl Harbor had been attacked.[35] During the 1950s and as late as 1968, there was an official university tree in Ohio Union.

Class Day

In the early years of OSU, much of student life revolved around one's class—freshman, sophomore, junior and senior. Each elected officers and typically had their own colors and a historian to record the accomplishments. Class Day originated in that era, probably beginning in 1881 and became closely linked to commencement.

---

35. Pollard, "Traditions," 10.

7.29 *Faculty and senior class having a baseball game as part of Class Day in 1892*

In 1885, Field Day, which had been a separate tradition, merged with Class Day and added foot races and other contests to the day of celebration.[36] The tradition continued to World War II, when graduating classes became too large (although there was a set of class day activities in 1973). Typically, Class Day events included ivy planting, a breakfast, athletic exercises, a parents luncheon, and a baseball game against the faculty.

Traditions Week/May Week

One of the most colorful traditions was May Week, a tradition that the Student Alumni Council has tried to revive since 2003. Beginning in 1909, the Women's Council held a simple May-pole dance to celebrate the spring. The next year, a May Fete replaced the May-pole dance. Typically, this event took the shape of a pageant depicting a theme of some kind and required much planning and coordination. The theme for 1919 was "Light of the Ages," which presented scenes ranging from the ancient Hebrews, Greeks, and Romans to the modern era, including the Great War (World War I). By 1925, a Traditions Day first and then a Traditions Festival replaced May Week. The Festival of 1932 featured initiations into the honorary societies, a tug-of-war, an egg fight between freshmen and sophomores, and even a circus. Participants enjoyed rides on a Ferris wheel and a merry-go-round, and

---

36. Pollard, "Traditions," 23.

attended a big top show and sideshows.[37] In 1939, Traditions Festival became May Week, which continued to the early 1970s. Activities in this fun-filled week included baseball games on the Oval, parades, dances, tugs-of-war, greased pig contests, a Merrie Olde England theme, water-fights, a Scarlet and Gray Day, and a Flower Day. However named, these spring events blended youthful enthusiasm with the excitement of the end of the academic year.

7.30 May Fete in 1916

University Day

As a tradition, University Day experienced a cycle of birth, decline, renewal, and death. In February 1883, students organized an event to be held on February 22 to celebrate President Washington's birthday and be an opportunity for students to give speeches, sing, and play music. Soon after that, a military parade became part of the festivities and featured a salute from cannon near University Hall.[38] In 1898, the day included a lunch with legislators as guests of honor. This tradition continued for several years, but fell into decline. The ringing of the chimes for the

---

37. *OSU Alumni Magazine*, June 1932, 326.
38. *OSU Alumni Magazine*, March 1933, 176.

7.31 *University Day event in 1924, celebrating the construction of an addition to the Ohio Historical and Archaeological Society building, later Sullivant Hall*

first time served to revive the tradition that continued until World War II. In its final years, University Day was the occasion for a speech or a radio address by the university president.

SOME THOUGHTS ABOUT TRADITIONS

OSU has lost some traditions but others have continued. From time to time there are new ones—such as jumping into Mirror Lake to evoke the spirit of Coach Woody Hayes before the football game with Michigan. At least two reasons explain the persistence of campus traditions. First, colleges and universities exist to transmit ideas and observations created by one generation to the next as well as to create new knowledge. Thus, attention to tradition may be part of the cultural identity of any university in celebrating and reliving the past. Second, a set of traditions can build a sense of community within a diverse population. Since colleges and universities change roughly one-fourth of their student populations each year, traditions serve to bind new members into the settled community or campus by providing opportunities for sharing time-honored rituals. Even if traditions serve no purpose, they are great fun and part of campus life and heritage.

CHAPTER EIGHT

FROM NEIL FARM TO OSU CAMPUS

College years are the closing years of the most receptive period of life. Let us send out our graduates into the busy walks of life with the undying memory of a beautiful University and with an insatiate desire to come back every year at Commencement with their good classmates, to renew the friendship of her wide lawns, her shaded walks, and her splendid halls.

—Professor Charles Chubb, *OSU Alumni Magazine*, 1910

8.1 *An airplane flies across OSU's principal campus in Columbus, Ohio, ca. 1995.*

O NE OF the most spacious campuses in the United States, the physical environment of The Ohio State University is impressive, equal to some cities. In 2009, the university owned 15,904 acres—nearly 25 square miles—and 911 buildings on its campuses in Columbus, Newark, Marion, Mansfield, Lima, and Wooster. Additionally, OSU has an airport, two golf courses, an island in Lake Erie, and "enough worked agricultural land to qualify as the world's largest farm in the middle of a city" belong to OSU.[1] On the densely populated campus in Columbus alone there are more than 55,000 students (approximately 8,000 additional students are at regional campuses), faculty, and staff who use and take care of 1,756 acres for 470 buildings and at least two hundred and five different species of trees and shrubs.[2] Under the ground run some ten miles of tunnels to provide support, from electricity to steam, to campus buildings.[3] All these physical elements—land, buildings, roads, utilities—are connected to serve a common purpose: to create and serve a special environment for teaching, service, and scholarship.

The story of how OSU grew from a farm to a megacampus is more than simply counting the buildings and acreage. Fundamentally, it was and continues to be the

---

1. Jane Ware, *An Ohio State Profile: A Year in the Life of America's Biggest Campus* (New York: William Morrow and Company, Inc., 1990), 19.

2. OSU Web Site osutoday/stuinfo.html; Ware, 20.

3. Ware, 21.

work of people who had ideas about what a successful university should look like in the layout of the campus. At many times in its history, OSU engaged trustees, architects, staff, and community groups in its planning efforts. Sometimes, plans changed to reflect differing visions of a learning environment. Ultimately the goal has always been to create a campus that is functional in meeting the diverse needs of a large institution and has memorable spaces and places that inspire, that welcomes solitary scholarship and contemplation, and also has picturesque opportunities for people to gather and exchange ideas.

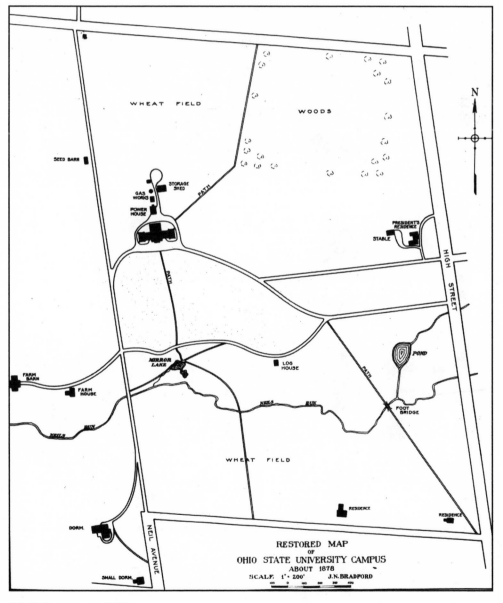

8.2 Campus map, ca. 1878

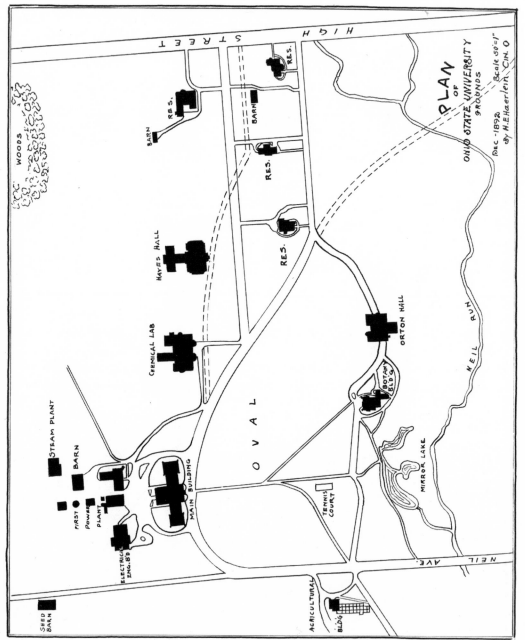

8.3 Proposed plan of campus by landscape architect H. E. Haerlein of Cincinnati in 1893

In 1870, the trustees purchased 331.11 acres known as the "Neil Farm," which had nine tracts of land, for $117,508. Most ($76,863) of this money came from bonds that residents of Franklin County had voted to support financially.[4] On the Neil Farm were a stream (Neil Run) that led to several bogs, and a wooded area known as "the woods" in the northeastern portion of the campus. Seven houses, some of brick, others of frame and one of log and frame, also stood there.[5] Three of the original houses served OSU for many years. For example, the Rickley House at 15th and High Street became the home of the president until a new president's house (now the Kuhn Honors House) was built in 1925. The old house continued in use for the School of Music until 1949. Professor Norton Townshend occupied a house at 11th Avenue and High Street that was demolished in 1959. Finally, there was a farmhouse behind Campbell Hall until it was torn down in 1962.[6] Absent in the beginning were such distinctive landmarks as the Oval and Mirror Lake.

After vetoing a proposal from the outspoken trustee Ralph Leete to locate the main building in downtown Columbus near the State Library, the trustees turned their attention to considering how to develop the Neil farm into a campus. In the winter of 1870–1871, the Executive Committee of the Board of Trustees visited Eastern agricultural colleges and garnered ideas for planning the new campus. In July 1871, the trustees hired F. R. Elliott, a landscape designer from Cleveland, to develop a plan for campus grounds to encompass not less than forty of the original roughly three hundred acres. That plan was "to show the location of all necessary avenues, walks and building places."[7] When Elliott presented his plans, they elicited much discussion among the trustees but no agreement.[8] Next, the trustees looked to Cincinnati, where they found Herman Haerlein. He had worked first in England as a landscape architect and then had achieved distinction by planning Spring Grove Cemetery in Cincinnati.

Haerlein's view was that the campus should look like an English manor, with a main building (University Hall) and then other buildings scattered about. Informality, not rigid planning according to some predetermined scheme, was Haerlein's philosophy. It was also the view of the foremost landscape architect of the time, Frederick Law Olmstead. In all likelihood, trustees liked informality because the new university did not have the means to consider long-term commitments to a fixed plan. Repeatedly, until 1903, the trustees consulted Haerlein in laying out roadways and in identifying places for new buildings such as Mendenhall Laboratory, Page Hall, Townsend Hall, the Armory (where Wexner Center stands) and even the care of trees and shrubs.[9]

---

4. William C. McCracken, "The History of the Physical Plant of The Ohio State University, 1870–1899," vol. I (Columbus: bound typescript, 1942), 9–10.

5. McCracken, vol. I, 11.

6. *The Ringing Grooves of Change* (Columbus: The Ohio State University / Office of Campus Planning, 1970), 7.

7. OSU Trustee minutes, July 6, 1871, 38.

8. OSU Trustee minutes, January 3, 1872, 46.

9. John H. Herrick, *OSU Campus Master Plans* (The Ohio State University / Office of Campus Planning and Space Utilization, 1982), 9–10.

Then as now, grandiose plans can change in unexpected ways. Anecdotal evidence exists that in those days campus planning had an informality that invited circumvention. According to an account written years later by OSU architect Howard Dwight Smith, one example of the frailty of planning was Brown Hall, which was razed in 2009. Haerlein wanted Brown Hall, which faced Bricker Hall (formerly known as the Administration Building), to be at an angle. Professors Thomas French and Joseph Bradford disagreed with Haerlein's siting. Just before digging the trenches, they moved the stakes so Brown Hall would run parallel to University Hall. The same account states that in planning the Physics Building, now Mendenhall Laboratory, the chair of the department of physics asserted a personal preference. He wanted the building placed so that when he lectured, the sun's rays would shine through an opening in the south wall of the main lecture hall, even though this orientation put the building out of line with other buildings.[10]

Sometimes an influential trustee decided a location. President William Henry Scott remembered that in the 1880s, when planning a new building, it was customary for the president and board to tour the campus and discuss possible sites. When the state legislature provided funding for a manual training (industrial arts) building in 1891, there was a disagreement among OSU's leaders. President Scott wanted it near the university's woodworking and metal working shops and in a less prominent part of the campus. Trustee Rutherford B. Hayes insisted that the building, soon named Hayes Hall, must have a prominent place on the Oval. Hayes argued that manual training would be the educational future of the University. Of

8.4 The University Archives has a comprehensive collection of air views of the campus. This one was taken in 1899, before airplanes, and from University Hall and looking east. Note how different the Oval looks.

---

10. Howard Dwight Smith, "Architectural Development of Ohio State," *Ohio Architect* (September 1955), 8–9

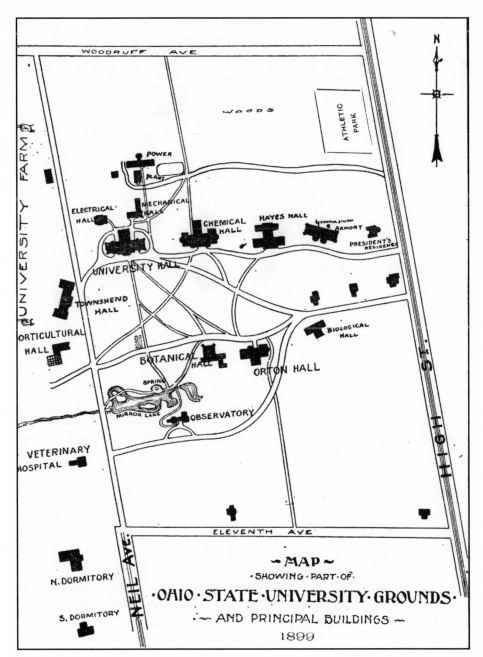

8.5 *Campus map, 1899*

course Hayes prevailed, and Hayes Hall is one of the picturesque buildings on the Oval.[11]

After Haerlein, another point of view in planning the campus took hold, one that favored locating new buildings not randomly but in accordance with a formal and systematic plan. In 1904, the trustees reviewed a master plan by Frank Pack-

---

11. *OSU Alumni Magazine* (October 1936), 9.

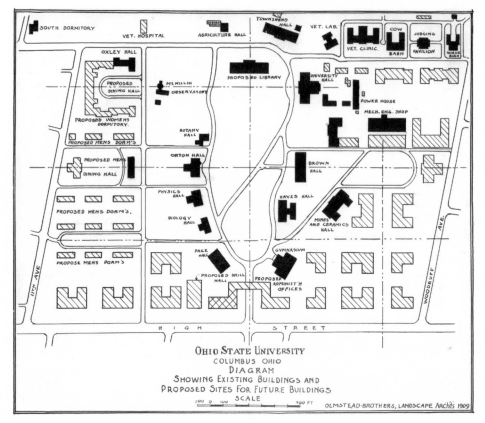

8.6 *The Olmstead Brothers had much influence on the planning of college campuses throughout the United States. In their plan for OSU of 1909, note that the proposed library is situated at the commanding spot on the Oval. Actually, it is the only building within rather than outside of the Oval. However, Professor Chubb of OSU objected to a proposed building at the eastern end that would block the majestic view of the library.*

ard, a prominent architect in Columbus. Packard's proposal called for buildings to be placed along an axis that ran through the campus. Lord Hall on 17th Avenue, designed by Packard, was the only building erected along the proposed axis. Until torn down in 2009, it stood at an odd angle and out of alignment with buildings near it. Although Packard's plan of an axis failed to endure, his proposal for a green lawn in the center of campus may be the origin of the Oval.[12] Certainly, a common feature of many colleges and universities is a central green space that is attractive for walking, meditating, and general leisure.

Next, the trustees turned to the famous firm of the Olmstead Brothers, who had achieved a national reputation in planning parks and campuses. Their report, entitled "The University of the Future," appeared in the student yearbook, the *Makio*, of 1909. The brothers concluded that the campus had grown much and was likely to grow even more in keeping with the increasing numbers of students and faculty. Large buildings and many of them should be expected, which was inappropriate for the informal layout favored for so many years: "We are forced by our study of the

---

12. Campus Master Plan, vol. 1, 1995, 7, OSU Archives.

problem to the conclusion that so many and so large buildings are hereafter to be located, that the informal style of grouping must be abandoned, and that the formal style should be followed hereafter."[13]

The Olmstead Brothers recommended that the trustees develop the campus more systematically by earmarking areas for different studies or services. Within those areas, the university should erect buildings that were formal and large. Open lawns or green space should be identified in advance and protected from planning for new buildings: "Keep permanently free from buildings a grand central lawn westerly from and perpendicular to High Street, starting at the proposed grand entrance at Fifteenth Avenue and ending at the proposed great Library on the hill south of University Hall. The width of the central lawn may be different at different places but it should eventually be symmetrical or as nearly so as possible."[14] Like Packard, the Olmstead Brothers recommended the idea that became the Oval.

This report, in turn, provoked an OSU professor in architecture, Charles St. John Chubb. In an article published in the *Alumni Quarterly* of April 1910, Chubb was critical both of OSU's architecture and the Olmstead plans for the campus. He thought that University Hall was an ugly building that was built in the worst period of American architecture (which he referred to as the "United States Spirit of 1870"). Also, Chubb called for the eventual demolition of Hayes Hall, now one of OSU's architectural landmarks, which he described as an unsightly building. In general, Chubb despaired of the OSU's campus: "I have now, like a doctor to his despairing patient, told you that our poor campus has most known architectural diseases."

Chubb took aim at the Olmstead plan. Specifically, Chubb argued that the central green space or Oval needed to be formal and that it should have straight walks of bricks and cement.

8.7 Charles St. John Chubb

---

13. Quoted in Herrick, *OSU Campus Master Plans,* Appendix G-1, 10.
14. Quoted in Herrick, *OSU Campus Master Plans,* Appendix G-1, 15–16.

8.8 *Prof. Joseph Bradford, first University Architect, had a lasting influence on the design of the campus*

He opposed an Olmstead proposal to build an administration building along the main entrance to the campus at 15th and High. This would block the unobstructed view from High Street across the Oval to the proposed library (the Main Library or Thompson Library, opened in 1913), which should be the climax of the architectural plan. Outspoken, even acerbic, Chubb wielded an extraordinary influence on OSU's architectural heritage.

To achieve consistency in the quality of planning, Chubb urged that the trustees create the position of University Architect. They in fact did so in April 1911. Professor Joseph Bradford, a graduate of OSU in Mechanical Engineering in 1883, had worked for the Pennsylvania Railroad and had also apprenticed as an architect. In 1891, Bradford returned to OSU as assistant professor of drawing and then advanced to associate professor of architecture and drawing in 1899. He became a full professor of architecture in 1906.

To assist Bradford, OSU's trustees created an architectural advisory board consisting of the University Architect, the Landscape Architect, the president, the superintendent of the University Power, Heat and Light Plant, and four members of the faculty "presumably engineers." They were to approve all architectural plans

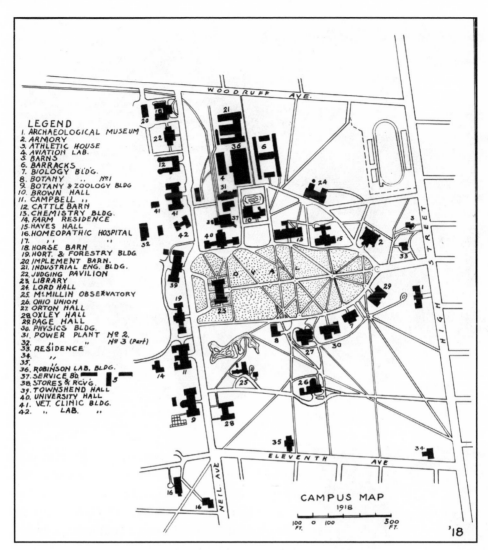

LEGEND
1. ARCHAEOLOGICAL MUSEUM
2. ARMORY
3. ATHLETIC HOUSE
4. AVIATION LAB.
5. BARNS
6. BARRACKS
7. BIOLOGY BLDG.
8. BOTANY „ Nº1
9. BOTANY & ZOOLOGY BLDG
10. BROWN HALL
11. CAMPBELL „
12. CATTLE BARN
13. CHEMISTRY BLDG.
14. FARM RESIDENCE
15. HAYES HALL
16. HOMEOPATHIC HOSPITAL
17. „ „ „
18. HORSE BARN
19. HORT. & FORESTRY BLDG.
20. IMPLEMENT BARN.
21. INDUSTRIAL ENG. BLDG.
22. JUDGING PAVILION
23. LIBRARY
24. LORD HALL
25. McMILLIN OBSERVATORY
26. OHIO UNION
27. ORTON HALL
28. OXLEY HALL
29. PAGE HALL
30. PHYSICS BLDG.
31. POWER PLANT Nº 2.
32. „ „ Nº 3 (Part)
33. RESIDENCE „
34. „
35.
36. ROBINSON LAB. BLDG.
37. SERVICE Bd.
38. STORES & RCV'G.
39. TOWNSHEND HALL
40. UNIVERSITY HALL
41. VET. CLINIC BLDG.
42. „ LAB. „

CAMPUS MAP
1918

100 0 100   500
FT.   FT.

'18

8.9 Map of campus by first OSU architect, Joseph Bradford, in 1918

before the board of trustees reviewed them. In October 1912, the trustees directed Bradford and Chubb to review the campus and propose locations for new buildings the university had requested from the state legislature.[15]

Both Bradford and Chubb favored the avant-garde Beaux Arts movement inspired by the 1893 Columbian Exposition in Chicago.[16] This philosophy of architectural planning featured impressive buildings and a formal plan for campus development. As University Architect, Bradford had an enormous impact on the university's buildings and grounds. As University Architect until 1929, he oversaw the design and construction of some forty university buildings.

15. OSU Trustee minutes, August 2, 1911, 6.

16. *A Framework for Change and Improvement: The Campus Master Plan,* vol. I (Columbus: The Ohio State University 1995), 10.

8.10 *A more developed campus appears in this air view from 1927. Note that Thompson Library does not have a tower.*

8.11 *Howard Dwight Smith, second University Architect and designer of Ohio Stadium and many campus buildings*

In 1913, Bradford presented a master plan that showed a distinctive and formal oval in the center of the campus.[17] In 1917, he led the opposition to placing a proposed stadium of a bowl shape at Ohio Field near Woodruff and High streets. There, it would have rivaled the library and disrupted the academic life of the campus. Instead, Bradford succeeded in persuading the trustees to reverse themselves and place the new stadium west of the campus and near the Olentangy River. In doing so, he extended the range of the active campus, and provided more area for athletics. In 1920, Bradford presented a campus plan for placing new buildings by academic groups "which determined largely the grouping of buildings today."[18]

Another of Joseph Bradford's accomplishments was recruiting Howard Dwight Smith, who suc-

---

17. Smith, "Architectural Development of Ohio State," 9.
18. John H. Herrick Historic Map Collection, 192–03, 2.

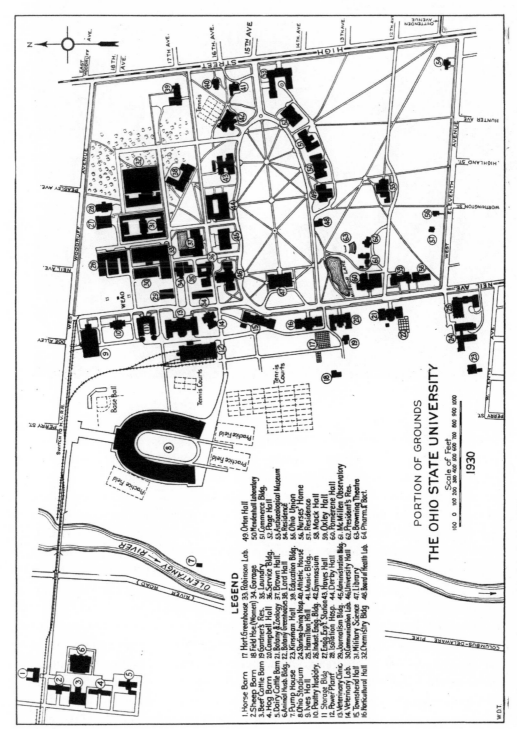

W.D.T.

8.12 Campus map by Howard Dwight Smith, 1930

8.13 *The campus in 1939. Note the cars on Oval Drive.*

ceeded Bradford as University Architect. After taking classes from Bradford as a student, Smith graduated from OSU with a degree of Civil Engineer in Architecture in 1907. Following years of study at Columbia and practice as an architect, Smith returned to OSU as professor of architecture in 1918. From 1918 to 1921, Smith designed Ohio Stadium, his first major project. After resigning to serve as architect for the Board of Education in Columbus, Smith returned in 1929 to become University Architect and a professor in the department of architecture. He remained at OSU until his retirement in 1956 and influenced the design of fifty university buildings, including Stillman Hall, the War Research Building (Smith Laboratory), the tower added to the Main Library (Thompson Library), and St. John Arena.

Bradford and the university architects who succeeded him created plans for managing the growth of the campus to accommodate ever increasing numbers of people and educational programs. Often, they employed consultants to draw plans, some of which they presented to OSU's board of trustees. In 1946, for example, the trustees approved a master plan for a new medical center presented by consultants Skidmore, Owings, and Merrill. Funded by multiple appropriations from the state legislature after a successful campaign of advocacy by OSU and health professionals, groundbreaking for the center took place on May 13, 1948. Since then, construction and expansion have been continuing characteristics of OSU's medical areas.

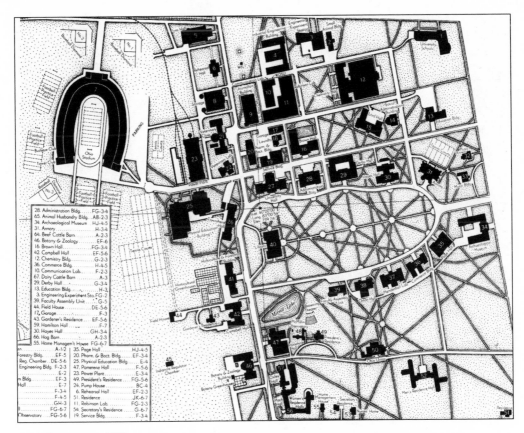

8.14 Campus map, 1939

After World War II, the press of returning veterans and increased enrollments led to more planning of campus growth. The university hired Hale Walker to concentrate on campus planning and he continued with the university until 1949. In this period, there were two major developments. First, plans for the campus showed an imaginary axis along which buildings were to develop. One ran east and west through the center of the Main Library and the Long Walk of the Oval; another cut though the center of Ohio Stadium and continued north and south.[19] Also, Hale recommended that land west of the Olentangy River be reserved for buildings that supported the academic programs of the College of Agriculture.[20]

In 1957, OSU appointed Professor John Herrick from the College of Education as Director of University Plant Studies. Herrick brought about significant changes both in the process of planning and in the resulting plans themselves. As a professor in the College of Education, Herrick had studied and recommended plans for school districts in Ohio that sought to establish new schools. As head of campus planning, Herrick made planning more open by issuing informational bulletins that kept faculty and staff informed and welcomed comments. Herrick was especially

---

19. Herrick, *OSU Campus Master Plans*, 5.
20. *A Framework for Change and Improvement: The Campus Master Plan*, 1995, 15.

8.15 In this air view from 1950, note the construction of the medical facilities in the upper left.

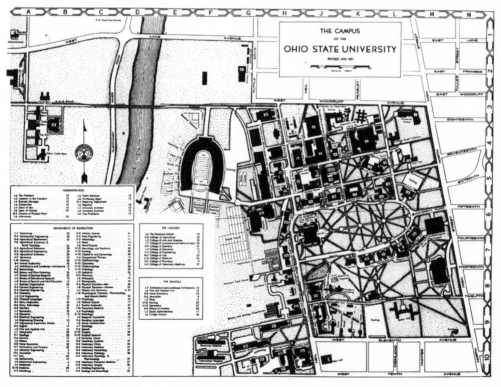

8.16 Campus map, 1950

sensitive about involving others in the planning process because of an incident early in his career at OSU. As a young and very junior professor, Herrick had requested campus planning documents and been deliberately ignored.[21] In a real sense, Herrick introduced the modern and continuing idea of campus planning in which faculty, staff, and students are all participants. A second and continuing change in the Herrick era was an emphasis on identifying, preserving, and improving the attractive places of the campus. Herrick and others felt that such places heightened the quality of the academic experience at OSU.[22]

One of the most important master plans for the campus was that of Caudill, Rowlett, and Scott (CRS) in 1959, which was approved in phases by the trustees in 1960 and 1962. This influential plan had four significant recommendations that had long-term consequences for the campus of today. First, it urged OSU to pay more attention to creating and maintaining well-proportioned and attractive outdoor spaces rather than to simply erecting more buildings along axial schemes. Second, it identified several buildings—such as Orton Hall, Hayes Hall, and University Hall—as having extraordinary architectural and historic significance and thus encouraged OSU to attend to their preservation. Third, the report drew attention to the Olentangy River as an aesthetic asset that deserved more development. Finally, CRS recommended that OSU lessen vehicular traffic in the central campus area and separate cars and people as much as possible. These recommendations focused on planning a campus that would be not only efficient but also attractive.

8.17 Dr. John Herrick, first director of OSU Campus Planning

Of all the master plans developed in the modern era, one could point to this one as the most significant in its effects. At its western end, OSU planned for dormitories along the Olentangy River. In 1967, Lincoln and Morrill Towers opened, although the plan by Caudill, Rowlett, and Scott had not called for such high-rise dormitories. A new student union, Drake Union, opened

---

21. See oral history interview of John H. Herrick, 1983, at The Ohio State University Archives.
22. Herrick, *OSU Campus Master Plans*, 6.

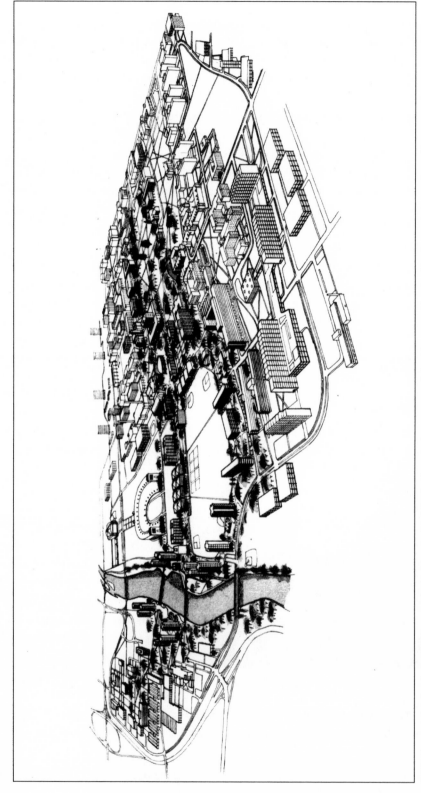

8.18 Concept drawing from the Campus Master Plan study of 1961. Note the importance of the Olentangy River in this view and the number of high-rise buildings envisioned. Only Lincoln and Morrill towers were actually built.

8.19 Taken in 1960, this air view illustrates that the OSU campus has become in appearance a city. A concern that began in the 1960s was establishing green spaces, facilitating pedestrians, and protecting the most distinctive architectural features of the campus.

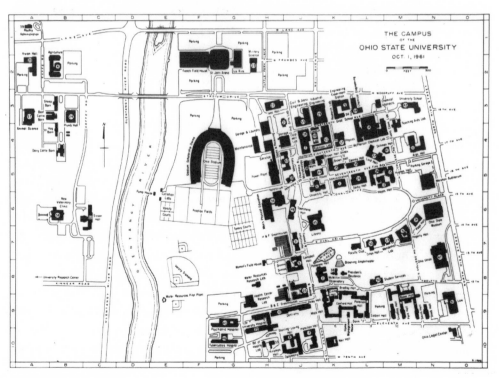

8.20 Campus map, 1961

in 1972 to serve the students near the river who were remote from the Ohio Union on High Street.

On the central campus, the CRS report had impact also. Spaces for open lawns—green spaces—and benches began to appear with more regularity. In the 1970s, the university closed the Oval to automobile traffic, much to the dismay of some faculty and students who missed being able to park close to their offices and classrooms. Beginning in the 1970s, the university began a major investment in historic renovations of buildings along the Oval. Hayes, Orton, Mendenhall, and Derby Halls have since been renovated. Finally, in 2009 the university completed a massive renovation of the Main Library (Thompson Library), which occupies the most prominent location on the campus.

Even the best of plans are not always reliable in shaping the future. Ever increasing enrollments for OSU—the social context of the plan by Caudill, Rowlett, and Scott—did not happen. As the State of Ohio built or acquired more public universities, such as at Bowling Green and at Kent, it limited the number of students for whom OSU would receive a subsidy so that other public universities could grow. Limiting the subsidy restricted the ability of the university to add the instructors and support necessary to admit the increasing number of graduates from high schools in the state who were eligible to enroll in Columbus. Thus, enrollment at OSU in Columbus stabilized at a high level.

The high-rise dormitories of Lincoln and Morrill Towers, with sixteen students crowded into each suite, proved unpopular with the students themselves and no more appeared along the river. These mishaps aside, the CRS master plan was as significant a benchmark and a point of departure for planning the modern OSU environment, as was the work of the Olmstead Brothers that officially ended the era of the informal campus.

Probably the best example of a plan that failed was West Campus, the OSU land across the Olentangy River. In 1964, President Fawcett proposed that OSU build a general college there that would help OSU educate an almost limitless number of undergraduates in the baby boom era. The general college would be part of OSU but would offer two-year educational programs and be managed separately.[23] Fundamentally, West Campus was to provide two years of education for high school graduates who did not have the academic preparation to succeed on the main campus of OSU. Thus, Fawcett attempted to deal with the pressures for admission and the state requirement that OSU had to admit every high school graduate in Ohio, if space were available.

Faculty, however, objected to creating a separate institution that, while affiliated with OSU, had lower academic standards than expected at a four-year university. A faculty committee, chaired by Professor Richard Zimmerman of the College of Engineering, transformed the idea of a separate general college into a college for

---

23. Francis P. Weisenburger, *History of The Ohio State University, Vol. IX: The Fawcett Years, 1956–1972* (Columbus: The Ohio State University), 52.

8.21 *Rendering of a scene of the Gateway Project envisioned by Campus Partners. Its goal is a more pedestrian friendly and attractive neighborhood for the campus.*

all freshmen and sophomores. Here, undergraduates would receive special academic advising and be on a campus less intimidating and more intimate than the one across the river. Separating freshmen and sophomores from the main campus would lessen overcrowding. Thirteen buildings were planned for West Campus, but only five, including a library (Pressey Hall), were built.

By the early 1970s, some assumptions regarding West Campus proved false. Enrollment at OSU stabilized rather than grew, as community colleges appeared in other parts of Ohio. Also, the students on West Campus had to meet faculty and seek services on the Main campus, thus needing extensive busing. Finally, in 1989 West Campus ended as a place for classes and became the home of several research centers and administrative buildings.

In 1995, OSU worked with consultants to develop a new Master Plan that added to the previous plans in several ways. First, the plan took the view that the OSU campus was an urban environment that blended large numbers of people with dedicated green space. Second, the plan called for avoiding excessive sprawl of buildings that wasted land; instead, OSU should favor an environment that made walking efficient, effective, and desirable. Parking garages and remote parking areas connected to the campus were to make a pedestrian-friendly campus possible. Finally, the future should preserve and highlight the historic appearance of the

8.22 A concern of the 1990s, when this photo was taken, was to improve the gateways to the university from the city as well as to make the campus more attractive by enhancing its green spaces and noteworthy buildings.

UNIVERSITY LIBRARIES

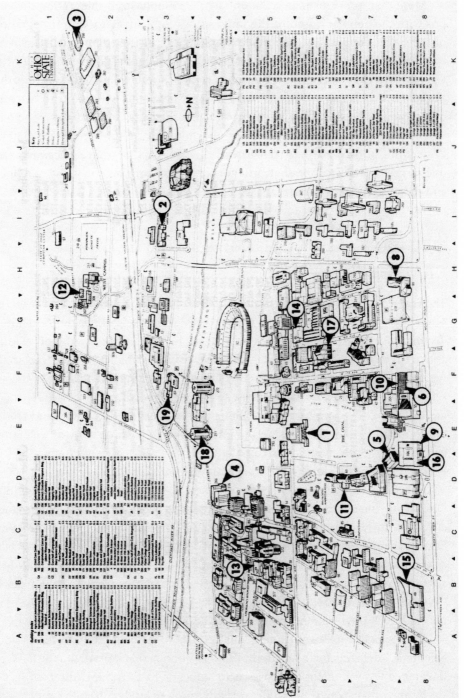

8.23 *Campus map, 1998*

campus. The Oval and Mirror Lake would continue to be centerpieces of the complex map of the campus.[24]

More than previous plans, the one of 1995 emphasized integrating the campus with the neighborhood of the university: "The University is an integral part of the larger community. The quality and vitality of the campus will affect and be affected by the character of the surrounding neighborhoods. The life of the University reaches well into the urban neighborhoods east, south, and north of the campus, with many students living in neighborhoods within one to two miles of the campus borders."[25] Since then, OSU has formed Campus Partners to work with Columbus in developing the neighborhood near High Street. The Gateway Project of Campus Partners transformed the southern entrance of campus from one largely of bars to one that brought new opportunities for living, shopping, and entertainment to the area.

OSU BUT NOT COLUMBUS: THE REGIONAL CAMPUSES

The regional campuses of OSU offer a different learning environment, more like a small college. Whether at Lima, Mansfield, Marion, Newark, or the Agricultural Technical Institute at Wooster, campuses typically have only a handful of buildings and are remote from large cities. Even the classes are smaller. In fact, each of the regional campuses takes pride in its teacher and student ratios and the career counseling and academic tutoring provided to students. Technical colleges independent of OSU share the campuses and such central services as the library and student union. Almost all the students are commuters, many of whom work as well as take classes. Most have ambitions of completing a two-year degree or completing their education at OSU-Columbus or at another institution in Ohio.

Although the regional campuses are different, they are OSU. In the beginning, OSU faculty members traveled from Columbus to provide instruction, but gradually took up residences in the local communities. Faculty at regional campuses achieve tenure and promotion through academic departments on the Columbus campus and must teach, accomplish works of scholarship, and do professional service. Credits earned by students at regional campuses transfer fully to OSU-Columbus. In fact, OSU has always said that its regional campuses are equal partners in the OSU educational enterprise and experience.

The regional campuses came about because of demographic pressures and a heightened demand for education. The baby boom that followed World War II threatened to overwhelm campuses with students. In 1957, OSU directed Professor Kenneth Arisman of the College of Education to study how OSU could set up

---

24. *A Framework for Change and Improvement: The Campus Master Plan,* 3.
25. *A Framework for Change and Improvement: The Campus Master Plan,* 20.

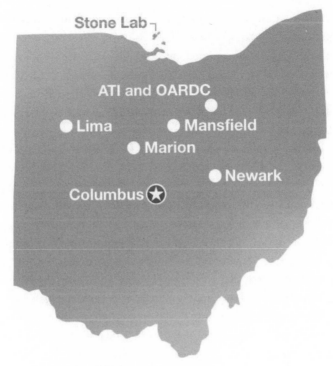

8.24 *Campuses of OSU*

instructional centers that were away from the Columbus campus. Arisman's report noted that between 1950 and 1956 Ohio gained 13 percent in population, both from births and migration into Ohio. In many places in Ohio, high school graduates had no choice but to move away from their communities to attend one of the colleges or universities elsewhere in the state because none were available locally. Often, distance adversely impacted educational opportunity. As an example, Arishman pointed out that 43 percent of college age youth in Franklin County, where opportunities for education were plentiful, were attending institutions of higher learning while only 4.6 per cent of those living in Lawrence County were enrolled. Residents of Franklin County could choose from nine colleges and universities while Lawrence County had none. Proximity to a college as well as the income of the parent—not academic ability alone—were decisive reasons for college attendance. Arisman concluded that some areas of the state—Central Ohio, Eastern Ohio, Western Ohio, and the North Central region—were without the institutions of higher education needed for economic and social advancement.[26] His report persuaded the trustees to set up branch campuses at Marion and at Newark in the autumn quarter of 1957. As OSU president Novice Fawcett put it, these were to be "in the spirit of helping to find answers to Ohio's growing need for educational opportunities for its intellectually competent young people."[27]

26. OSU Press Release, Archives vertical file, May 13, 1957.
27. OSU Press Release, Archives vertical file, May 13, 1957.

In a historical sense, the regional campuses continued and extended the land-grant mission and history of OSU. The Ohio Agricultural and Mechanical College (renamed OSU in 1878) opened its doors in 1873 and its low tuition—funded from the federal Morrill Act of 1862—lowered the cost of higher education in Ohio. Similarly, the effort to expand OSU-Columbus throughout Ohio brought higher education to communities and counties that lacked access to low-cost higher education.

The regional campuses also reflected the history of OSU-Columbus in other ways. Even as the residents of Franklin County pledged bonds and competed with other counties to host the Ohio Agricultural and Mechanical Colleges, OSU encouraged and required community support and investment. In 1957, when OSU began its study of educational needs, some sixty communities applied for consideration.[28] At first, only two were selected. At Marion, for example, local industry provided funds to refurbish existing laboratories; its Chamber of Commerce agreed to underwrite the first year's operation while local organizations and companies provided more than $7,000 for scholarships.[29] Similarly, Newark offered rooms in the city schools and local groups raised money for scholarships.

Other regional campuses soon followed. OSU began serving Mansfield in 1958 by offering evening classes at a local high school. Two years later, another branch of OSU opened in Lima. Like OSU in Columbus, where the university began as a single building that served all purposes, the regional campuses developed slowly, typically as an evening program in a local high school.

Community support and opportunities in state funding enabled OSU's regional campuses to buy land and expand their learning environments. A state bond issue in 1965 made possible the building of campuses at Marion and Newark, where local groups had helped to buy campus sites. At Mansfield, a fund drive by a local advisory board and state support led to the purchase of a 500-acre wooded area at the northwest edge of Manfield in 1965. At Lima, private donations from the Galvin Foundation and a statewide bond issue brought about a campus of 565 acres. Newark used moneys raised privately and a state appropriation to buy land for its campus in 1968.

A different and more specialized regional campus developed at Wooster. In 1892, the Ohio Agricultural Research and Development Center, begun as the Ohio Agricultural Experiment Station on the Columbus campus in 1882, had moved there. Its presence led to an effort by OSU and funding from the State of Ohio to build a special institute that would provide specialized and technical training for youth interested in careers in agriculture. Thirty acres near the Center became the campus of the Agricultural Technical Institute, which opened in 1972. Students earned an associate degree by completing courses in agricultural research and laboratory techniques, agricultural chemicals, soil fertility, and plant nutrition as well

---

28. "University College: Newark" in *OSU Centennial History*, 1969.
29. "University College" in *OSU Centennial History*, 1969.

as horticulture and wood science. The Institute was to be an educational model for specialized education that integrated research and teaching in agriculture.

Sometimes the pressures for geographical expansion led to efforts that did not continue. In 1962, OSU opened a regional branch at a high school in Lakewood, near Cleveland. That effort ended in 1966 when it became part of the newly created Cleveland State University. Another outreach effort took place in 1964 when OSU, in cooperation with Miami University, offered courses near Dayton. That enterprise resulted in the independent Wright State University, which became a separate institution in 1967.[30]

All in all, the growth of the physical setting of OSU points to several conclusions. Certainly, the increase in physical size evidenced the importance of the university in teaching, research, and service and its cultural and economic significance. As it added land and buildings, planning the campus became increasingly complex. Growth in physical size needed to complement, not contradict, teaching and learning. An intellectually stimulating—and memorable, as Professor Chubb stressed—environment had to be preserved while adding unprecedented numbers of people and buildings. Finally, extending the Columbus campus to other parts of Ohio enabled the university to provide different learning environments, smaller and more intimate. All the while, OSU continued its land-grant mission of providing the OSU branded quality of education at a low cost to the people of Ohio.

30. Weisenburger, 51.

CHAPTER NINE

SOME SPECIAL PLACES AT OSU

The places we have known do not only belong to the world of space in which we situate them for the sake of simplicity.
—Marcel Proust, *Remembrance of Things Past*

AS A CAMPUS, The Ohio State University has special places—buildings and spaces—that inspire and that linger in memory and that make the campus both unique and attractive. Knowing these places, landmarks that they are, is a fundamental part of the campus experience. Learning about their history, how they began and how they changed, helps one appreciate these places even more.

ENARSON HALL (154 W. 12TH AVENUE)

Enarson Hall was the first student union at a public university in the United States. Students themselves, not faculty or administrators, led the effort for the building. As early as 1892, students had complained that OSU lacked a building where the numerous student organizations could meet and where students could spend leisure hours before and after classes. On three occasions, the Ohio State YMCA attempted to raise money for a student building. Finally, in 1907, students and alumni conducted writing and speaking campaigns to influence state legislators to provide state support. In 1908 they succeeded, with an appropriation of $75,000. Students themselves, at the request of the trustees, formed the Ohio Union Committee and raised additional money to furnish and equip the building.

Constructed in 1909 in the Jacobean architectural style, the Ohio Union included dining rooms, a lounge, a ballroom, reading rooms, billiard tables, writing rooms, and offices. In the beginning, the Union was a male only club; each male student paid a membership fee. Women could only enter as a man's guest or to attend meet-

9.1 Enarson Hall in 1918 (Student Union Building)

9.2 A 1970s view

ings and events of coeducational student organizations until around World War II. Until then, women students used nearby Pomerene Hall.

After World War II, the extraordinary numbers of students and organizations overwhelmed the building as a place for meeting, studying, and relaxing. In 1951, student petitions and student fees led to a new Ohio Union on High Street. However, the first Ohio Union continued to house student services, including the Student Health Center and was known as the "Student Services Building" as well as the "Old Union."

As the building aged and as student services moved to other places, the university considered tearing it down. Students, however, saved their old building. Two students drew attention to the historic significance of the building and succeeded in placing it on the National Register of Historic Places on April 20, 1979. In 1985, the university remodeled and restored the building as a home for University College and in 1986 renamed it Enarson Hall, in honor of President Harold Enarson and his contributions to students. In 1996, OSU created a Visitor Center in Enarson Hall to centralize and improve campus visits by prospective students and their families.

HAYES HALL (108 NORTH OVAL MALL)

Completed in February 1893, Hayes Hall is the oldest building on campus. Unlike Orton, which has remained a building for geology, Hayes Hall has had an unusual

9.3 Hayes Hall

9.4 Hayes Hall Foundry

history in its origins and use. Those who enter the building will notice the inscription above the entrance arch, "The Trained Mind, the Skilled Hand." From this they will assume, falsely, that this building has always been a place for the Fine Arts.

Actually, Hayes Hall originally served a much different purpose. Named after President Rutherford B. Hayes while he was a trustee of OSU, the building was to house manual education or industrial training. Hayes had admired Booker T. Washington, the famous African American educator who was a national figure after the Civil War. In fact, Hayes shared Washington's view of the importance of skilled labor in maintaining social harmony. He believed passionately that training in skills useful to industry—metal working, carpentry, foundry work, and more—was the way to bridge what he saw as a widening gulf between capital and labor in an industrial society. According to Hayes, land-grant colleges, which had low tuition and were more financially accessible than the private colleges, should provide industrial or manual education to the average workingman.

Hayes lectured and lobbied tirelessly for vocational or industrial education. When the state legislature provided money for a building, the trustees resolved on November 17, 1891 to name the structure Hayes Hall, "in recognition of the untiring labors of President Hayes towards its establishment and his devotion to the cause of industrial education." Hayes himself had responsibility for working directly with Columbus architect Frank L. Packard and recruiting faculty for industrial education. Unfortunately, Hayes died before Hayes Hall opened.

In its first year of operation, the equipment needed for manual education occupied most of Hayes Hall. The first floor contained a machine shop, a forge, and a foundry. The second floor had carpentry and pattern shops. On the third floor was the department of drawing, which provided classes in mechanical and free-hand drawing. Photography classes were also taught there.

With the death of Rutherford Hayes, campus interest in industrial education waned. Soon, Hayes Hall began to serve purposes other than industrial education. Students had classes in mathematics, rhetoric, and philosophy in what must have been a noisy building. The Home Economics program established a laboratory in the building. After completion of the Shops Building (later renamed Welding Engineering Laboratory) in 1916, the foundry, machine shop, and other mechanical departments moved from Hayes Hall, and thus the building lost its industrial character. During World War I, Hayes Hall became the headquarters for the military department and provided a dormitory for aviation cadets. In the early 1920s, the School of Fine Arts began holding classes there and eventually art departments, especially the History of Art department, made use of the building.

As a work of architecture, Hayes Hall is also important enough to have a place on the National Register of Historic Places. Built of brown sandstone and red pressed brick, it represents the Romanesque Revival style of architecture. Its most prominent feature is the arch over the entrance. The inner arch has stone carrions of flora and fauna. In 1978, the university completed a major renovation and restoration of the building as an effort to preserve OSU's architectural heritage.

9.5 Mirror Lake

MIRROR LAKE AND MIRROR LAKE HOLLOW

In 1951, the student newspaper, the *Lantern,* commented: "It is said that a coed has not really been to the University unless she has been kissed in Mirror Lake Hollow to the accompaniment of twelve strokes of Orton Hall's Chimes."[1] Like the Oval, these areas are beautiful places of nature that people and the university have shaped. In 1873, when the university opened, a stream, Neil Run, provided water to the campus. The campus also had a few springs, streams, and bogs, but there was nothing known as Mirror Lake. Captain Haerlein, who did the first planning for

---

1. Quoted in John H. Herrick, *The OSU Mirror Lake Hollow* (Columbus: OSU Office of Campus Planning, 1984), 23.

the campus, took the first step in developing Mirror Lake when he sited the Botany Building (which stood near where the Faculty Club is) about 1889. Haerlein had in mind that faculty and students who studied botany, would use the Neil Run Hollow behind the Botany Building as an outdoor laboratory for nature studies.[2]

In 1895, Mirror Lake began to take shape because of the construction of McMillin Observatory (torn down in 1976). Mr. Emerson McMillin, president of Columbus Gas and Coke Company in New York City, was an enthusiastic astronomer who admired OSU professor Henry Lord. McMillin offered to provide money to build and equip an observatory if the university would provide a handsome site. That gift led to improving the area to create what became known as Mirror Lake, a place name first used in 1896.[3] In response to McMillin's offer, OSU made a driveway for the observatory, tripled the size of the lake, and erected bridges.[4] Although OSU tore down the observatory in 1976, a marker near Enarson Hall reminds all about the observatory, although it does not associate McMillin Observatory with Mirror Lake.

People and nature combined to further change Mirror Lake and its Hollow. The spring that fed Mirror Lake had such remarkably good tasting water that in 1886 OSU created a special grotto that made it easier for people to reach the water, enjoy its taste, and relax. In 1918, a storm uprooted many large trees around the lake. Two years later, OSU took out the islands and bridges and changed the lake's size and

9.6 *Mirror Lake, with observatory in background*

---

2. OSU Campus Master Plan 1995, vol. 1: 6.

3. *The Ringing Grooves of Change* (Columbus: the Ohio State University/ Office of Campus Planning, 1970), 14; Herrick, OSU Mirror Lake Hollow.

4. Herrick, *OSU Mirror Lake Hollow*, 13.

9.7 Grotto at Mirror Lake in 1910. Note the dippers to the left of the woman in this photo.

9.8 May Fete at Mirror Lake Hollow, 1922

shape.[5] In 1925, the streams feeding Mirror Lake dried up because of a new storm sewer for a growing Columbus and OSU. Students raised money for a fountain in Mirror Lake, completed in 1930, which spouted water from a sulfuric well at first and then from the Olentangy River. Finally, in 1977, OSU began using Columbus city water for the fountain and Mirror Lake.

That students gave their own money for a fountain in Mirror Lake points to the important place of Mirror Lake and its nearby Hollow in student life. Like the Oval, Mirror Lake and Hollow has been the site of many and various student events. The first graduating class, the class of 1878, posed at the bogs that became Mirror Lake. In 1887, students began a tradition of May Week in the Hollow. Student honor societies, such as Sphinx, Links, Romophos, and Bucket and Dipper have held initiations rites in the area. Beginning in 1908, the Browning Society presented plays and about the same time musical concerts sounded in Mirror Lake Hollow. Dunkings of freshmen in Mirror Lake were common until about 1930. Finally, students and faculty even played golf in a course that was partly in Mirror Lake Hollow.

OHIO STADIUM

In some ways, the history of Ohio Stadium is similar to that of the Main Library. Both represented major transformations in the university's status. Ohio Stadium memorialized the prominence of OSU in athletics even as the Main Library stood for the progress of the university's in academics. Like the Main Library, the Stadium grew initially from the vision of a few dedicated people who convinced others to join them.

Originally, places for football were as modest as athletics at Ohio State itself. When in 1890, OSU assembled its first football team, games took place at Recreation Park in Columbus, at South High and Whittier, miles from the campus. Two years later, students played on a field near North Dorm, the North Athletic Field which students used until 1898. In that year, growing interest in football and a petition from students led to a new athletic field, northeast of the Oval and near the University woods. Known as University Field, it had a seating capacity of around five hundred. That year OSU joined the Ohio Athletic Conference along with Western Reserve, Case Institute, Wooster College, Ohio Wesleyan, and Oberlin. As attendance grew, the university added more seats. Finally in 1908, the university renamed its athletic field as Ohio Field and increased seating to 6,100.

In 1912, OSU joined the Western Athletic conference which included the larger schools of the Midwest. Unprecedented crowds jammed Ohio Field, which even the increase in the seating could barely contain. As the university tried to accommodate the increasing popularity of football, one of its faculty, Thomas Ewing French, had a major role in visioning and bringing about Ohio Stadium. (In fact, French

---

5. Herrick, *OSU Mirror Lake Hollow*, 14.

9.9 Ohio Stadium

was known as the "father of Ohio Stadium." See chapter 4.) In 1915, French spoke before the Columbus Chamber of Commerce and predicted that someday 50,000 people would witness a football game on campus. An undefeated season in 1916 and the OSU's first football star, Chic Harley, made French's ambitious prediction seem reasonable to many. Near Ohio Field, fans climbed trees because they could not find enough seats for a good view.

In January 1917, the trustees approved a proposal to build a bowl-shaped stadium in the woods west of University Field. A few weeks later, when architect Joseph Bradford and others complained that the new stadium would be too close to the new library (opened in 1913) and out of symmetry with other buildings, the trustees reversed themselves. They voted to move the site of the stadium to farmland near the Olentangy River, on a field of about forty acres. This more expansive location afforded a larger shape as an alternative to a compact bowl.

World War I interrupted progress, but not for long. When the war ended in 1918, OSU hired an OSU alumnus and young architect, Howard Dwight Smith, to design a stadium, his first major assignment as a professional. French, Bradford, and Clyde T. Morris, University Engineer, helped in the project. Smith took the lead in the design and drew on his studies of classical architecture, especially of the Coliseum of ancient Rome. A horseshoe-shaped and doubled-decked stadium, with bowed and curved sides that enabled spectators to be closer to the playing field than at other stadiums, became the final and extraordinary design.

Meanwhile, planners for a stadium raised money. The trustees and university administration refused to jeopardize OSU's priorities for new academic buildings by placing the stadium on its list of requests for state funding. Supporters of the stadium, who included President William Oxley Thompson, turned to fans for support. Previously, OSU had had no experience in seeking private funding. However, Columbus had experienced successful public efforts to raise money privately for Liberty Bonds that paid for World War I, and those campaigns or drives served as a model.

Athletic director Lynn St. John headed a committee of three to organize a campaign. Leading the campaign itself was Sam Summer, graduate of the class of 1905 and vice president of the Joseph Scenthal Company. Summer and his colleagues identified Ohio State graduates across the country and organized committees in counties and cities. They argued that the university, the city, and the state needed the stadium as a place not only for football but as a landmark that would draw national attention. The unofficial campaign slogan was that Ohio Stadium was the magnet that would draw the nation and the world to Columbus.

A kick-off in October 1920 began "Stadium Week," a time of pageants, parades, and speeches in Columbus that coincided with festivities in many other places where OSU alumni lived. By November 26, donors had pledged more than $900,000 of the one million dollars sought. By January 20, 1921, $1,001,071 had been raised. Eventually, the stadium would cost roughly $1,300,000, the shortfall covered by loans paid from athletic profits.

On August 3, 1921, Governor Harley Davis and OSU president Thompson led a groundbreaking ceremony to begin construction. Eighty-five thousand tons of concrete poured into the site. As the stadium rose, the massive project attracted much attention, especially from professional engineers and architects. Its unusual design and graceful lines prompted the American Institute of Architects to award Smith recognition in 1921 for "excellence in public works."

On October 7, the team played their first game there and won 5–0 against Ohio Wesleyan. Stadium Dedication Day was the third game played in the stadium, against Michigan on October 21, 1922. An overflow crowd of 71,385 enjoyed the festivities, although the home team lost 19–0.

Since its opening in 1922, Ohio Stadium has undergone several renovations. Press boxes, scoreboards, and even the field have changed from natural grass to artificial turf and then back to grass. In the 1930s a dormitory added in the South Tower provided student housing until its relocation in the 1990s. By far, the most significant renovation took place from 1998–2001. Funded with revenue largely from the sale of hospitality suites and club seats, this renovation put the old stadium into compliance with modern building codes. It added an exterior shell to the original walls, increased the size of the stadium, added seats (including permanent ones at the south end), lowered the field, removed the running track and the dormitory (Stadium Scholarship Dorm), and renovated locker rooms and band rooms. Most, but not all, will agree that the renovation made the stadium a more modern place while preserving its historic character.

9.10 *Ohio Stadium under construction*

9.11 *Dedication Day game for Ohio Stadium, a loss to Michigan*

ORTON HALL (155 SOUTH OVAL MALL)

Designed by Columbus architect J. W. Yost and completed in the summer of 1893, Orton Hall may be the most distinctive and most recognized building at OSU. In fact, it has a place on the National Register of Historic Places. Named in honor of President Edward Orton (1873–1881), who remained active as professor of geology, the building serves as a classroom building and offices for the department of geology and the Geology Library.

More than any other building on campus, Orton Hall tells a story. Its architecture represents the geological history of the State of Ohio. All the forty types of stones used to build Orton Hall came from Ohio, many of them donated. They appear in the building as they occur in the bedrock of the state: the oldest stones form the lower part of the building and the youngest ones are at the top. Around the top of the chimes tower, twenty-five gargoyles look down upon the campus, sandstone representations of the heads of extinct animals. In the interior , the capitals of the columns contain carved representations of fossils. In all ways, the building was planned to be, and serves, as a learning laboratory for geology. Meanwhile, the chimes that sound across the Oval first rang in 1915, the gifts of seven graduating classes.

9.12 *Orton Hall*

Orton himself served as State Geologist. In the early days of the university, Ohio citizens sent soil samples to his office for analysis. As specimens of rocks and fossils arrived, there was a growing interest in having a separate building for geology and in a museum that could display them. In their proposal to the legislature, the trustees included space to relocate the University Library because they knew it needed more room to grow and because a multi-purpose building would be more likely to win support from the state legislature. Although the OSU Library left Orton Hall in 1913, Orton Hall still contains a library, the Geology Library, which President Orton's son, Professor Edward Orton, Jr., donated and planned.

9.13 Orton Hall, at completion in 1895

THE OVAL

As the center of campus, the Oval has also been pivotal to the life of the university. In its long history, the Oval has been the place for events and games. Military drills, commencements, alumni reunions, homecoming parades, freshman orientations, a record-breaking game of musical chairs in 1980, student fairs, itinerant preachers, and protest rallies have all been staged on the Oval. For many at OSU, the Oval has served simply as a place of refuge for napping, sunbathing, dog walking, throwing Frisbees, or eating lunch.

At first, the Oval was an informal place, an area of open lawn that did not even have sidewalks. One year, the *Makio,* the student yearbook, included a humorous report that students had slipped and even disappeared in the mud. University Architect Joseph Bradford deserves credit for improving the Oval. One of his earliest plans, in 1914, proposed a set of geometrically designed walks within the Oval, an ambitious design for which there was no funding.

Particularly remarkable is the "Long Walk" which extends 1,275 feet down the center of the Oval. This was in Bradford's plan for the campus in 1914.[6] So prominent is the walk that traditions and folktales surround it. One tradition prominent in

---

6. John H. Herrick, *The OSU Oval* (Columbus: OSU Office of Campus Planning, 1982), 9.

9.14 A classic view of the Oval

9.15 The Oval in the 1880s

9.16 The Oval, ca. 1905

the 1920s and early 1930s restricted freshman from walking on the "Long Walk" on penalty of being tossed into Mirror Lake by upperclassmen. Today, some students believe that if they hold hands, walk the entire "Long Walk" and hear the chimes from Orton Hall as they are walking, they will marry.

9.17 Demonstration on the Oval in 1970

POMERENE HALL (1760 NEIL AVENUE)

Pomerene Hall began as a student union for women even as nearby Enarson Hall served as a student union for men. Completed in 1922 as the "Women's Building," it housed the dean of women; classes in physical education for women, including swimming and basketball; and lounges and meeting rooms used chiefly by women and their organizations.[7] There was a close association with the School of Home Economics, which managed the Pomerene Refectory, a food service on the ground floor for many years until it became part of OSU's Food Services.

In 1927, the trustees named the building in honor of a man, Frank Pomerene, even though this was a women's building. Pomerene had been a graduate of OSU (undergraduate degree 1891 and law degree in 1895) and had served fourteen years as a trustee until his death in 1919. In 1957, when the dean of men's offices moved to Pomerene Hall, it became coeducational and lost its original identity as a woman's building.

---

7. Herrick, *OSU Campus Buildings*, # 067, OSU Archives.

9.18 Pomerene Hall, a view from Neil Avenue in 1927

9.19 Pomerene Hall viewed from Mirror Lake

THOMPSON LIBRARY

The Thompson Library (also known as Main Library) may be one of the most frequently photographed places on campus. Certain it is that of all the buildings on the campus, the Library best reflects the development of OSU from a small college into a major university. The building itself has changed three times to meet the increasing need for more books and journals as well as space for study to support teaching and research at the university.

9.20 Thompson Library

When the university opened in 1873, the library occupied a room in University Hall. At first, there was no regular librarian; faculty rotated in taking responsibility for its management. Initially, this was no great hardship because the library had few books and was only open a few hours a day. Within a decade or so, circumstances had changed greatly. Professional organizations in history, economics, sociology, and many other academic professions had organized in the 1870s and 1880s and published journals and new books to share the results of research and new knowledge. By 1892, so important had the state of the library become that OSU faculty passed a resolution: "That the most pressing want of the University and one the consideration of which ought to take precedence over any other is the appointment of a professional librarian. There is nothing that hampers so much the work of professors and students as the condition of the library. . . . "8 The trustees agreed that an impending move of the library from University Hall to the newly built Orton Hall required a full-time librarian to take charge of the planning and administration. In 1893, the trustees appointed a student, Olive Branch Jones, as the first full-time librarian. She continued as librarian until 1927, when she became associate professor of bibliography, a position she held until her death in 1933.

When the library moved to Orton Hall, it was to be there only temporarily as that building was to serve geology, not the entire university. Jones championed

9.21 *Olive Branch Jones*

the cause of a new building from the beginning of her career. In letters and annual reports to President Canfield and later President William Oxley Thompson, Jones set forth her views. Fundamentally, she wanted a library on the Oval but away from its apex. The best spot, according to Jones, was on South Oval, near where the Fac-

9.22 *Main Library in 1913*

---

8. OSU Faculty minutes, December 1892.

9.23 *The majestic reference room in the Main Library, ca. 1920–1925. In the 1960s a floor was inserted to create more user space.*

ulty Club stands. There, the building could expand into Mirror Lake Hollow, as its needs increased.

Others disagreed. President Canfield insisted that the library was the heart of the university and should be in the center of the Oval. The Olmstead Brothers, whom the trustees had hired to plan the campus, recommended the apex of the Oval. Their recommendation became a fact in 1910. In that year, Alonzo Tuttle, an OSU professor from the College of Law who served as a member of the Ohio Senate, persuaded the state legislature to set aside $250,000 in each of two years to build a library building.

Although Olive Jones lost the argument for location, she joined a team to plan the Main Library that included university architect Joseph Bradford and his colleague in architecture, Professor Charles Chubb. This committee recommended a design suggested by Allen and Collins of Boston in the classical Renaissance style. Built of limestone and occupied in 1913, the library with its exterior facing east to the main entrance of the university at 15th and High streets presented an impressive, even monumental, presence.

Spaces inside the three floors of the original library were equally impressive. The first floor had a study room, a lecture room, two seminar rooms, and a checkroom for hats and coats. On the second floor, the most remarkable place was the reference hall. The ceiling was 30 feet high and the walls were 120 feet long and lined with

10,000 books. On the third floor were eight seminar rooms and a map and chart room. So impressive was the Main Library that in January 1913 the *OSU Alumni Monthly* dedicated the entire issue to the newly opened building. A student wrote that "the building had grown up under our eyes, to be sure, and yet we had not dreamed the verity of its beauty."

Soon, the building proved to be too small as the university increased in numbers of faculty and student users and as printed materials for teaching and research multiplied. As early as 1920, the *Lantern* reported that fraternities were sending pledges to hold places in the Main Library for their fraternity brothers. The Great Depression and World War II delayed efforts to add to the Main Library.

The end of the war and the swelling of student enrollments caused major changes to the library. In 1948, OSU renamed the building the William Oxley Thompson Memorial Library and undertook a massive program to add space. To provide an economical way of storing an ever-growing body of printed materials, a stack tower was added that, in time, would become a campus icon. Initially and until the late 1960s, this was a place of storage, not study; pages brought requested items from the stack tower to the circulation desk for the waiting students. When construction ended in 1951, the changes also included wings to the front of the building. All in all, the changes were so significant that OSU held a dedication ceremony in 1951, which the Librarian of Congress attended.

As enrollments and printed materials continued to increase, the William Oxley Thompson Memorial Library changed also. In 1965, a floor was inserted into the Reference Hall to provide more space. A few years later, students gained direct access to the stack tower rather than have to wait for pages to bring materials to the circulation desk. In 1977, the university completed an addition to the west side of the Main Library that added square footage but ended access from the west.

All these changes—so necessary for the library to adjust to the size of the university and its needs—lessened the monumental character of the building. In 1998, a faculty committee concluded that "All the several visions of decades of well-meaning architects have wrought such havoc on the original building that what was once the university's greatest pride is now the university's greatest humiliation." So important was the condition of the Main Library to the well-being and future of OSU that it was the only building mentioned in the Academic Plan of 2000. In 2003, OSU hired architects and committed itself to renovating the Main Library in ways that would restore its historic places. At the same time, the goal was to make the building more able to meet the increasingly diverse needs of its faculty and students and to add new spaces, such as a new western wing entrance facing Neil Avenue.

After closing for three years, the Thompson Library reopened in 2009. The renovated building greatly expanded the number of seats available (from 800 to 1,800 while still holding 1,000,000 volumes) and presented some inspirational spaces. Upon entering, two spacious atria in the east and west let light into the building and inspire visitors. While the stack tower has remained, it is now better lit, provides

9.24 *View of the new addition on the western side of the Thompson Library, completed in 2009*

9.25 *Shown here is the Buckeye Reading Room inside the western addition.*

9.26 This is the western atrium at ground level. Note the glass encased book tower.

9.27 The best view of the campus is from this room on the 11th floor of the Thompson Library.

better seating, and is partially encased in glass, making it a spectacular feature on the inside of the building. A second-floor reading room in the east has restored the grandeur of the original; meanwhile, another spacious room to the west on the second floor has become a favorite place for events as well as casual reading. A room on the eleventh floor provides not only comfortable seating in a paneled room but also the best view of the campus. So popular has the Thompson Library become that in its first five months after the reopening there were more than 700,000 visitors.

UNIVERSITY HALL (230 NORTH OVAL MALL)

Actually, OSU had two buildings named "University Hall." The University Hall that occupies the site today is a near replica of the original building of 1873 and opened in January of 1976. Within the front entrance are a portion of the old entrance arch and displays about the history of the university.

The original University Hall was the work of J. Snyder of Akron, who did not finish the building until January 7, 1874, even though classes had begun there the previous September. The base courses, windowsills, and window and door trim came from Berea sandstone sawed into the shapes and sizes needed. The bricks themselves took shape from clay dug near Woodruff Avenue and then fashioned into bricks at kilns north of the building. Because the dormitory building had not been completed, students lived at the east end of the first floor, in an area they called "purgatory." Four professors had apartments in the building. In the east end of the basement was a dining room. Other rooms served as classrooms, a library, a museum, and offices until more buildings became available on the campus. In 1896, an addition added more space to the back of the building to increase the size of the chapel or assembly room.

Generations of faculty and students wore out the original University Hall. Only ten years after its completion the trustees had the original cupola inspected for safety and in 1886 the tower was rebuilt. In 1913, bricks fell from the tower, and it was rebuilt again. In 1918, a windstorm ripped away the turret at the northeast corner, and in 1929 the tower had to be rebuilt. Periodically, students and faculty complained of the interior conditions within the building. In 1947, a student publication carried an article entitled "Our Favorite Fire Trap: University Hall is Ready to Go Up in Flames."[9]

In 1966, a civil engineering firm commissioned by the university evaluated the building, listed many flaws, and concluded that it would not be possible to renovate the building to meet modern needs. A few months later, an advisory committee of faculty urged that the University raze the interior of University Hall, save the outer shell, and create a new building within, provided the costs did not exceed that of constructing a new building.

---

9. University Hall, BMOC, vertical file of OSU Archives, March 1947.

9.28 New University Hall

9.29 The old University
Hall in 1874

Even as discussions took place, University Hall continued to weaken. In March of 1967 a piece of sandstone more than three feet long and weighing nearly 800 pounds fell some fifteen feet to the ground at the entrance to the building. Fortunately, no one was injured. On May 2, 1968, the university closed the north wing of University Hall because the floors sagged so severely. However, many faculty and students protested that the building should continue as a museum or historic site, if not a functioning classroom or office building. In 1970, students formed a "Save University Hall" campaign, an effort that gained a boost when University Hall was placed on the National Register of Historic Places on July 16, 1970.[10] Concerned alumni formed the Committee for Rehabilitation of University Hall and sought to block efforts at demolition.

Eventually, OSU trustees and administration brokered a compromise between the modernists and the preservationists that pleased many, but not all. A new building would replicate much of the original University Hall exterior. However, its interior would be modern and useful as a classroom building and offices. As little as a month before the demolition in September 1971, opponents tried to block the destruction by filing a lawsuit.[11]

In the end, many of the original bricks were sold to alumni, faculty, and students and these still exist, especially as book ends. The pillars and archway at the main entrance on the south side came from the original building and reappeared in the new one. A curious fact is that John Conrad supplied the bricks for the new building; his grandfather, another John Conrad, owned the company that made the bricks for the original University Hall.[12]

WEXNER CENTER FOR THE ARTS / THE ARMORY (1871 NORTH HIGH STREET)

Located on the Oval, the Wexner Center inherited features of the Armory, a building that had occupied the site for nearly a century. In 1891, the trustees requested state funding for a multipurpose building that could be an armory for courses in military science, a gymnasium, and an assembly hall. Completed in 1898 by architects Yost and Packard, the building resembled a medieval French castle. Inside were an 80 x 50-foot drill hall, an indoor basketball court, a canvas track and two swimming pools, one for men and another for women.[13] Until fire destroyed the building in 1958, the Armory had been a place for graduations, intramural athletics, physical education, and dances. As one professor recalled, "Since the Armory

---

10. John H. Herrick, *OSU Campus Buildings* (Columbus: The Ohio State University / Office of Campus Planning, 1988), # 088.

11. OSU Archives Vertical File.

12. *Columbus Dispatch,* October 24, 1976 in OSU Archives Vertical File.

13. *OSU Lantern,* September 24, 1987; OSU Archives Vertical File.

9.30 Wexner Center for the Visual Arts

was the site for many social events, the building carried great sentimental value for people who were at OSU many years ago."[14]

The site of the original Armory, near to buildings that served the College of the Arts, stood vacant for more than twenty-five years. In 1982, OSU determined to have an arts center on the site and held a national competition of architects. The successful architects, Eisenman/Robertson of New York and Trott and Bean of Columbus incorporated the turrets of the Armory into their design. In the words of Richard Trott, who had been a student at OSU and had seen the Armory as an undergraduate: "Our design represents a belief that there ought to be a history of that site. It's not a virgin field. The Armory stood there for over 60 years."[15]

The rest of the building radically challenged conventions in architecture, even as universities stand for both continuity and change. Besides the towers, a central characteristic of the place is the monumental scaffolding that looms over both Mershon Auditorium and Weigel Hall. In theory, the building aligns with an imaginary axis that links it to the main runway of Columbus airport and to the football stadium. Unusual spaces and extraordinary use of different types of glass and steel and concrete made the building a national attraction, winning it an award from *Progressive Architecture* in 1985. Meanwhile, the new building brought added controversy

14. Quoted in *Lantern*, September 24, 1987; OSU Archives Vertical File.
15. Quoted in *Lantern*, July 1, 1985; Archives Vertical File.

9.31 *The Armory in 1902, draped in mourning for the death of President William McKinley*

by transforming the main entrance to the campus at 15th and High Streets into a pedestrian mall.

So radical and thought-provoking was the design that it inspired a twenty-five million dollar donation from OSU graduate and business executive Leslie Wexner toward its forty-three million dollar cost. The building, named in honor of his father, opened in 1989. It provided exhibit galleries, offices, theaters, shops and storage areas for the Arts on campus.

CONCLUSION

All in all, the buildings on the Columbus campus represent an eclectic collection of architectural styles, ranging from Romanesque to deconstructive modern. Some of the buildings are the work of prominent architects whose works are significant accomplishments and objects of study. The Wexner Center stands as Peter Eisenman's largest work to that time. Earlier, prominent architects included Frank L. Packard of Columbus and the nationally known Allen and Collins, who designed the Thompson Library. No one style characterizes the campus, and such diversity enriches the campus architecturally. Thus, the campus itself is a kind of architectural laboratory for OSU's School of Architecture.

OSU has so many buildings, some of which are more than a century old, that maintaining them and deciding about restoration and renovation is a major challenge. All of the buildings around the Oval have undergone major renovations and updates. Particularly dramatic was the renovation of Page Hall, completed in 2004, that preserved the historic front but inserted entirely new and attractive spaces in the interior. In 2008, OSU completed a project to restore and improve the old Botany and Zoology Building on Neil Avenue, which it renamed Jennings Hall, in honor of OSU President Edward Jennings, for whom evolutionary biology was a personal interest.

From time to time, however, OSU decides that a building should be removed for more "green space" or to make way for a newer building. Examples include the original College of Veterinary Medicine building on 17th Avenue, which became a park, and Ives Hall, originally a barn, that became the site of the modern Knowlton Hall, the School of Architecture. Such decisions invariably provoke much discussion, arguments in favor of architectural heritage versus cost and functionality. In 2004, OSU completed a project funded by the Getty Foundation that resulted in a historic building survey which identified buildings of historical significance and recommended strategies for preservation. Nevertheless, all of OSU's buildings, old or new, are part of its educational mission and must both inspire and support learning.

CHAPTER TEN

OUR UNIVERSITY THROUGH TIME

A Selective Chronology of OSU

Time is a sort of river of passing events, and strong is its current; no sooner is a thing brought to sight than it is swept by and another takes its place and this too will be swept away.

—Marcus Aurelius, *Meditations*

There is a time for some things, and a time for all things; a time for great things, and a time for small things.

—Miguel de Cervantes Saavedra, *Don Quixote*

1862 · (July 2) U.S. Congress passes the Morrill Act, and it is signed by Abraham Lincoln. It provides for the creation of land-grant colleges endowed from the proceeds of public lands owned by the federal government. Their mission was to provide higher education that included programs in engineering and in agriculture.

1864 · (February 4) The Ohio legislature agrees to participate in the land-grant college program, but does not decide where it will be located or if the land-grant money would be divided among existing colleges and universities in Ohio.

1870 · (March 22) Cannon Act provides for the creation of the Ohio Agricultural and Mechanical College to become Ohio's only land-grant college. It empowers the trustees to make decisions about curriculum and location.

1870 · (September 21) The trustees vote to accept the offer of Franklin County as the site of the college. Next the trustees vote to purchase the Neil Farm as the site of the campus for the new college.

1871 · (March 10) The trustees accept architectural plans for the first classroom building, University Hall.

1873 · (January 2) The trustees decide to have the college offer a broad curriculum from the first year and proceed to hire the first faculty.

1873 · (September 17) the Ohio Agricultural and Mechanical College (later OSU) opens for registration, with 24 students, including two women, the daughters of Professor Norton Townshend.

1875 · The first dormitory, North Dormitory, located at 1659 Neil Avenue (between

10.1 Scene of student cadets in front of University Hall in 1878. Note how rough the landscape is.

10.2 *Student members of the Sketch Club on an outing in 1888. The somber student at the far right is Ralph D. Mershon, for whom Mershon Hall would be named. Mershon was an active alumnus, successful engineer, and generous donor to the university.*

10.3 *Alice Williams*

10th and 11th Avenues). It could accommodate a maximum of 65 students. Previously, students who wished to live on campus stayed in University Hall, the only building. Others lived in rooming houses off campus. In 1908 the North Dormitory was razed.

· In 1875 Alice Williams becomes the first woman faculty member as a tutor in romance languages. In 1881, she is made an instructor, and then in 1887 an associate professor in French, resigning in 1889.

1876 · The number of students rises to 120.

1877 · The trustees vote to reduce faculty salaries until enrollment has reached 200, which occurs the next year.

· The department of mining and metallurgy is established by act of the state legislature, which also provided funding for equipment—$4,500. This was the first gift of money from the state.

1878 · An act of the state legislature changes the name of the Ohio Agricultural and Mechanical College to The Ohio State University. This is supported by President Edward Orton, who believes that the term "university" better reflects OSU's broad and diverse mission.

- Students select the official colors of The Ohio State University as scarlet and gray for ribbons with which to wrap the diplomas of the first graduating class. Originally, the student committee had selected orange and black, until they learned these colors were already in use by Princeton.
- The first class of six is graduated on June 19.

1879
- The university offers free lectures on farming, the first example of extension service at OSU.

10.4 Mary Frank Morrison

- The OSU Alumni Association is founded when first graduating class of 1878 returns to campus to observe commencement and holds an organizational meeting.
- Mary Frank Morrison is the first woman to receive a BS degree from OSU. Morrison Tower on West 11th Avenue, originally a women's dormitory, was named in her honor in 1962.

1880
- Entrance requirements are lowered to boost enrollment. The trustees tem-

10.5 Morrison Tower

porarily drop algebra over the objections of President Orton.

- Enrollment is at 302, of whom 39 are women.

1881
- The trustees order that attendance at daily chapel exercises be compulsory for all students. Edward Orton and other faculty had opposed this because of their view that it was inappropriate for a publicly supported institution.

- Walter Quincy Scott becomes the second president of The Ohio State University, following the resignation of Edward Orton.

1882
- The state legislature creates the Agricultural Experiment Station, which will become the Ohio Agricultural Research and Development Center and later relocate in Wooster, Ohio. Legislators and many farmers maintain that OSU should do more to foster agriculture in Ohio.

1883
- The trustees decide not to renew Walter Q. Scott's appointment as president. He is succeeded by William Henry Scott, who had been president of Ohio University.

1885
- The School of Pharmacy and chair of veterinary science are created.

1886
- The first MA degree is awarded to Annie Ware Sabine of Columbus. Having achieved a BA in 1884, Sabine passed an examination for the graduate degree administered by three OSU professors.

1887
- Former U.S. President Rutherford B. Hayes becomes a trustee and succeeds in bridging the rift between agriculture and OSU and raises the stature of OSU with the state legislature.

- The federal Hatch Act aids land-grant colleges by establishing agricultural experiment stations. The control of the federal subsidy is contested by OSU's trustees and the board of control of OSU's Ag Experiment Station. Hayes is instrumental in resolving the dispute.

- OSU faculty abolish the student demerit system, which had assigned points as penalties when students misbehaved. Automatic expulsion could result if students accumulated too many demerits. This had been a point of friction between students and faculty.

1888
- OSU adds a manual training department (industrial arts) to its curriculum, a favorite topic of Rutherford B. Hayes.

1890
- OSU awards its first Doctor of Science degree to Clarence Moores Weed for his dissertation, "A Monograph of the Harvest Spiders of America, North of Mexico." A distinguished entomologist, Weed became president of Lowell State Teachers College before his death in 1947.

Football begins as a varsity sport, although it had been played on the dormitory fields west of North Dormitory as early as 1881. The first game was played against Ohio Wesleyan at Delaware, Ohio on May 3. The team ordered uniforms before the game, which ended in victory.

President Scott has noted "a new and unprecedented" student interest in athletics, that led to teams in baseball, lawn tennis, and football. Responding to a petition from students, the trustees allocated money for an athletic field near North Dormitory that included space for baseball, football,

10.6 *Bertha Lamme Feicht as a student. She became the first woman in the United States to graduate with a degree in engineering in 1893.*

and a grand stand.

1891 · The Hysell Act of the state legislature yields a special tax levy in support of the university. This act was significant in that it was the first time that the State of Ohio had committed to providing financial support for OSU on a regular basis.

· The trustees vote to establish a School of Law.

· Enrollment at OSU exceeds 500 for the first time (664).

1893 · Hayes and Orton Halls are completed, both of which became campus landmarks listed on the National Register of Historic Places.

· Trustee and former U.S. president Hayes dies.

· Olive Branch Jones is appointed as the first full-time librarian and serves until 1927. Previously, the management of the library was the responsibility of one of the faculty. Jones had a major role in designing OSU's William Oxley Thompson library and in developing one of the foremost research libraries in the United States.

· The trustees accept the resignation of William Henry Scott as president, although he continues as a professor of philosophy

1894 · The department of ceramics, first in United States, is created. Leadership came from Professor Edward Orton, Jr., the son of OSU's first president.

1895 · The McMillin astronomy observatory is given as a gift to OSU by philanthropist Emerson McMillin. The gift results in improvements that create

Mirror Lake as landscaping for the observatory.

- James H. Canfield, chancellor of University of Nebraska, is elected OSU president.
- Edith Cockins (later Cockins Hall) becomes the first registrar.

OSU celebrates the twenty-fifth anniversary of its founding in 1870.

1896 · OSU ends its preparatory school, which offered instruction to those who could not pass the admissions test. The preparatory school ended because the growing numbers of high schools in Ohio adequately prepared students for higher education.

- The first foreign student (from Jamaica) receives a BA from OSU.

OSU reorganizes into six colleges: Agriculture, Arts, Philosophy and Science, Engineering, Law, Pharmacy, and Veterinary Medicine.

- The departments of pedagogy and domestic science are established. They would later become the College of Education and Human Ecology.
- OSU dedicates McMillin observatory on West 12th Avenue. It overlooked Mirror Lake until the building was razed in 1976.

1897 · The first OSU-Michigan football game takes place, with Michigan winning.
- Students number more than one thousand for the first time (1150).
- Contracts let for Townshend Hall.

1898 · An athletic board is organized to regulate student athletics and provide for faculty control. OSU wanted to make certain that irregularities of finance, unfair competition, and interference with the educational mission would be avoided.

- Townshend Hall is dedicated. It is named for Norton S. Townshend, the first professor of agriculture and a member of the board of trustees that established the Ohio Agricultural and Mechanical College in 1870.
- The first OSU basketball game is played against North High School in Columbus.

1899 · President Canfield resigns to become librarian at Columbia University.
- William Oxley Thompson, president of Miami University, is elected president of OSU.
- Enrollment stands at 1,252.

1899 · The College of Dentistry is authorized.

1902 · The trustees name new law building in honor of Henry F. Page, who bequeathed to OSU his estate of more than $200,000. Page did not attend OSU, and his gift was a surprise.

1904 · The library of former president Edward Orton is bequeathed by his son, Edward Orton Jr.

1904 · "Carmen Ohio," written by Fred Cornell, is first sung in public by the University Glee Club, of which Cornell is a member.

1905 · Enrollment passes two thousand for the first time.
- Dedication of the sundial on the Oval, a gift of the class of 1905, takes place.

- The first regular summer school is held.
- A. B. Graham, founder of 4-H, become superintendent of the Agricultural Extension at OSU. Graham had founded the first boys and girls agricultural club in Springfield Township in 1902. When he became superintendent, he was thought to be the first full-time superintendent in the United States. Graham remained at OSU until 1914, when he joined the New York State Agricultural College. Later, he was responsible for the agricultural extension for the U.S. Department of Agriculture until his retirement in 1938. Graham returned to Columbus, where he died in 1961.

10.7 A. B. Graham

1907
- The College of Education is created.
- Sphinx, the senior honorary fraternity, is inaugurated.

1908
- Alonzo J. Bowling became the first known African American to receive an MA from OSU.
- Ohio Field at North High Street and West Woodruff Avenue is dedicated. It served as the site for football and other athletic contests until the completion of Ohio Stadium in 1922.

1909
- Student union completed, the first at a public university. Located on West 12th Avenue, it became Enarson Hall in 1986 and is listed on the National Register of Historic Places.

10.8 Ohio Field at Woodruff and High Streets as it looked in 1916

- Oxley Hall becomes the first women's dormitory at OSU. Located at 1712 Neil Avenue, it was named in honor of the mother of President William Oxley Thompson.
- OSU Alumni Association commences publication of what would become *Ohio State University Magazine*.
- Student enrollment stands at 3,439.

1912
- The graduate school begins as an effort to formalize and to foster graduate education and research. However, graduate degrees had been awarded prior to its organization.

1913
- Caroline Breyfogle is made first dean of women at OSU. The creation of this position acknowledged the importance of administrative leadership to support women students and their programs. In 1913, women students comprised about one-fourth of the student population (1,043 of 4,435).
- Main Library opens, the first building on campus to be built exclusively as a library (the previous ones being in University Hall and Orton Hall).
- The Engineering Experiment Station begins at OSU by act of the state legislature. Its purpose was "To make technical investigations and to supply engineering data which will tend to increase the economy, efficiency, and safety of the manufacturing, mineral, transportation, and other engineering and industrial enterprises of the State, and to promote the conservation and utilization of its resources."

10.9 *Engineering Experiment Station scene*

1914
- Starling-Ohio Medical College joins OSU as its College of Medicine. Discussions had begun as early as 1898, but progress had been difficult due to concerns about financial obligations to the university and the reluctance of the medical college to become a public institution.
- Mortarboard, the women's student honorary society, begins.

1915
- The chimes are dedicated in Orton Hall, a gift of the classes of 1906 through 1914.

1916
- College of Commerce and Journalism (the predecessor of the Fisher College of Business) is established.

1917 · US enters World War I. More than four hundred students officially withdraw from studies to volunteer for military service. OSU participates in national training programs, and OSU, through President Thompson, Professor Edward Orton, Jr., and alumnus Ralph Mershon, create "the Ohio Plan" which leads to the national Reserve Officer Training Program.

1918 · Chimes, the junior women's honorary, begins.

1919 · The Bureaus of Governmental, Business, and Social Research are established to garner social and economic data in Ohio for research. This evidenced the growing importance of OSU to Ohio for social research in the development of social and economic policy.

1920 · OSU celebrates its fiftieth anniversary.

10.10 Two coeds walking in front of University Hall in 1910

10.11 Panoramic view of campus and students in 1912

10.12 *Military parade in June 1918*

10.13 *WEAO (later WOSU)*

WEAO (later WOSU) begins broadcasting and becomes a pioneer in education by radio.

- Enrollment stands at 8,313.

1922
- The Four Quarter Plan begins. The change from semesters to quarters was an effort to make more efficient use of university buildings by reducing the length of the summer break.
- The dedication of Ohio Stadium takes place.
- The Bureau of Educational Research is established to garner data about education in Ohio.

1923
- The Sullivant Medal is awarded to Benjamin Garver Lamme, a distinguished engineer. In 1920, former OSU professor Thomas C. Mendenhall endowed a fund for OSU to provide a gold medal in no less than five-year intervals. As the highest award of OSU, it still recognizes notable achievements that could be inventions, discoveries, practical solutions to a significant problem, or the production of a valuable literary, artistic, historical, philosophical, or other work.
- Enrollment exceeds 10,000 for first time.

10.14 Sullivant Medal awarded to Benjamin Garver Lamme

1924
- Alma W. Paterson becomes the first woman trustee of OSU, serving until 1933. A graduate of OSU in 1904, Paterson became president of the OSU Alumnae Council and was a co-founder of the Alumnae Scholarship House for women students.

1925
- OSU accepts the gift of Gilbraltar Island, in Lake Erie, from trustee Julius F. Stone as a home for the Center for Lake Erie Area Research, which had been at Cedar Point.
- William Oxley Thompson resigns as president after twenty-six years, the longest term of any president at OSU.
- Acting president George Washington Rightmire and a committee of

10.15 Benjamin Garver Lamme

OSU trustees investigate charges voiced by Ohio governor Donahey and state legislators that some OSU students and faculty were Communists and used alcohol in this era of Prohibition. The investigation found that the rumors were much exaggerated and largely baseless.

10.16 *Professor Pressey and his teaching machine in 1960, which is now at the Smithsonian Institute*

- Professor Sidney L. Pressey (College of Education) creates the first teaching machine (now at the Smithsonian Institute).
1926 · George Washington Rightmire becomes the sixth president of OSU, the first OSU president to have been a student here.
- Enrollment stands at 12,296.
- "Maudine Ormsby," a Holstein cow, is elected queen of Homecoming.
- Browning Amphitheatre is dedicated in Mirror Lake Hollow. The amphitheatre was built as a place for the Browning Dramatic Society to hold plays. The first was *A Midsummer Night's Dream.*
1927 · The Women's Building, completed in 1922, is renamed. In 1919, a day before the groundbreaking ceremony, trustee Frank Pomerene died and the building was renamed in his honor. At the ceremony, senior Jessie Masteller turned the first earth and declared "Here shall women reign supreme and strew fresh flowers of wisdom on the narrow paths of life."[1] Pomerene Hall was the place for the Dean of Women and for organizations of women students to meet, to hold events, and to exercise.
1927 · Joe Park is appointed as OSU's first Dean of Men. A graduate of OSU, Park would achieve a national reputation for leadership of student services until his death in 1952. He was responsible for bringing about the Student Senate, the Student Court, and a fraternity system looked upon as a model in the nation.

---

1. *OSU Monthly,* December 1927, 103.

10.17 *Browning Amphitheatre as it was when dedicated in 1926*

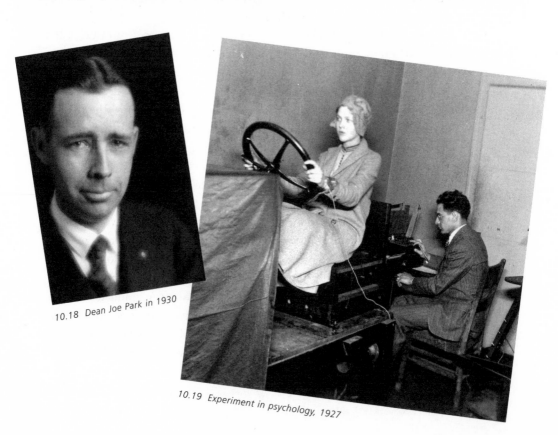

10.18 *Dean Joe Park in 1930*

10.19 *Experiment in psychology, 1927*

1927 · Freshman Week begins as the first university-wide and sponsored orientation of new students to OSU. Previously, colleges and student organizations had oriented freshman, but many, especially President George Rightmire, who had been a student, felt that OSU needed a better organized and more pervasive effort at welcoming new students.

1928 · Junior deans are appointed in each college as an effort to help undergraduate students. These deans provided academic advice to freshmen.

1929 · The Great Depression begins in the US and continues until World War II in 1939. It presented great challenges to OSU and other institutions in higher education. State appropriations declined, resulting in reduced numbers of courses and programs. The New Deal that began in 1933 brought federal support for higher education that included financial aid to students and support for building projects and for faculty research.

1930 · Students number 15,126.
   · The statue of William Oxley Thompson is unveiled in front of the Main Library facing the Oval. The monument was the gift of student classes of 1923, 1925, 1926, and 1928. They raised approximately $13,000 to create the fourteen-foot statue. Thompson himself posed for the sculpture.

1931 · The Depression causes sharp reductions in state budgetary support; faculty salaries fall. Faculty and students try to eliminate compulsory military drill.

10.20 *Professor Arthur Klein*

   · A committee of OSU faculty, chaired by Professor Arthur Klein (College of Education), reduces the number of courses taught at OSU to cope with the economic crisis.
   · OSU is involved in controversy when an African American student is denied the right to live at Home Economics house, even though such residence is a requirement of majors in Home Economics. The university makes alternative arrangements.
   · The trustees reaffirm compulsory military drill over the opposition of many faculty and students.
   · The board of trustees dismisses controversial but tenured Professor Herbert A. Miller of the sociology department. Miller had been a vocal opponent of OSU's compulsory drill and had angered some parents when he took classes of students to Wilberforce University in Ohio to socialize

with African American students there. The decision not to renew Miller's contract drew much criticism on campus and off and brought an investigation and censure from the American Association of University Professors.

· OSU opened University School in Ramseyer Hall as a laboratory school for the College of Education. It taught grades kindergarten through 12 in an effort to test new educational methods. The school continued until 1967.

· Salaries are again reduced because of the budgetary crisis.

10.21 *Professor Herbert A. Miller*

1933 · Stadium dormitory opens in Ohio Stadium as economical housing for students during the Depression. Located in the southwest corner of Ohio Stadium, the dormitory originally housed seventy-five men at a cost less than regular housing. In exchange for inexpensive housing, the students had to maintain a good grade point average and assist in the operations of the dormitory. As part of the extensive renovation of Ohio Stadium, the dormitory moved to Mack Hall on Neil Avenue in 1999.

1934 · The OSU Research Foundation begins as an effort to find sponsors for faculty research projects.

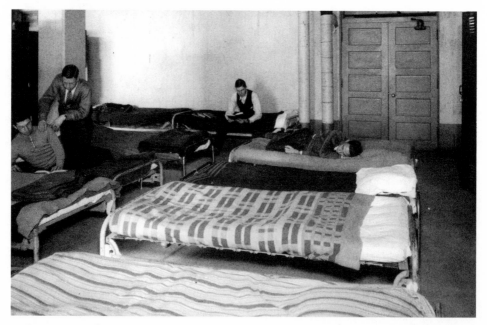

10.22 *Stadium dormitory scene*

10.23 *Jesse Owens*

- The Federal Emergency Relief Administration provides financial support for students by financing student employment.

1935 · Ohio Staters, a prominent student service society, is established. It continues today to undertake useful projects that benefit the OSU community.

1936 · The first "Script Ohio" formation is performed by the OSU Marching Band.

- OSU establishes the Office of Student Financial Aid to coordinate financial support for students during the Depression.
OSU student Jesse Owens stuns the world by winning four gold medals in track at the Olympics in Berlin. In 1960, his daughter, Marlene, would become the first African American Homecoming Queen at OSU.

1938 · "Disciplina in Civitatem" (education for citizenship) becomes part of the University's coat-of-arms.

- The Development Fund is organized in an effort to raise money from individuals, corporations, and foundations to make up for the reductions in state support.

1938 · Block O begins under the leadership of Clancy Isaacs, head cheerleader. Isaacs felt that cheering needed to be more organized and so developed this student organization for cheering OSU athletes. It has become one of the largest of student organizations.

1939 · World War II begins in Europe.

1940 · Howard Landis Bevis is elected the seventh president of OSU.

· Enrollment stands at 17,568.

· The Faculty Council is organized to represent OSU faculty in OSU affairs.

· Baker Hall is named in honor of Newton D. Baker, distinguished statesman and trustee of OSU.

1941 · The U.S. joins the Allies in World War II.

1942 · The Committee on War Activities is established to coordinate programs for the war effort.

· The trustees provide for the War Research Laboratory (now Smith Laboratory) as a building to conduct war related research.

· The Navy establishes Recognition School on campus to enable the rapid identification of aircraft as friendly or enemy.

1943 · The trustees approve the Army Specialized Training Program to provide instruction in subjects needed for the war effort.

· Enrollment falls below 8,000.

· OSU creates the Committee on Post-War Problems to plan for the impact of the end of the war upon OSU.

· The trustees rename OSU airport in honor of former football star Don

10.24 *Block O, ca. 1939*

10.25 *Busy scene on the grand staircase of the Main Library, 1939*

10.26 *OSU's President Howard Bevis in a campus scene from 1943*

Scott, who died while serving in Great Britain.

1945 · A trailer camp is set up at the State Fairgrounds as housing for returning and married veterans.

· OSU adopts a five-point priority system to handle increased admissions, with the highest priority going to returning veterans.

1946 · The trustees pass the first Speaker's Rule forbidding the use of university property by candidates for political office.
Enrollment exceeds 26,000.

· The cold war begins, as the U.S. and Europe seek to contain the expansion of the Soviet Union and communism.

1948 · OSU celebrates its seventy-fifth anniversary, commemorating the opening of classes rather than the official beginning of the university. To celebrate the seventy-fifth anniversary of the actual opening in 1945 would have been too close to the war.

· OSU stands fourth in U.S. college enrollment.

· Ground is broken for a new medical center at OSU.

1950 · Sculptor Erwin F. Frey, whose works include the statue of William Oxley

Thompson, receives the Sullivant Medal for outstanding achievement.

- Enrollment stands at 25,948.

1951
- The trustees imposed a second Speaker's Rule, requiring that speakers external to the university be approved by the president ten days prior to the event. Communists or members of other subversive groups, who sought to undermine the basic liberties of Americans, were prohibited from using OSU facilities as public meetings. Enforcement of the rule caused decades of controversy. In 1965, the rule was changed so that only the approval of the faculty advisor was required for student groups to invite speakers to campus.

10.27 Don Scott

10.28 Don Scott Airport, ca. 1967

1951 · The new Ohio Union on High Street is dedicated. Students had petitioned the trustees for the new building and paid for it from fees.
Wayne Woodrow "Woody" Hayes becomes football coach.

· OSU dedicates and opens the expanded Main Library, renamed in honor of William Oxley Thompson. Among the additions was the stack tower.

1952 · Alumnus Ralph D. Mershon dies. His will provides a gift of more than seven million dollars to OSU.
Former trustee and cheerleader Herbert Atkinson dies and his ashes are buried in a wall of Bricker Hall, where they remain.

· OSU adopts an official flag.

1953 · Dr. Byron T. Darling, tenured in the physics department, is first suspended and then terminated by OSU for refusing to testify before the U.S. House Committee on Un-American Activities. He had been accused of being a member of the Communist Party. The action by the president and the trustees led to censure from the American Association of University Presidents in 1956.

· A junior college is established on Guam with cooperation of the College of Education.

· Millionth volume was added to the stacks of Thompson Library.

10.29 Campus scene about 1950. Note the bobby sox and the saddle shoes!

1954 · The victory bell is rung after OSU wins football games in Ohio Stadium.

1956 · Following the retirement of President Bevis, the trustees authorize a faculty commit-tee of eleven to recommend nominations for OSU presi-dent, the first time faculty participate in the selection process.

· Novice G. Fawcett becomes the eighth president of OSU, following his career as super-intendent of Columbus pub-lic schools.

· Enrollment increases to 28,455.

· WOSU-TV begins regularly scheduled television broad-casts.

10.30 Queen of May Week shown in parade of floats, 1959

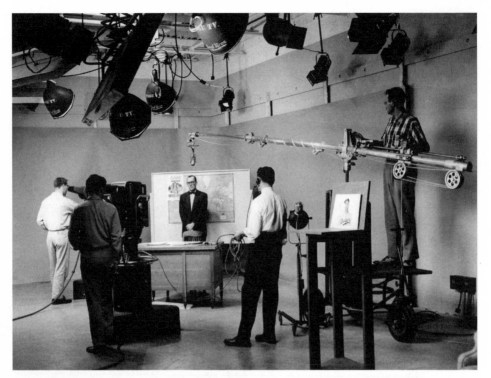
10.31 *WOSU-TV in its early days*

1957 · St. John Arena and Mershon Auditorium are dedicated.
Regional campuses of OSU begin at Marion and Newark.
OSU Press is established to publish works of scholarship.

1958 · Trustees approve establishment of an OSU campus at Mansfield.
· Dr. Howard Sirak performs the first open heart surgery at OSU.

1959 · The Armory, one of the landmarks on the campus, is torn down following a fire the previous year. In 1989, the Wexner Center for the Arts was built on the site. The towers in the Center represent the Armory that had stood there.

1960 · The trustees approve establishment of an OSU campus at Lima.

1960 · The basketball team wins the NCAA championship.
· The first awards for distinguished teaching are granted.
· President Fawcett tours India to inspect the work being done by OSU faculty in agriculture and education.
· Enrollment reaches 31,535.
· Distinguished writer, cartoonist, and former OSU student James Thurber dies. His papers become a prominent feature of Rare Books and Manuscripts in the OSU libraries.
· The trustees approves a master plan for the physical development of the OSU campus.
· OSU opens a campus in Lima, Ohio.

- Marlene Owens, daughter of Jesse Owens, becomes the first African American Homecoming Queen.
- The Faculty Council votes not to accept an invitation to play football in the Rose Bowl because of the absence of a contract with the Rose Bowl and previous dissatisfaction with Rose Bowl arrangements. Mass demonstrations take place on campus and on High Street.
- The Thompson Library adds its 1,500,000th volume, thus becoming seventeenth in size among research libraries in the U.S.

1963
- The establishment of the President's Club greatly enhances OSU's Development Fund program. It involved the OSU president more directly in the work of raising money from private sources.

10.32 James Thurber as a student in 1917

1964
- The U.S. Congress passes the Gulf of Tonkin Resolution. North Vietnamese fired upon a U.S. warship in this area near North Vietnam and the U.S. Congress passed a resolution authorizing the president to use force to protect American interests and U.S. allies in the area. This resolution became the legal premise for the U.S. war in Vietnam and led to much unrest on college campuses, including OSU.

1965
- The Speaker's Rule, a point of controversy between administration and faculty and students since 1946, is ended with a change that no longer requires the OSU president to review requests for off-campus speakers.
- The university hires its first archivist and the OSU Archives is formally established.

1966
- University College is organized to serve as the "portal" of entry for all freshmen. It provided educational advising and classes until students sought majors in other colleges of OSU.
- The baseball team wins the NCAA championship.
- Enrollment reaches 40,277, an increase of 85 percent from 1956, as "baby boomers" born during and after World War II reach college age.

1967
- The Lincoln and Morrill towers are opened.
- OSU libraries acquire their two millionth volume. (By 2007 the libraries contained more than 4 million volumes.)
- The football team wins the national championship.

1968
- Numerous students march and demonstrate against the Vietnam War and charges of discrimination against minorities and women. They seize control of the Administration Building (now Bricker Hall).

1969
- The Black Studies Division is approved by the College of the Humanities.

10.33 Scene in front of the Administration Building (now Bricker Hall) in 1969. Some students held a moratorium vigil and a peace teach-in to protest the controversial war in Vietnam.

10.34 Dormitory room in Norton House, 1966

10.35 Entrance to OSU Campus, 1970. This photograph was taken by a student for a photographic contest sponsored by Ohio Staters and The Ohio State University Association.

1970 · The Office of Affirmative Action is established.

1970 · May Student protests and violence lead to occupation of the campus by the Ohio National Guard and state troopers. The campus is closed following the deaths of students at Kent State University.

OSU celebrates the hundredth anniversary of its founding. The occasion included medals awarded for achievement, lectures, exhibits, and a special film "Centennial" concerning the history of OSU.

· The Office of Minority Affairs is established.

· Student enrollment reaches 63,203.

1971 · The original University Hall is razed and replaced with a replica.

1972 · Harold Enarson, president of Cleveland State University, becomes the ninth president of OSU.

Drake Union, which overlooks the Olentangy River, is opened.

The University Senate begins, the first governance structure to include students, faculty, and administrators at OSU.

1973 · Professor John D. Kraus, a pioneer in astronomy, develops the "Big Ear "telescope with two 360-foot mesh screens and begins listening for extraterrestial sounds.

1974 · The Nobel Prize in chemistry is awarded to OSU alumnus Paul Flory.

1975 · OSU establishes the Office of Women's Studies.

· Archie Griffin wins his second Heisman Trophy, the only player to do so.

1978 · A blizzard closes the OSU campus for two days.

1978 · Dedication of the Hilandar Room in the Thompson Library, a research collection of Slavic and Byzantine manuscripts.

10.36 The fashions of the early 1970s included leisure suits and Afro hairstyles, as depicted in this photograph from the era.

10.37 Professor Kraus shown in 1956 with his helical or corkscrew radio telescope, situated on the University Farms north of Lane Avenue and west of Kenny Road in Columbus

1979 · OSU adopts the Medical Practice Plan, which redirects some income from physicians practicing at OSU Hospitals toward supporting medical education and research.

· In the Journalism Building, a room is dedicated to OSU alumnus and cartoonist Milton Caniff. This was the beginning of the Library for Communication, Graphic and Photographic Arts (later, the Cartoon Research Library, now in the Wexner Center) in which the work of Caniff and other cartoonists is preserved for research and teaching.

1980 · The track in Ohio Stadium and the University Recreation Centers is renamed in honor of Jesse Owens. (Later, in a renovation of Ohio Stadium, the track is relocated at Jesse Owens Stadium.)

1981 · Edward Jennings, president of the University of Wyoming, becomes the tenth president of OSU.

1983 · The Nobel Prize in chemistry is awarded to OSU graduate William Fowler.

1982 · Stadium Drive is renamed in honor of Coach Woody Hayes.

1984 · A task force recommends that all classes be consolidated on the Main Campus and that West Campus cease being a classroom campus for freshmen and sophomores.

1985 · The University Campaign begins with the goal of raising $350 million dollars from private sources—and actually succeeds in raising $401.2 million by 1990. Aside from the Stadium Campaign in the 1920s, this was the first major fund-raising effort by OSU.

· The University Honors Program is established. Previously, honors programs had been centered in colleges.

· OSU acquires the papers of polar explorer and aviator Admiral Richard E. Byrd and renames its Institute of Polar Studies the Byrd Polar Research Institute.

· Dr. Richard Olsen in the College of Veterinary Medicine develops a feline leukemia vaccine.

1986 · OSU approves a selective admissions policy, to begin in 1987.

· Dr. P. David Myerowitz performs first heart transplant at OSU.

1987 · OSU holds its three hundredth commencement in June.

1988 · Faculty approve new undergraduate curriculum requirements.

· The Young Scholars Program is founded to identify promising boys and girls from low-income, minority groups, and target them for special guidance in preparing for admission to the university.

1989 · The Wexner Center for the Arts is completed

1990 · The Arthur James Cancer Hospital opens.

· E. Gordon Gee, president of University of Colorado, becomes eleventh president of OSU.

1991 · Renowned choreographer Twyla Tharp donates her archives to OSU's

10.38 Preacher on the Oval in the 1980s

Lawrence and Lee Theatre Research Institute.

1993 · The Science and Engineering Library opens, first library to be open 24 hours per day, seven days a week.

1993 · Max Fisher donates $20 million to OSU's College of Business to build a new complex of facilities.

1995 · OSU celebrates its 125th anniversary and begins another fund-raising campaign, with the goal of $850 million. Festivities of the celebration include a time capsule in the Main Library and the development of a historical documentary.

1996 · WOSU creates and broadcasts "Echoes Across the Oval," depicting the history of OSU by means of historical photographs, films, and interviews.

1997 · President Gordon Gee announces his resignation from OSU to become president of Brown University.

1998 · Dr. William E. Kirwan, president of the University of Maryland, becomes the twelfth president of OSU.

· The Jerome Schottenstein Center and the new Max Fisher College of Business open.

· Dr. Randall Wolf, Dr. Robert Michler, and Dr. David Brown are the first U.S. team to perform robotic heart surgery.

2000 · The Dorothy Davis Heart and Lung Research Institute opens.

2001 · OSU creates the Academic Plan, with the goal to "become one of the world's great public research and teaching universities." Its strategic goals would continue to shape OSU's programs in 2008.

10.39 The Main Library and the Long Walk on the Oval in the 1990s

2002 · President Kirwan announces his resignation to accept the post of chancellor of the University of Maryland, effective June 30.

· Karen Holbrook, provost at the University of Georgia, becomes the thirteenth president of OSU.

· Mirror Lake renovation is completed.

· Don Scott (OSU's airport) celebrates its sixtieth anniversary.

2003 · The Freshman Success Series begins, featuring small seminars in which all freshman students learn from faculty in small classes as a way of enhancing the undergraduate experience and preparing new students for the academic rigor and excitement of OSU.

· The football team wins the national championship.

· The Orton Hall chimes are rededicated.

· Archie Griffin becomes president of the OSU Alumni Association.

· OSU commencement is rescheduled from Fridays to Sundays as a convenience to graduates and their families.

2004 · WOSU-TV broadcasts its first digital signal.
· The Ross Heart Hospital opens.
2005 · The South Campus Gateway Center opens on High Street, the fruition of a project to improve the OSU campus neighborhood by bringing private residences, restaurants, and small business establishments to the area.
· OSU's Sullivant Medal is awarded to Liang-Shih Fan for his research into the clean use of coal.
· The National Science Foundation reports that OSU is among its top ten public research institutions.
· OSU breaks ground for an Early Childhood Development Center in Columbus, the result of a major gift from Betty Schoenbaum.
· The renovation of the Oval is completed, a project that included new turf, walks, and an irrigation system.
2006 · OSU Libraries partner with the Undergraduate Student Government to loan free textbooks for general education courses.
· Metro High School opens a collaborative venture with Battelle Memorial Institute and OSU that focuses on education in math, science, and technology.
· OSU's Thompson Library closes for a massive renovation that will add a new wing to the west and a restoration of its historic rooms. It reopens in 2009.
· President Holbrook announces that she will not seek renewal of her contract as president of OSU.
· The Colleges of Human Ecology and Education merge to form the College of Education and Human Ecology.
2007 · OSU is accredited for another ten years and given high marks by a review team.
· The Ohio Union is torn down to make way for a new building that will replace it in 2010.
· E. Gordon Gee, chancellor of Vanderbilt University, returns to OSU as its fourteenth president, the first to return for a second term of office.
2008 · OSU opens Urban Arts Space, a major facility for the exhibit and display of art, in downtown Columbus at the former Lazarus department store.
· The W. K. Kellogg Foundation gives OSU an Engagement Award for its efforts to revitalize the Weinland Park neighborhood of Columbus.
Ohio State's Wilma H. Schiermier Olentangy River Wetland Research Park, established in 1992 as a fifty-two acre site for ecological research, is named as the 24th Wetland of International Importance in the USA, the first in Ohio be so designated by the U.S. Fish and Wildlife Service.
2009 · The university senate votes to change the academic calendar from quarters to semesters, beginning in 2012. A major reason is that joining other public universities in a semester-based year will enable students in Ohio to transfer credits more easily from one institution to another.

- The Thompson Library reopens after three-year closure. It wins design and construction awards and welcomes more than 700,000 visitors between August and December.

2010 · New Ohio Union opens on High Street.

CHAPTER ELEVEN

BIBLIOGRAPHIC ESSAY

Historical Research
at The Ohio State
University

THIS BOOK drew on the writings—books, articles, theses—and even the curatorial work of others. Therefore, it is proper, necessary, and useful to credit those authors, most of whom were not professionally trained historians but had an appreciation and an interest in OSU's past. Readers who wish to know more about the history of OSU should consult the works and historical collections cited below.

OSU has several general histories, each different in nature and content. The first was *History of The Ohio State University (formerly Ohio Agricultural and Mechanical College)* that was published in 1878 by the trustees. A slim publication, it reviewed the enabling legislation, federal and state, that created the university, and contained the bylaws and rules of the board.

Official histories sponsored by OSU itself nearly fill an entire bookshelf. The fiftieth anniversary of OSU in 1920 inspired a celebration and led to publishing *History of The Ohio State University, Volume I, 1870–1910,* that Alexis Cope, who had been secretary of the board for many years, had started. This was the first of thirteen volumes that OSU would publish over nearly nine decades as its official history. Since President Bevis (1940–1956), the end of each presidential administration has led to another volume that served to review the challenges and accomplishments of the president's administration. In fact, the trustees have commissioned a campus professor, Christian Zacher, to write a history of OSU in the years of President Karen Holbrook (2002–2007).

Another series of official history appeared in 1970. As part of OSU's celebration of its centennial, each college and department of the University compiled histories. The resulting volumes, bound in a series, came to the OSU Archives and the OSU Libraries. Typically, the histories focused on the origins and milestones of each academic and administrative area. They provide a different, less presidential, view by reviewing the teaching of subjects, the development of major fields of study, and the accomplishments of professors in teaching and research. Unfortunately, the histories vary in quality and have not been kept up to date.

For the general reader, the work of James Pollard is still useful. A journalist by profession, his *History of The Ohio State University: The Story of Its First Seventy-Five Years, 1873–1948,* appeared in 1952. Largely based on annual reports of trustees and presidents, the book is informative. However, it contains so many details that it is more of a work of reference than a book for casual reading, except for the most determined of readers.

Pollard, who was OSU's first University Historian, added several books about the university. No one can claim to know OSU's past without having read Pollard's accounts. He wrote two volumes about President Howard Bevis in the official history series and two more works. First was *William Oxley Thompson: "Evangel of Education"* that appeared in 1955. This biography of President Thompson provides much insight into his background, character, and accomplishments.

A few years later, Pollard published *Ohio State Athletics, 1879–1959* (1959), which discussed the development of OSU's athletic program as well as the evolution of individual sports. There have been many histories of OSU's sports, such as Jack Park's *The Official Ohio State Football Encyclopedia* (2001) and Bob Hunter's *Buckeye Basketball* (1981). However, Pollard's book remains a significant starting point for any reader.

One of the most interesting histories of OSU is William A. Kinnson's *Building Sullivant's Pyramid: An Administrative History of The Ohio State University, 1870–1907*. Published in 1970, the book explores the intellectual climate of the founding and early years of the university. Land-grant universities, such as OSU, were innovations in higher education and raised many questions. How different were public, land-grant institutions from private and largely denominational colleges? Should land-grant institutions concern themselves mainly with agriculture and engineering as priorities or should they offer a diverse curriculum that would draw enrollment from many different interests? What were suitable roles for faculty and for trustees? Was student life at land-grant colleges to be less trivial than at private institutions? Kinnison studied the intellectual ferment, the exchange of views, between those who offered answers to those questions.

There are many histories of colleges and departments besides the Centennial series. OSU's College of Medicine has a three-volume history, the last completed by George Paulson in 1998; for the College of Education there is H. G. Good's *Rise of the College of Education* (1960). University School, a program of the College of Education, has been the subject of several books, including Robert Butche's *Image of Excellence* (2000).

OSU's students have written some histories as theses and dissertations. Particularly useful for this book were Pouneh Alcott's *Women at The Ohio State University in its First Four Decades, 1873–1912* (1979) and Pamela Pritchard's *The Negro Experience at The Ohio State University in the First Sixty-Five Years, 1873–1938: With Special Emphasis on Negroes in the College of Education* (1982). Critical for understanding the little publicized history of women's athletics at OSU is Mary A. Daniels, *The Historical Transition of Women's Sports at The Ohio State University, 1888–1975 and Its Impact on the National Women's Intercollegiate Setting during That Period* (1977). Ironically, a history of OSU Libraries was done as a thesis for the University of Michigan, James E. Skipper's "The Ohio State University Library, 1873–1913" (1960).

The university has many studies of the buildings and the physical development of the campus. *Ringing Grooves of Change,* published by OSU's Office of Campus Planning, was intended for OSU's centennial in 1970 but has continuing value. It chronicles the growth of the Columbus campus and has photographs of buildings finished in each era.

John Herrick, who headed Campus Planning during the centennial, and for whom a street that connects Stadium Drive with Cannon Drive is named, contributed a lasting legacy of research and scholarship about the physical history of the campus. As a retirement project that continued until his death in 1990, Herrick wrote brief histories of each building that had been on the Columbus campus. Typically, entries contain multiple names of buildings, architect, contractors, cost, and additions to the buildings. Herrick's history has been digitized and published on the Web by OSU's Knowlton School of Architecture.

In addition to his five-volume OSU *Campus Buildings* (1979), Herrick wrote three special histories that are consulted often. One is *The OSU Oval* (1982) and the other is *The OSU Mirror Lake Hollow* (1984). Both include information about the origins, changes, and use of these special places. Finally, his *OSU Campus Master Plans* provides a survey of the history of the planning process.

Paul Young, a professor of architecture, also added much to the knowledge and the development of the OSU campus. His historical work and perspective are reflected in the first volume of the OSU Campus Master Plan of 1995. Professor Young was one of the founders of the course "OSU: Its History and Its World" that inspired this book. He continued to help teach the course until his death in 2008.

Fundamental to historical research are historic documents, and inevitably students and scholars of OSU's past find their way to the OSU Archives. There, researchers have available all the books cited above. In addition, the Archives has official publications, such as course catalogs and annual reports, files of administrative offices ranging from presidents and vice presidents, deans and department chairs, minutes of university committees, records of student organizations, and documentation of distinguished professors in teaching and research. Much useful information, including digital exhibits and photo galleries, is on the website of the University Libraries, a department of The Ohio State University Libraries.

Some resources at the Archives are so often used that they deserve special mention. There is an index to the *OSU Alumni Magazine* that began publication in 1909. Also in the Archives are several file drawers of biographical and topical information culled from newspapers and press releases. Finally, the Archives has transcripts from its oral history program that has interviewed each president since Novice Fawcett (1956–1972) as well as retired faculty and administrators. Those interviews add personal reflections and recollections to the official documentation at the Archives.

Probably the most distinctive resource at the Archives is its photographic collection. Nearly two million photographs and slides show the people, buildings, and activities of OSU from the 1870s to the present. Roughly half of the collection refers to athletics and its players, teams, and games because athletics attract photographers. In addition, the Archives has a collection of historic films that appeared as documentaries on WOSU television, such as *Echoes across the Oval* and *Birth of Ohio Stadium*.

Rarely is the history of any institution complete. Colleges and universities can, and some do, span centuries. In fact, they have been among the most durable institutions in the history of civilization. Activities on campuses, from scholarship to service, are so diverse in nature and so global in reach that they defy any single study. With the resources available and as the history of OSU continues, *The Ohio State University: An Illustrated History* is intended to both orient readers to the university and inspire others to add to the historical scholarship.

INDEX

(Page numbers in *italic* refer to illustrations)